Current Practices
in
Quantitative Literacy

© 2006 by
The Mathematical Association of America (Incorporated)

Library of Congress Catalog Card Number 2005937262

ISBN 10: 0-88385-180-6
ISBN 13: 978-0-88385-180-7

Printed in the United States of America

Current Printing (last digit):
10 9 8 7 6 5 4 3 2 1

Current Practices in Quantitative Literacy

edited by

Rick Gillman
Valparaiso University

Published and Distributed by
The Mathematical Association of America

The MAA Notes Series, started in 1982, addresses a broad range of topics and themes of interest to all who are involved with undergraduate mathematics. The volumes in this series are readable, informative, and useful, and help the mathematical community keep up with developments of importance to mathematics.

14693492 $20

MAA Service Center
P.O. Box 91112
Washington, DC 20090-1112
1-800-331-1MAA   FAX: 1-301-206-9789

Introduction

Rick Gillman
Valparaiso University, Valparaiso IN

Quantitative Literacy is one of those things about which we say "I know it when I see it", but is difficult to describe precisely and concisely. It includes numeracy (an understanding of numbers and magnitude); some geometric, algebraic and algorithmic skills; some problem solving ability; an understanding of probability and statistics; and the ability to quickly capture information, summarize it, and make a decision.

The working definition I find most convenient is the following, extracted from the bylaws of the MAA's SIGMAA on Quantitative Literacy. (There are alternatives provided in the various essays included in this volume and in related works.)

Quantitative literacy (QL) can be described as the ability to adequately use elementary mathematical tools to interpret and manipulate quantitative data and ideas that arise in individuals' private, civic, and work lives. As with reading and writing literacy, quantitative literacy is a habit of mind that is best formed by exposure in many contexts.

As mathematicians, it is very tempting to say that being quantitatively literate is equivalent to being more proficient at mathematics, and therefore the solution to developing quantitatively literate citizens is to have them study more mathematics. But this is inherently a poor solution since mathematics is fundamentally about developing and understanding deeper abstractions and connections. Mathematics uses many tools and techniques that, to put it bluntly, do not have much value in the daily world of our fellow citizens. A quantitatively literate citizen will be able to use fairly elementary mathematical tools in sophisticated manners in a wide variety of contexts.

While developing a quantitatively literate citizenry is the responsibility of a much larger community, it is the obligation of the collegiate level mathematics community to take leadership in (a) identifying the prerequisite mathematical skills for QL, (b) finding innovative ways of developing and implementing QL curricula, (c) assisting colleagues in other disciplines to infuse appropriate QL experiences into their courses, and (d) stimulating the national dialogue concerning QL.

With this perspective in mind, the purpose of this volume is to present a wide sampling of the specific efforts being made on campuses across the country to achieve our common goal of having a quantitatively literate citizenry.

As you read these essays, you will see the difficulties these colleges and universities have grappled with to define quantitative literacy within their own communities and to implement appropriate curricula. You will also see a wide range of solutions that result because of differing pressures created by the student population being served, the definition that the community accepts, and the pre-existing curricula.

The volume begins with a series of essays that help to develop and set the context for the curricular programs that follow. The first essays by **Sons** and **Ganter** lay the historical framework for the current attention being given to quantitative literacy. In particular, Sons' essay describes the context of quantitative literacy over the past two decades, while Ganter's essay describes the current initiative to make quantitative literacy a priority. The essay by **Briggs** helps to bring these ideas into immediate application when he describes ten problems that every college graduate should be able to solve.

The majority of this volume consists of examples of institutions working to implement quantitative literacy curricula. All of these writers have been asked to speak about issues concerning student placement, program history, curriculum content, and program assessment; individual writers have chosen to focus on different elements of this list. Because quantitative literacy is inherently part of the general education curriculum and of interest to many other individuals on their campuses, they have also been asked to describe input from individuals outside of the mathematics department and the relationship of their program to the overall general education curriculum.

Each program can be compared with the model described in *Quantitative Reasoning: A Complement to the Standards*, published by the MAA in 1995. This volume makes it very clear that any specific quantitative literacy program must be responsive to the local conditions of an institution including its mission, its student clientele, its history and its resources.

However, with this understanding, the volume is able to describe the general form of a complete quantitative literacy program. Such a program would include an appropriate placement exam so that students are able to move efficiently to a course in which they will succeed and which will support their academic interests. The program may very well have a remedial component for those students who are not prepared for the collegiate level work being offered at their institution. The core of the program is a two-tiered system consisting of a "foundations" course usually taken during the first or second year and "infusion" or applied courses taken in the latter years of undergraduate study. It is anticipated that the foundation course or courses would usually, but not necessarily, be offered by the mathematics department. The courses in the second tier of the program would be offered by disciplines outside of mathematics (frequently within the students' majors) which would utilize the foundational skills previously developed to address problems of interest to the students in context.

These essays are organized into three sections. The first describes programs that have significant components outside of the mathematics department. **Bressoud** describes a program unique to his institution's mission. **Diefenderfer, Doan & Saloway, Taylor, Fink & Nordmoe**, and **Hartzler & Leoni** describe programs in which quantitative experiences are embedded in a wide range of courses throughout the institution. **Bukowski, Coe & Ziesler, Haines & Jordan, Gordon & Winn, Johnson, Kantrowitz & O'Neill**, and **Mast & Pawlak** describe programs in which a finite set of specific courses satisfy the quantitative literacy requirement.

The third section of the volume describes courses explicitly designed to satisfy a quantitative literacy requirement. These essays include those by **Ellington & Haver, Jabon, Jimenez & Zack, Sevilla & Somers,** and **Sons**. It is interesting to read how different institutions have resolved issues of curriculum, staffing, and placement.

The final section addresses issues that don't neatly fit into the other two. Most of this section of the volume consists of a series of essays that focus on placement, advising, assessment, and remediation. However, essays by **Al-Hasan** and **Maher** are included which describe current efforts to establish a quantitative literacy program. While their campuses are very different, their essays reveal similar issues involved in this process: effective placement, student interests, involving other departments, and adapting current courses to serve this purpose. The essay by **Muir** speaks directly to placement and advising, while the essay by **Lichtman** presents some interesting insights into the effect of high school preparation on placement. **Gillman** and **Çömez & Martin** speak to the problem of assessment.

Many of the essays speak to particular issues. The essays by **Bressoud, Gordon & Winn,** and **Mast & Pawlak** address the manner in which the quantitative literacy program is particularly tied to their institutional missions. In addition, the **Gordon & Winn** and **Çömez & Martin** papers demonstrate that the level of quantitative proficiency expected of students can vary by institutional mission.

Not only does the essay by **Hartzler & Leoni** describe a quantitative literacy program at a community college, but it also describes the amount of time and energy required to prepare faculty to include QL topics in their courses. **Bressoud** and **Diefenderfer, Doan & Salowey** address this same issue in their essays. Similarly, **Ellington & Haver** and **Sons** address the same issue of preparing TA's, part-time faculty, and regular faculty in the mathematics department to teach QL specific courses.

The issue of faculty development, both within the department and among the faculty of the institution more generally, leads naturally to the related topic of pedagogy. This is described specifically in several essays (**Jimenez & Zack, Sevilla & Sommers**) and implied in many others. As you read these essays, you will see that either explicitly or implicitly, they say that the student is expected to be actively engaged in his or her learning experience by reading, writing, working in groups, collecting and manipulating data, and interpreting answers.

The use of student centered pedagogy as described in many of these essays reflects another belief implicit in all of these essays. This is the belief that learning is an integrated experience. We cannot effectively teach our students in compartmentalized courses, but each course should be connected to others either formally in the curriculum or more simply through explicit recognition by instructors that material in one course in one discipline can, and will be, used in other courses in other disciplines.

Although the programs and courses described in this volume only represent a sample of what is happening in the community, some trends do seem to be apparent. For example, the approach that an institution takes to address the quantitative literacy of its students seems to depend significantly on the size and type of institution.

Smaller, more liberal arts oriented schools tend to develop more extensive infusion based models for their programs which involve many faculty and courses outside of quantitative intensive disciplines. Mid-sized or small comprehensive schools tend to use traditionally quantitative courses outside of the mathematics department, as well as courses within the department, to teach quantitative reasoning. Large schools tend to rely almost exclusively on the mathematics department to provide appropriate courses, with very little effort to infuse quantitative material into courses outside of the quantitative intensive disciplines. There are many reasonable explanations for these tendencies, but it does indicate how far we are from the model described in *Quantitative Reasoning* in which students have many opportunities to develop the "habit of mind" required to be quantitatively literate citizens.

The essays do indicate that there is a consensus on the mathematical skills necessary to be quantitatively literate. These include elementary logic, the basic mathematics of financial interest, descriptive statistics, finite probability, an elementary understanding of rates of change, the ability to model problems with linear and exponential models, estimation and approximation, and general problem solving. In addition, the essays suggest that many of our students enter college with minimal mastery of these skills and their applications. The goal of quantitative literacy is to raise student mastery of these skills and their use, but a very significant gap in the literature is an articulated statement of standards for what "mastery" means.

There seems to be consensus that students do not master this set of skills, nor develop the habit of utilizing them to solve problems, in a traditional college algebra course. It is generally assumed that students completing a calculus course, statistics course, or finite mathematics course do achieve these two goals, but the evidence is not provided in these essays; possibly because the set of standards has not been articulated as of yet.

The "liberal arts mathematics" courses and textbooks deserve particular attention here. While many of them are intentionally designed to foster quantitative literacy, it seems that many truly wonderful courses and books are not so designed. For example, it is unclear if a course that teaches the "great ideas" of mathematics to help students appreciate the "beauty and wonder" of mathematics advances a student's quantitative literacy.

Even with the concerns that have been raised in the last several paragraphs, this collection of essays suggest that we have moved a long way in the past ten years in our understanding of quantitative literacy, our ability to implement effective programs to promote it, and the interest in many types of institutions across the country to address the issue.

As a closing remark, I would like to say thank you to Joan Steffen, and the MAA *Notes* Editorial Board without whose help compiling and editing these essays would have been much more difficult and time consuming.

Contents

History
and
Context

Some Historical Notes

Linda Sons

Northern Illinois University, DeKalb, IL

Introduction

The classic children's book "The Little Engine that Could" provides an interesting framework to use in reflecting on the movements in the past which have led up to the quantitative literacy programs at colleges and universities today. Whether there was a "happy" train to begin with which was trying to haul "toys and food to the other side of the mountain" is an unanswered question, but certainly there were some "well-intentioned" trains which had engines that either stopped "with a jerk" or slowed to a crawl while yearning for the aid of other engines.

In looking at quantitative literacy through the years, this essay seeks to familiarize the reader with some of the books and proceedings related to quantitative literacy (past and present), define some terms regularly used in discussing quantitative literacy, trace the development of the content and pedagogy for quantitative literacy programs as it evolved through the work of the Mathematical Association of America (MAA) and the National Council of Teachers of Mathematics (NCTM), note connections of the quantitative literacy "movement" with other curricular movements being advocated or occurring in the mathematical community, and link these movements with changes in text material and pedagogical sources.

Early Movements by the MAA

For the past fifty years the natural MAA curricular group to consider mathematics for general education in college has been its Committee on the Undergraduate Program in Mathematics (CUPM—first called just CUP). In the summer of 1954, even before Sputnik, the committee sponsored a writing group for the development of an experimental general mathematics text for all "normally" prepared first year college students. The text *Universal Mathematics* appeared in two parts with writing continuing from 1954 to 1958. The work presupposed students having at least two, and preferably two and one-half units of high school mathematics (a rather common attainment for college-bound students in the 1950s). It seems that the intent, even by its title, was some minimal expectation for all college students, but the term quantitative literacy was not used.

While there was some pilot-testing of *Universal Mathematics*, CUPM's attention was diverted to other matters in the years that followed. Its efforts led to the booklet *A General Curriculum in Mathematics for Colleges* (GCMC), aimed at describing "a basic mathematics program ... to accommodate today's diversity of students and their objectives." In connection with a section in that report called "One-year mathematics to satisfy a B.A. requirement" remarks are made that say no description is given of a special year-course in mathematics appreciation for students at liberal arts colleges, because the Committee felt it better for such students to pursue either a year of calculus or a semester of calculus followed by a course in probability which used the calculus. The report section then provides a few remarks pertaining to college students in general, but makes the disclaimer that these "remarks do NOT have the force of a recommendation, since CUPM has not yet considered in detail this important curricular problem" (page 25). Further, the report is punctuated with concerns for the huge increase in the number of students going to college in the 1960s and the shortage of faculty available to cover the students' needs in mathematics.

In 1969 CUPM presented *A Transfer Curriculum in Mathematics* and advocated that Math A described therein have as an objective the development of mathematical literacy. Such literacy was defined as "the ability to read and understand mathematical statements and the ability to translate into mathematical language (making proper use of logical connectives) statements and problems expressed in ordinary English. Continual practice should be given to solving 'word problems' and in analyzing mathematical statements, with particular emphasis on developing the ability to understand and to use deductive reasoning." Math A was intended for those who needed reinforcement of their high school mathematics as well as preparation for calculus. It was not prescribed for all college students, nor was any specific course with a literacy objective set out for all college students. Math A was essentially a slower-paced version of the "old-fashioned" algebra, trigonometry, and analytic geometry. The 1969 report "deferred the consideration of lower-level or non-university parallel courses as a matter for further study." In January 1970, CUPM formed a Panel on Basic Mathematics to provide the "further study". The considerations of the Panel were presented in January 1971 in the booklet *A Course in Basic Mathematics for Colleges*. The thrust of the January 1971 report was to describe a single flexible one-year course, known as Math E, together with a linked mathematics laboratory.

Math E was proposed to replace some of the courses being taught below college algebra. The course's main aim was stated to be "to provide the students with enough mathematical literacy for adequate participation in the daily life of our present society." The associated laboratory was intended to be used to remedy deficiencies in arithmetic and provide opportunity for drill in algebraic manipulation. A secondary aim of the course was to provide enough algebraic skill and use of mathematical language so as to enable students who desired to do so to continue on to Math A. The course was expected to reach out to students of a higher age level and greater maturity than those coming immediately out of high school, ones for whom it might be their terminal course in mathematics. Still, the course was not viewed as defining literacy for all college students.

Continued efforts by CUPM on the curriculum for four years of college mathematics led to the publication in 1972 of *Commentary on A General Curriculum in Mathematics for Colleges*. The intent of the Commentary was to note that many of the 1965 suggestions were still relevant, but to also modify some 1965 suggestions because of recent developments. The 1965 statement about a special one-year course in mathematics appreciation for students in liberal arts colleges was repeated with the further view expressed "that mathematics is best appreciated through a serious effort to acquire some of its content and methodology and to examine some of its applications"(page 43).

Turmoil in the nation in the early 1970s led to many colleges and universities in America abandoning general education programs, "core" curricula, and even minimal competencies. The climate certainly was not ripe for CUPM to be making recommendations regarding mathematics for ALL college students. However, by 1978 there was revived interest in general education programs and minimal requirements for students, and CUPM formed a committee to consider the mathematical needs of ALL college students.

Connections with Influential Forces in School Mathematics

Concern for school mathematics and its teaching became a national concern when Sputnik streaked across the sky in 1957. The call went out for improved teaching of mathematics and an improved curriculum. CUPM had an active panel on teacher training for the schools, and a number of professional organizations went together to obtain National Science Foundation support for the School Mathematics Study Group (SMSG). In the summers of 1960 and 1961 SMSG writers produced materials for an improved K–12 curriculum. These were field-tested (many at university lab schools) and a longitudinal assessment was carried out in the period 1966 until 1970.

The SMSG materials were part of what came to be called "the new mathematics"—a movement at its best aimed primarily at teaching for greater understanding of the mathematical concepts at the school level where too often total rote had taken over as a teaching methodology. Unfortunately, the new materials were thrust by well meaning educational administrators on teachers who were not prepared to properly use them. The consequences of such actions led to a "back to the basics" counter movement seeking to reinstall the once prevalent rote memorization teaching methodology and intending to remedy the concern the public held because of problems evidenced largely on test results. These happenings came in the early 1970s when colleges and universities in America were abandoning general education programs and minimal competencies.

As the 1970s rolled on, the thrust of the two movements in school mathematics which appeared to be counter to each other was to be taken up by the leadership of the National Council of Teachers of Mathematics (NCTM) and its affiliated groups to articulate realistic and responsible directions mathematics programs should take in the 1980s. Using a series of studies funded by the National Science Foundation, two mathematics assessments of the NAEP, and an extensive survey of diverse sectors of the society (a project called PRISM), the NCTM made its recommendations in April, 1980 labeled *An Agenda for Action*. The Agenda consisted of eight recommendations--three of which were: 1) Problem solving must be the focus of school mathematics in the 1980s; 2) The concept of basic skills in mathematics must encompass more than computational facility; and 3) Public support for mathematics instruction must be raised to a level commensurate with the importance of mathematical understanding to individuals and society. Accordingly, the early 1980s yearbooks of the NCTM provided material supportive of the Agenda's implementation.

Actions of the Early Eighties

The report of the CUPM panel formed in January, 1978, was published in the American Mathematical Monthly in 1982. It noted that "In a relatively severe, but all too common form, ignorance of mathematics amounts to a form of 'functional illiteracy'." It sought to answer the question: What mathematics should every graduate of an American college or university know?

In response to surveys to determine the current status of minimal mathematics expectations at American colleges and universities, the panel found such great diversity that it could not describe an everywhere attainable goal. Its primary recommendation was: All college graduates, with rare exceptions, should be expected to have demonstrated reasonable proficiency in the mathematical sciences.

To implement this recommendation the panel stated that every college or university should formulate, with adequate concreteness, what this "reasonable proficiency" should mean for its students; define how students should demonstrate this proficiency; and establish this demonstration as a degree requirement. It noted that: "The idea that all college graduates should be expected to have acquired a certain familiarity with mathematics rests in part on the well-founded belief that such a familiarity is necessary for effective functioning in contemporary life, and certainly for life in those spheres college graduates are most likely to enter." The ignorance the panel deplored, and the belief it expressed for students being able to function mathematically, were soon to receive national attention.

Both the MAA and the NCTM were working on reform in the teaching and learning of mathematics when *A Nation at Risk* was published by the National Commission on Excellence in Education in 1983. The publication of *A Nation at Risk* led to a flurry of activity including a retreat sponsored by the Conference Board for Mathematics at which the group endorsed the establishment of a set of standards to be drawn up by the NCTM and the formation of the Mathematics Science Education Board, an umbrella organization with representatives from the mathematical sciences, education, and industry and business that could provide overall direction for a broad reform movement in mathematics education.

Calls for Change and Reform

One by one reports issued at the national level pointed out that mathematically illiterate individuals would not be able to participate fully in the life of our contemporary society. Among such reports were: 1) *The Mathematics Report Card: Are We Measuring Up?* (Educational Testing Service, 1988); 2) *Everybody Counts: A Report to the Nation on the Future of Mathematics Education* (National Academy Press, 1989); 3) *50 Hours: A Core Curriculum for College Students* (National Endowment for the Humanities, 1989); and 4) *Moving Beyond Myths: Revitalizing Undergraduate Mathematics* (National Academy Press, 1991).

In March of 1989 while some of these reports were at the printers or still in preparation, the NCTM released its *Curriculum and Evaluation Standards for School Mathematics* (usually shortened to *The Standards*). These were to be followed in 1991 by NCTM's *Professional*

Standards for Teaching Mathematics. Also appearing in 1991 was a report from the MAA Committee on the Mathematical Education of Teachers named *A Call for Change: Recommendations for the Mathematical Preparation of Teachers of Mathematics*.

Begun in 1980 the Educational Equality Project of the College Board aimed to strengthen the academic quality of secondary education and to ensure equality of opportunity for post-secondary education for all students. In 1983 (the year *A Nation at Risk* appeared) the Project published its *Academic Preparation for College: What Students Need To Know And Be Able To Do*. The basic competency in mathematics and the specific preparation in mathematics for a college entrant detailed in the booklet defined a level of knowledge and skills expected for all high school graduates intending to do college work.

Also in the early 1980s, the American Statistical Society joined forces with the NCTM to provide curriculum materials and in-service training so that mathematics teachers in the secondary schools could effectively incorporate basic concepts of statistics and probability into their teaching. Published in 1987, the resources carried the (unfortunate) title *Quantitative Literacy Series*. Their usefulness formed some background for the heavy data analysis perspective prevalent in strands of the NCTM *Standards*.

Another call for change in the 1980s was one to reform the teaching of calculus. After a remarkable session of discussion at the national professional meetings, the Sloan Foundation sponsored a conference/workshop at Tulane University in January of 1986 to develop alternative curriculum and teaching methods for calculus at the college level. The report on that conference *Toward A Lean and Lively Calculus* appeared in the MAA Note series late in 1986. In 1987 the Sloan Foundation funded a convocation *Calculus For a New Century* at the National Academy of Sciences, and the National Science Foundation supported the work of many calculus reform projects from 1988 through 1994.

Two other movements were prevalent in the 1980s which also impacted quantitative literacy issues. On the one hand there were those developing new liberal arts courses--many funded by the Sloan Foundation and aimed for elective use by students at four-year somewhat selective institutions, and on the other hand, there were those seeking to foster a new view of mathematics by the public. In the latter area, John Paulos published the book *Innumeracy*, whereas the television series funded by the Annenberg Foundation and the 1988 book *For All Practical Purposes* (now in Second Edition) simultaneously contributed to both movements.

Late in 1989 with *The Standards* now published by the NCTM, CUPM formed a committee on quantitative literacy requirements (hereafter referred to as the 1989 QL Committee) to frame recommendations which would mesh with the new pre-college standards and be realistically achievable in the college years. The Committee studied the many documents and books noted in this essay (and more), gathered input by conducting a series of well-attended sessions at the national mathematics professional meetings (including a debate on the use of college algebra as a requirement which was attended by about 200 people), gathered input and fostered debate through essays and announcements in national professional newsletter publications, considered the views of societies such as the Sigma Xi, sponsored a Focus Group discussion session reported in the 1992 publication *Heeding the Call for Change*, and studied writing on overcoming math anxiety, studied research available from mathematics educators—especially on problem solving—and conducted a massive poll of colleges and universities across the United States to determine the then current objectives and requirements concerning mathematics for all students.

The 1989 QL Committee's report which CUPM adopted in January 1995, was NOT a distillation of the current status in the mathematical community regarding quantitative literacy, but a visionary document with recommendations supported by suggestions and approaches intended to enable the recommendations to be ACHIEVABLE. In some ways the current volume is a testimony to their usefulness.

QL Terms Defined

The 1989 QL Committee agreed that every college graduate should be able to apply simple mathematical methods to the solution of real-world problems. It further defined a quantitatively literate college graduate in terms of five capabilities. That is, such a graduate should be able to:

1) Interpret mathematical models such as formulas, graphs, tables, and schematics, and draw inferences from them.

2) Represent mathematical information symbolically, visually, numerically, and verbally.

3) Use arithmetical, algebraic, geometric and statistical methods to solve problems.

4) Estimate and check answers to mathematical problems in order to determine reasonableness, identify alternatives, and select optimal results.

5) Recognize that mathematical and statistical methods have limits.

While these capabilities could be attained at varying levels, the 1989 QL Committee further explained its intent and how these capabilities would mesh with *The Standards* of the NCTM for the college graduate. It noted that the college graduate should be expected to have deeper and broader experiences than those who only graduate from high school and that the level of sophistication and maturity of thinking expected should extend to reasoning which is commensurate with the college experience. "College students should be expected to go beyond routine problem solving to handle problem situations of greater complexity and diversity, and to connect ideas and procedures more readily with other topics both within and outside mathematics." Quantitative literacy for college students is seen in one sense as extending the concept of "mathematical power" in *The Standards*, including some mathematical content, but especially involving the ability to *use* concepts, procedures, and intellectual processes with a greater degree of versatility in approaching and solving problems or understanding quantitative information.

The British use the word "numeracy" to mean mathematical literacy, but in the American mind this word conjures up the notion of just number sense at its lowest levels and not the broader implications set by the definition above.

The 1989 QL Committee recognized that the introduction of a single course would not enable a college student to move from the high school attainment of mathematical power to the college level of quantitative literacy. Research by mathematics educators noted that there were five aspects of intellectual competency which provided a framework for problem solving. These included knowledge of concepts, fact, procedures, and strategies or heuristics, but also knowledge of how and when to use these in a manner which is effective and efficient. Further, students require practice in the acquisition of the habits of sense-making, interpretation, and exercise of control. Advocated in the 1989 QL Committee report was thus a PROGRAM in quantitative literacy. A quantitative literacy PROGRAM normally has the following components:

1) Explicit requirements of quantitative experience for college entry or for entry into courses or experiences which can be credited towards the baccalaureate degree;

2) Placement testing intended to help determine appropriate entry into the quantitative literacy program;

3) Foundation experience(s) to be accomplished ordinarily within the first year of the student's college work;

4) Further quantitative experiences in diverse contexts to be accomplished during a student's sophomore, junior, and senior college years so as to be interspersed throughout the work of these years.

The foundation experiences have generally been specific courses designated by colleges. They are intended to provide some resources in mathematics, but, more importantly, the knowledge of strategies and heuristics and guidance on when to use these in conjunction with the mathematical knowledge. FOUNDATIONS courses are intended to introduce students to the complexity of thought and maturity of thinking expected in the college experience; such courses should provide a background on which a student can draw as the student encounters mathematical thought and quantitative reasoning throughout the undergraduate curriculum. A quantitative literacy PROGRAM also includes CONTINUATION experiences. CONTINUATION experiences may be courses or projects or other aspects of the undergraduate curriculum which enable the student to PRACTICE the patterns of thought introduced in the FOUNDATIONS experiences. CONTINUATION experiences are an important component for enabling the student to genuinely extend the concept of mathematical power, and to more fully acquire the capabilities intended for the college graduate. Ideally, quantitative reasoning should permeate the undergraduate curriculum the same way quantitative data permeates society.

Content and Pedagogy

What should be the content of a "foundations course" or the nature of the so-called foundations experience? Whatever the actual mathematics involved in the foundations work, the content would be a solid introduction to the type of quantitative reasoning expected of the student. Thus the content involves the student actually DOING quantitative reasoning and not just being exposed to it. Depending on the accomplishment in mathematics of students as they enter college, the foundations work provides resources in mathematical knowledge, problem-solving strategies, interpretive forms, formulation of problems, and engagement in the use of these in genuine applications. As noted in the 1989 report, "there are plenty of mathematical topics with both utility and beauty, so beauty need not be sacrificed." The mathematical topics chosen should link with the prerequisite knowledge assumed. The content chosen also provides a basis for instructors in other fields to show students how to apply the foundation knowledge in gaining understanding in that field through quantitative reasoning. Certainly a FOUNDATIONS course cannot be the "old-fashioned" intermediate algebra or college algebra course or the "old-fashioned" liberal arts mathematics appreciation course.

The pedagogical approach for a quantitative literacy foundations course or experience is the study of mathematics in context. And the context is expected to relate to student interest, daily life, and possible future work settings even when the character is remedial. Of course, the expectation for a college student is to extend study to the completion of work beyond that of remedial character.

Teaching methods for quantitative literacy courses are not lecture and listen, but they may involve group work, projects, writing, and many of the approaches advocated by those in the calculus reform movement. In particular, teaching methods generally enable students to be actively involved in building their understanding while connecting with their prior ideas.

Historically, quantitative literacy courses have not been prevalent in colleges and universities across the United States. Instead there have been many remedial and many algebra courses taught which often aimed only at computational skills, and usually by means of rote learning. Or there have been liberal arts courses required which often covered the topics faculty WANTED to teach and/or provided a survey of mathematical ideas while doing little to develop the student's reasoning powers. In fact, they provided a hurdle to jump for degree requirements, but little "carry away" value.

Some selective four-year institutions seemed to be content with the mathematical knowledge their students had upon entry--namely four years of high school mathematics. These institutions appeared to be unconcerned with whether their students could use the mathematics they had studied in everyday quantitative settings or in their study of other disciplines in their college careers. The development of quantitative reasoning commensurate with the development of the college mind was not an agenda item for such colleges.

At the time the 1989 QL Committee gave its report there were very few foundations courses in the United States and certainly a real lack of text material or other course material available to support the introduction of such courses. Indeed, because of the varying levels of entry into foundations courses brought on by the varying level of mathematics required for admissions at colleges and universities, a wide variety of material was required. Since 1996 however, a number of colleges have introduced foundations courses for students whose college programs require no hierarchy of mathematics, and some text materials are now in second or third edition. Further, at a number of colleges, the liberal arts course, traditionally focused on aesthetic topics, has taken on a shift towards having at least a quantitative literacy component, and some "old" liberal arts mathematics books in latest editions have shifted to having such a component too. In fact, for some lower division courses commonly taught which might be entry points for students in a multiple entry quantitative literacy program, "reformed" text material provides a quantitative literacy component.

Whatever the entry point into a foundations experience, the 1989 QL Committee noted that the experience by definition should be a natural transition from the processes now listed as the new *Standards* towards the depth expected in a college career. These processes of problem solving, reasoning, connections, communication, and representation are to be introduced with appropriate mathematics in context in the foundations experience encountered early in college study and developed in continuation experiences as the college years unfold.

Conclusion

So where IS "the little engine that could"? Since the adoption by CUPM in January 1995 (and the publication in 1996) of the 1989 QL Committee report, a large number of colleges and universities have at least started on a quantitative literacy program by developing a foundations course. In the State of Illinois the adoption by the so-called Illinois Articulation Initiative of the viewpoint that a foundations course be included in its general education program has led many institutions to develop such a course. With foundations courses firmly in place, work can be done to foster continuation experiences.

Nationally, various efforts supporting quantitative literacy, noted in another essay in this volume, have kept the little engine moving a little faster. While some national reform efforts in mathematics at the collegiate level may be playing the role of having passed by a slow moving train, the little engine IS moving.

Among other movements the little engine is being helped by the work of the new NCTM *Standards*, and SIGMAA QL, the new special interest group formed at the January 2004 national MAA meeting should be greasing the wheels even more.

This volume itself should be helpful to colleges and universities in developing a quantitative literacy program more fully. In doing so, it will enable the little switch engine to haul "toys and food to the other side of the mountain" for many more college students!

References

Summer Writing Group of the Dept. of Mathematics, Univ. of Kansas, Universal Mathematics. (1954). *Part I: Functions and Limits*. Univ. of Kansas, Student Union Book Store.

Bennett, J. & Briggs, W. (2002). *Using and Understanding Mathematics: A Quantitative Reasoning Approach*, (2nd ed.). Addison-Wesley.

Cheney, L. V. (1989). *50 Hours: A Core Curriculum for College Students*. National Endowment for the Humanities.

College Board, Academic Preparation For College: (1983). *What Students Need to Know and Be Able to Do*. The College Board.

CUPM, (1971). *A Course in Basic Mathematics for Colleges*, MAA.

——, (1965). *A General Curriculum in Mathematics for Colleges*. MAA.

——, (1969). *A Transfer Curriculum in Mathematics*. MAA.

——, (1972). *Commentary on "A General Curriculum in Mathematics for Colleges"*. MAA.

——, (1982). "Minimal Mathematical Competencies for College Graduates." *Amer. Math. Monthly* 89, 266–272; reprinted in Steen, L., (1989). *Reshaping College Mathematics* (MAA Notes Number 13, pp. 103–108). MAA.

Davis, R.L. , ed. (1958 CUPM). *Universal Mathematics, Part II: Elementary Mathematics of Sets with Applications*.

Douglas, R. G., ed., (1986). *Toward a Lean and Lively Calculus* (MAA Notes Series #6). MAA.

Educational Testing Service (1988). *The Mathematics Report Card: Are We Measuring Up?* ETS.

Garfunkel, S.. ed., (1991). *For All Practical Purposes*, (2nd ed.). W. H. Freeman.

Goldberg, S., ed., (1990). *The New Liberal Arts Program: A 1990 Report*, Alfred P. Sloan Foundation.

Harrison, A. (1990). *Entry-Level Undergraduate Courses in Sciences, Mathematics, and Engineering: An Investment in Human Resources,* The Scientific Research Society.

Leitzel, J., ed., (1991). *A Call for Change: Recommendations for the Mathematical Preparation of Teachers of Mathematics*, MAA.

National Commission on Excellence in Education, A Nation At Risk (1983). *The Imperative for Educational Reform*, U.S. Government Printing Office.

NCTM, (1980). *An Agenda for Action: Recommendations for School Mathematics of the 1980s*, NCTM.

——, (1989). *Curriculum and Evaluation Standards for School Mathematics*, NCTM.

——, (2000). *Principles and Standards for School Mathematics*, NCTM.

——, (1981). *Priorities in School Mathematics*, NCTM.

——, (1991). *Professional Standards for Teaching Mathematics*, NCTM.

NRC, (1989). *Everybody Counts: A Report to the Nation on the Future of Mathematics Education*, National Academy Press.

——, (1991). *Moving Beyond Myths: Revitalizing Undergraduate Mathematics*, National Academy Press.

Paulos, J. (1988). *Innumeracy: Mathematical Illiteracy and Its Consequences*, Hill and Wang.

Piper, W. (1998 reteller). *The Little Engine That Could,* Platt and Munk. (original entitled "I Think I Can" published in 1930).

Quantitative Literacy Series (1987). (A project of the American Statistical Association) Dale Seymour Publications.

Schufelt, G., ed., (1983). The Agenda in Action, *1983 Yearbook of the NCTM*, NCTM.

Sons, L. R., ed., (1996). *Quantitative Reasoning for College Students: A Complement to the Standards*, MAA.

——, (1992). "Reaching for Quantitative Literacy" in L. Steen, ed., *Heeding the Call for Change* (MAA Notes Number 22), MAA, pp. 95–118.

——, (October 1990). "What Mathematics Should Every College Graduate Know?" *UME Trends*.

Sons, L. R., Nicholls, P. J., & Stephen, J.B., (2003). *Mathematical Thinking and Quantitative Reasoning*, (3rd ed.). Kendall/Hunt.

Steen, L. A., ed., (1987). *Calculus for a New Century* (MAA Notes Series #8), MAA.

Issues, Policies, and Activities in the Movement for Quantitative Literacy

Susan L. Ganter
Clemson University, Clemson, SC

Introduction

We live in a society filled with quantitative information about social, economic, and medical issues that are critical to decisions we make. In this technological age, the average citizen is confronted with a wealth of quantitative knowledge that can be overwhelming and often misleading or incorrect (Cox, 2000). Many examples exist in areas as diverse as developing a budget for the AIDS crisis in South Africa, religion, sales profits, college rankings, and politics.

This fundamental change in how our culture shares information requires that every citizen attain a high level of quantitative literacy (QL). Yet students still learn quantitative skills in settings that are isolated from real world experiences, and therefore complete their education with inadequate quantitative abilities, unable to deal with the numbers that appear in everyday life (Steen, 2001).

As much as 20 years ago, national reports were calling for higher standards in mathematics and a curriculum that would help students learn to "apply mathematics in everyday situations" (U.S. Department of Education, 1983). The National Council of Teachers of Mathematics (NCTM) emphasizes the importance of QL in Principles and Standards for School Mathematics (NCTM, 2000), stating that technology and quantitative information have become commonplace for today's American citizen, significant change from life just a few decades ago. In addition, the level of mathematical thinking and problem solving required in the current workplace has increased dramatically. The Standards state that QL in the form of applications and problems from the world around us should be part of the mathematics curriculum at every level in elementary and secondary schools.

Unfortunately, most students tend to avoid highly quantitative courses in mathematics and science once they enter secondary school (Carnevale & Desrochers, 2003). And who can blame them? The importance of mathematics in the curriculum is not made obvious to students, and there is certainly no explicit vision for QL (Kirst, 2003). The decontextualized nature of the traditional mathematics curriculum, and its use as a filter for other courses, is a system that has failed many students, especially women and minorities (Steen, 2001). Therefore, it is critical that QL be seen as critical not only to quantitative disciplines outside mathematics, but also as critical to effective comprehension and communication when solving a multitude of problems (Brakke, 2003; Steen, 1998; 2000; 2001).

And what about college graduates? The importance of QL is now equal to that of verbal literacy, and both have become qualities of an educated person in today's society (Steen, 2001). Unfortunately, the current level of QL among college graduates is low (Madison, 2003). The foremost objective of higher education should be to produce well-educated, enlightened citizens who can reason, communicate, solve problems, and be leaders in their communities. Thus, quantitative literacy for college graduates should imply different knowledge and skills, both in depth and quality, from that expected of secondary school graduates. However, the typical college student enrolls in mathematics courses that focus on different mathematical content than is actually needed by the student (Carnevale & Desrochers, 2003). Significant mathematical ideas and techniques should be developed within applied contexts that motivate the use of mathematics as an obvious and powerful tool for understanding and problem solving; i.e., a student strong in trigonometry and calculus does not necessarily comprehend data and numbers as used in society (Steen, 2001).

As mentioned in Son's article in this volume, a quantitatively literate college graduate should be able to:

1. Interpret mathematical models such as formulas, graphs, and tables.

2. Interpret mathematical information that is presented symbolically, visually, numerically, or verbally, and be comfortable using these formats in his/her own mathematical representations.

3. Use appropriate combinations of arithmetic, algebra, geometry, statistics, and technology to solve problems.

4. Estimate and check answers to mathematical problems in order to determine reasonableness, identify alternatives, and select optimal results.

5. Recognize the limits of mathematical and statistical models and be able to explain those limitations in context (Steen, 2001; 2003).

College graduates should be expected to go beyond routine problem solving to handle problem situations of greater complexity and diversity than secondary school graduates, and to connect ideas and procedures more readily with other topics both within and outside mathematics.

The ability of higher education to impact this learning process, however, is often limited by the inconsistent messages sent to K-12 educators about what quantitative skills are important (Kirst, 2003). Better articulation and common goals between K-12 education, higher education, and the larger political and economic environment would help to solve this problem. However, uncoordinated decision making between these constituencies have made effective articulation virtually impossible (Carnevale & Desrochers, 2003; Kirst, 2003; Madison, 2003). The current secondary mathematics curriculum rushes students to calculus, stating that the primary reason for this rush is to better prepare students for the college mathematics curriculum. In fact, the majority of courses taught at the college level, even at many major research universities, are well below calculus (Somerville, 2003).

A similar disjuncture occurs in the testing process used for student placement in college mathematics courses. College placement tests in mathematics focus on standard precalculus material, while tests with similar placement goals that are administered by individual states to 12th graders focus on elementary algebra and geometry (Somerville, 2003). With the exception of the Advanced Placement (AP) Program, there are no major efforts to provide a smooth transition between secondary school and college, leaving students to wonder what it all means in their general education experiences in mathematics during the first two college years (Kirst, 2003). And, of course, none of these exams send a message that QL is important, at any level (Somerville, 2003).

Defining QL and the Surrounding Issues

"QL is a major hole in the undergraduate curriculum."

—Doyle Daves, Rensselaer Polytechnic Institute

Quantitative literacy is the ability to understand and interpret numerical information encountered in all areas of life, a skill that has become important primarily because of the technology boom of the late 20th century (Steen, 2001). The current secondary school and college curricula, largely the same as that of the 1960s, focus heavily on mathematical literacy; i.e., the mathematical skills needed for future courses, especially in mathematics and science. However, most graduates will have a much greater need for QL which, unlike mathematics and many other traditional school subjects, cannot be separated from context (Steen, 2001). Specifically, quantitative information presented as statistics is everywhere and although QL and statistics are not the same, they are intricately linked (Steen, 2001).

Congress defines literacy as "an individual's ability to read, write, and speak in English and compute and solve problems at levels of proficiency necessary to function on the job and in society, to achieve one's goals, and to develop one's knowledge and potential" (Colwell, 2003). Using this definition as a backdrop, QL can be loosely characterized by examples at three levels:

1. *Citizens reading the newspaper.* In a technological society, citizens are constantly confronted with numerical data and information. Decisions that they make concerning this information can dramatically change quality of life and personal well-being, for better or worse. In addition, to be a productive and contributing member of society, citizens must be informed jurors, voters, and workers, implying the need to understand the issues presented about policy, economics, and a host of other areas that utilize quantitative data.

2. *Reporters interpreting data.* The initial interpretation of quantitative information is often made by the media, newspapers, radio, and the like. Therefore, it is important that reporters understand the information well enough to first make an accurate interpretation, and then to write about the data in a way that conveys the intended message to the reader.

3. *Staffers developing bills for Congress.* Data from a variety of sources are used in the development of national policy in all areas. Congressional representatives and their staff must be able to decide what data are relevant and important, and then interpret their use in the writing of bills. Such writing involves a high level of comfort and ability in working with numerical information, with enormous ramifications for incorrect use of the information.

Individual citizens are most concerned with issues that have an effect on their daily lives (Colwell, 2003). Examples of societal events for which the average citizen needed QL include the anthrax crisis, the unprecedented fluctuations in the stock market and the resulting influence on interest rates, and the SARS epidemic (Colwell, 2003). Decisions made by individuals about how to act or react in these situations were directly impacted by the degree to which data presented by the media were understood and challenged. These examples and a host of others make clear the need to teach quantitative literacy as part of our educational system at all levels.

In addition, major needs of the workplace in the U.S. are not being met by the current mathematics curriculum (Carnevale & Desrochers, 2003; Madison, 2003). For example, a mathematics curriculum that is more accessible to more individuals is critical to the creation of better job opportunities for a larger percentage of the working public, since those with stronger quantitative skills secure higher paying jobs than their less quantitatively-minded peers (Carnevale & Desrochers, 2003). In fact, $63 billion is invested annually by businesses for technical training, most of which is remediation for K–16 educa-

tion. However, the public does not seem to understand the growing importance of QL, or the consequences of ignoring it, a situation that, ironically, may be due to the innumeracy of the average citizen (Steen, 2001).

In contrast to quantitative literacy, mathematical literacy can be defined as the "basic skills of arithmetic, algebra, and geometry that historically have formed the core of school mathematics" and which are necessary for the study of advanced mathematics. (Kirst, 2003). The need for QL does not imply the elimination of mathematical literacy as an important educational skill, but instead a need to balance mathematical and quantitative literacy. In fact, basic mathematical skills and the ability to use these skills in versatile ways is generally much more important than advanced mathematical knowledge (Carnevale & Desrochers, 2003).

Therefore, three dimensions necessary for QL, in combination with mathematical literacy, emerge as follows:

1. *Elements of QL such as*: confidence with mathematics, cultural appreciation of the role of data in society, interpreting data, logical thinking, making decisions, mathematics in context, number sense, practical skills, prerequisite knowledge, and symbol sense;

2. *Areas of life utilizing expressions of QL, such as*: citizenship, culture, education, professions, personal finance, personal health, management, and work; and,

3. *Skills needed for QL, such as*: arithmetic, data, computers, modeling, statistics, chance, and reasoning (Steen, 2001).

All three of these dimensions must be addressed if we are to achieve QL for every citizen.

The Academic and Political Realities of QL

The scope of QL needs to respond to the fact that students must deal with real contexts and real data. QL must be everywhere in the curriculum, in all disciplines and all courses, implying that each institution must find its own solution to the problems of identifying the level of QL required of its graduates and the mechanism by which they attain this literacy.

In an academic environment, this means that QL is a shared responsibility. Mathematics faculty, non-mathematics faculty and administrators are responsible for consciously keeping QL in classroom conversations (Madison, 2001; Steen, 2001). Currently, quantitative skills are not well integrated with other disciplines, in spite of many mathematical and statistical applications in virtually every discipline (Brakke, 2003). Instructors should take advantage of the frequent opportunities to promote quantitative understanding.

In addition, QL does not have a department or "slice" of the academic schedule, so it is at a disadvantage when competing with the traditional curriculum. Therefore, it is important to develop a supportive structure that will help to promote buy-in by all disciplines. Since the types of quantitative courses that are taught, and how they are taught, is heavily influenced by the mathematics curriculum, such a structure must include strong support and leadership from the mathematics community, especially college faculty, generated via discussions at national meetings, articles in mathematics publications, and professional development opportunities (Somerville, 2003).

Currently, QL is not part of the priorities in the development of educational policies, both within the K-12 system and in higher education (Somerville, 2003). There must be recognition and appreciation of the need for quantitative knowledge (Colwell, 2003). However, there are many pressures on the educational system that make the changes necessary to achieve QL for all students very difficult (Madison, 2003). So, in the end, it is textbook publishers and private testing firms that have the greatest influence on the curricula for quantitative courses at all levels, although the list of organizations and individuals that have an influence on the policies that guide these curricula is extensive and unwieldy (see Kirst, 2003, page 111). Not only should these influential groups be encouraged to emphasize QL, but educational policies should be developed to tip the scales of power so that all parts of the educational system contribute to QL curriculum development as appropriate (Steen, 2001).

Activities That Support QL

Somerville (2003) states that a big part of the solution may be as simple as agreeing upon what we mean by "college ready" in terms of quantitative skills. Discussions with professionals from a variety of disciplinary areas indicate that virtually everyone agrees on the importance of QL. However, there is little consensus on exactly what that means (Steen, 2001).

Madison (2003) points to two other needs if the QL movement is to have the widespread support necessary for success:

1. Systematic evidence to support the call for stronger QL education; and

2. Clear descriptions of the levels of QL and of strategies for how they can be assessed (page 6).

Specifically, we need standards for what constitutes QL at different ages and educational levels if we are to know that there has been progress. Establishing levels of QL is even more important as the influence of science and technology on our society grows (Colwell, 2003).

Successfully educating a quantitatively literate citizenry also calls for the "democratization of mathematics," or the process of making mathematics "more accessible and responsive to the needs of all students, citizens, and workers." Curricula must coincide with the current cultural, political, and economic goals (Carnevale & Desrochers, 2003, page 29), while also helping every citizen attain a level of QL appropriate to everyday life (Colwell, 2003). The many constituencies for which QL is important; medicine, business, politics, and education, just to name a few, must be motivated to act (Steen, 2001). And, professionals in the higher education arena, especially mathematicians, must stand united in their definition of the skills that constitute quantitative literacy, their support for QL in grades 11–14, and their notion of how and where it fits in the mathematics curriculum (Kirst, 2003; Somerville, 2003; Steen, 2001). "Mathematics is everywhere" should be the message (Colwell, 2003, page 244).

References

Brakke, D.F. (2003). "Addressing Societal and Workforce Needs." In B.L. Madison and L.A. Steen (Eds), *Quantitative Literacy: Why numeracy matters for schools and colleges.* Princeton, NJ: The National Council on Education and the Disciplines.

Carnevale, A.P. & Desrochers, D.M. (2003). "The Democratization of Mathematics." In B.L. Madison and L.A. Steen (Eds), *Quantitative Literacy: Why numeracy matters for schools and colleges.* Princeton, NJ: The National Council on Education and the Disciplines.

Colwell, R. (2003). "Quantitative Literacy Goals: Are we making progress?" In B.L. Madison and L.A. Steen (Eds), *Quantitative Literacy: Why numeracy matters for schools and colleges.* Princeton, NJ: The National Council on Education and the Disciplines.

Cox, P. (2000). http://www.psn.net/~xocxoc/math/glossary.htm

Kirst, M.W. (2003). "Articulation and Mathematical Literacy: Political and policy issues." In B.L. Madison and L.A. Steen (Eds), *Quantitative Literacy: Why numeracy matters for schools and colleges.* Princeton, NJ: The National Council on Education and the Disciplines.Madison, B.L. (2001). "Quantitative Literacy: Everybody's orphan." *Focus* 6:10-11. Washington, DC: Mathematical Association of America.

Madison, B.L. (2003). "The Many Faces of Quantitative Literacy." In B.L. Madison and L.A. Steen (Eds), *Quantitative Literacy: Why numeracy matters for schools and colleges.*

Princeton, NJ: The National Council on Education and the Disciplines.

National Council of Teachers of Mathematics (2000). *Principles and Standards for School Mathematics*. Reston, VA:

Somerville, J.I. (2003). "Say What You Mean (and Mean What You Say)." In B.L. Madison and L.A. Steen (Eds), *Quantitative Literacy: Why numeracy matters for schools and colleges*. Princeton, NJ: The National Council on Education and the Disciplines.

Steen, L.A. (1998). "Numeracy: The new literacy for a data-drenched society." *Educational Leadership,* 57:2.

—— (2000). "Reading, Writing, and Numeracy." *Liberal Education.*

—— (2001). "The Case for Quantitative Literacy." In L.A. Steen (Ed.), *Mathematics and Democracy: The case for quantitative literacy.* Princeton, NJ: The National Council on Education and the Disciplines.

—— (2004). *Achieving Quantitative Literacy: An urgent challenge for higher education.* Washington DC: Mathematical Association of America.

U.S. Department of Education, The National Commission on Excellence in Education (1983). *A Nation at Risk: The imperative for educational reform.* Washington, DC: U.S. Government Printing Office.

What Mathematics Should *All* College Students Know?

William L. Briggs
University of Colorado at Denver, Denver, CO

Marie and Alex just paid $250,000 for a house. They made a down payment of $50,000 and assumed a 30-year $200,000 mortgage with a fixed annual interest rate of 7.50% compounded monthly. The house will serve as a residence for several years, but Marie and Alex also view it as an investment, as property values in the neighborhood are projected to increase at a rate of 5% per year in the near future. Suppose the couple sells the house after eight years. Neglecting income tax deductions, do they come out ahead on their investment?

This question doesn't sound like one encountered in most mathematics courses. First, while it is a problem in words, it is not the dreaded word problem that many of us remember from high school mathematics courses. Second, the problem is relevant and immediate; it is unlikely that a student would respond to this question with the familiar "what does this have to do with my life?" Third, while the solution involves fairly elementary mathematics, it is a multi-step process that requires organizing several pieces of information. Fourth, the solution requires some understanding of home mortgages and appreciation of property values; these topics are not considered mathematics, but they represent applications of mathematics. Finally, the problem invites discussion and extensions: What assumptions were made in arriving at an answer? How would the answer change if Marie and Alex are in a 28% tax bracket and income tax deductions are considered? How would the answer change if the interest rate was 8.00% or the appreciation rate was 4% per year? What is the minimum time that Marie and Alex must live in the house before they break even?

We will return to Marie and Alex' story shortly, but some background would be helpful first. For the past twenty years, mathematics educators have been in the midst of a reform. Driven by a series of influential reports concerning the deteriorating state of mathematics education, many mathematics teachers have changed the way they teach. For example, they appreciate the diversity of learning styles in a single classroom; they use computers and calculators in wise ways to extend, rather than replace, students' quantitative skills; and they balance the practical uses of mathematics with more abstract topics. It may be too soon to assess the ultimate outcome of these reform efforts; but many educators believe that they will have a lasting impact on the teaching of mathematics.

However, this reform has been directed largely at students who are in the "calculus pipeline," students taking calculus or precalculus courses. These so-called STEM (science, technology, engineering, and mathematics) students comprise a relatively small fraction of all college and university students who take mathematics courses. Easily half of all post-secondary students who take mathematics courses are not calculus-bound and do so only to satisfy a core curriculum or general education requirement. Therefore these non-STEM students have not benefited greatly from the recent calculus reforms. A pressing question remains: What sort of mathematics course should we offer our liberal arts students? How should they be designed and taught? Or, what mathematics should all college students know?

There are several observations that bear on the teaching of liberal arts mathematics and explain why it is so challenging. First, teaching such courses is not a high priority of many mathematics departments and it is not the concern of many full-time faculty members. Second, students who take liberal arts mathematics courses often are hindered rather than helped by previous mathematics courses and instructors. Not surprisingly, they harbor genuine fears of mathematics, have lost confidence in their quantitative skills, and have little belief that mathematics might be of use in their future. It is unfortunate that because of poor advising or lack of alternatives, many of these students mistakenly end up in the calculus pipeline, taking a college algebra course. The outcome is invariably catastrophic. Third, because of the second observation, providing liberal arts students with a worthwhile experience in their last mathematics course requires overcoming significant psychological obstacles. It cannot be done by subjecting students to more of the same experiences they have had in previous mathematics courses. It can be done by demonstrating the breadth and utility of mathematics with compelling examples of how it affects students' lives in immediate ways. Finally, most mathematics educators have a shared understanding of the content of an algebra course or a calculus course. By contrast, there is no common agreement, at the moment, about the content and expectations of a liberal arts mathematics course. Indeed, transferring such courses between institutions is often difficult.

The task is further complicated by the algebra dilemma, one side of which is the belief that a minimally educated person must be proficient with the abstractions and manipulations of algebra. Risking analogies with other disciplines, this claim might be compared to the belief that a student must be able to identify a diminished seventh in order to have a lifelong appreciation of music, or that Sartre must be read in French in order to understand his philosophy. For calculus-bound students, there is no question that algebra is a gatekeeper and its thorough mastery is essential. For a more general audience, such as liberal arts students, selected algebraic skills are important, but there are other, equally vital skills.

For those of us who have spent much of a lifetime studying, using, and teaching mathematics, it is difficult to concede that when it comes to algebra, less could be better. However, this concession is an important key to designing a successful liberal arts mathematics course. As the story of Marie and Alex and the examples below illustrate, it is possible to identify a wealth of fascinating mathematics and relevant applications that do not rely on extensive algebra and symbolic manipulations. A useful principle is to avoid doing algebra when there is no ulterior purpose and to let the applications determine the necessary mathematics. If an important application requires some algebra, then it is always possible to isolate that particular skill and focus on its mastery, without introducing unnecessary generalizations.

Achieving a reasonable balance with respect to the role of algebra leaves room in a one-semester course for other truly essential topics. These topics should prepare students for careers and lives that will be filled with quantitative information and decisions. For example,

- students must be equipped with strong critical and logical thinking skills, so they can navigate the media and be informed citizens;

- they should have a strong number sense and be proficient at estimation, unit conversions, and the uses of percentages;

- they should be able to read a statistical study — or at least a summary — and evaluate it critically;

- they should possess the mathematical tools needed to make basic financial decisions; and

- they should understand exponential growth and know that it governs everything from populations and prices to tumors and drugs in the blood.

Any remaining time (or a second semester) can be filled with a wealth of breadth topics, such as risk analysis, voting, apportionment, mathematics and the arts, and graph theory, to name only a few.

The consequence of being selective about algebra and including a variety of practical topics is not a watered down mathematics course. The tradeoff is that mathematics becomes part of a larger set of skills, often called quantitative literacy or numeracy, which involves critical thinking, problem formulation, and written and oral communication. The quantitative reasoning approach allows students to see mathematics in a larger interdisciplinary setting that provides new problem-solving and decision-making powers. It presents mathematics in context, as a discipline that is connected to the world around them and essential to an understanding of that world. It also provides students with a much broader survey of mathematics and statistics than afforded by other courses.

As the story of Marie and Alex demonstrates, typical problems in an effective quantitative reasoning course involve the application of relatively elementary mathematics to practical situations. They are often open-ended problems that disabuse students of the belief that answers to mathematics problems are unique and always given in the back of the book. They may involve the use of library or Internet resources for background information. And they have the goal of strengthening students' problem solving confidence and communications skills. Here are five examples (numbered 2 through 6) that further illustrate the nature of quantitative reasoning. These examples involve no mathematics or prerequisite material beyond what is easily covered in a liberal arts course.

2. Suppose that the United States government decided to institute a national lottery, the proceeds of which would be used to retire the federal debt. Based on information that you gather about lottery finances, estimate how much money could be raised (after expenses and prizes) each week in a national lottery. How long would it take to pay off the federal debt assuming that the budget is exactly balanced every year in the future? Do you feel that this is a feasible strategy to pay off the federal debt?

3. Suppose that 1000 people are given a drug test that is 98% accurate and that 50 of the people actually are drug users. What percentage of the positive tests are false positives (nonusers who test positive)? Discuss the implications of this calculation for the practice of drug testing.

4. Recent studies have shown that the probability of a woman getting a false report on a mammogram is 7 in 100 (or 0.07). If a woman has annual mammograms, what is the probability that she has at least one false report in 10 years?

5. The following ballot initiative appeared before Colorado voters in 1992:

   Shall there be an amendment to the Colorado constitution to prohibit the state of Colorado and any of its political subdivisions from adopting or enforcing any law or policy which provides that homosexual, lesbian, or bisexual orientation, conduct, or relationships constitutes or entitles a person to claim any minority or protected status, quota preferences, or discrimination?

   What does a *yes* vote mean?

6. The world population is increasing at a rate of 1.3% per year. At this rate, how long will it take the population to double in size? Estimate the world population near the end of your lifetime.

The development of effective mathematics courses for liberal arts students is happening, albeit on a slow time scale. However, the "client departments" that comprise the liberal arts can hasten the pace. These departments must insist that liberal arts mathematics courses be given the attention lavished on more advanced mathematics courses. They must express to the mathematics faculty their expectations of a valuable mathematical experience for their students. In the end, the development of these courses should be a collaborative and interdisciplinary effort, in which mathematics departments either participate or take the lead. The effect will be to raise the tide of quantitative skills among all students, which is a worthy cause to be sure.

Problem Solutions

1. After 8 years, they have paid approximately $120,000 in interest and their property has appreciated by $119,360. So 8 years is very close to the break-even point.

2. Assuming a federal debt of $6 trillion and lottery revenues of $50 million per week, it would take about 2300 years to pay off the debt.

3. About 28% of the positive tests are false positives.

4. The probability is 0.52 or about 1 in 2.

5. A yes vote is a vote against protected status for homosexual, lesbian, or bisexual people.

6. The doubling time is roughly 55 years. Assuming a current population of 6 billion people, a 20-year old today would see a world population of roughly 13 billion 60 years from now.

References

Bennett, J., Briggs, W. (2004). *Using and Understanding Mathematics: A Quantitative Reasoning Approach* (3rd ed.). Addison Wesley.

National Academy Press, 1991. *Moving Beyond Myths: Revitalizing Undergraduate Mathematics.* National Academy Press, 1990. *A Challenge of Numbers: People in the Mathematical Sciences.*

National Academy Press, 1989. *Everybody Counts: A Report to the Nation on the Future of Mathematics Education.*

National Council on Education and the Disciplines (2001). *Mathematics and Democracy: The Case for Quantitative Literacy*, Lynn Arthur Steen.

Interdisciplinary
and
Interdepartmental Programs

Quantitative Methods for Public Policy

David Bressoud

Macalester College, St. Paul, MN

Introduction

What is quantitative literacy? How do you teach it? How do you measure it? How can you develop a program that will ensure that all undergraduates have it by the time they graduate? During the academic year 2001–02, faculty from Macalester College wrestled with these questions and found answers. These have led to a pilot program, Quantitative Methods for Public Policy (QM4PP), that is currently running at Macalester with funding from the Department of Education's Fund for the Improvement of Post-Secondary Education and the National Science Foundation's Course, Curriculum, and Laboratory Instruction program.

The QM4PP program is interdisciplinary. It involves courses from the sciences, social sciences, and humanities. It is also cohesive. The focus is on public policy, and all courses use the same policy issue as a source of illustrations and applications. All students from all of the participating courses come together one evening per week to hear experts debate the policy issue and to talk about their own use of quantitative methods in analyzing options. The policy topic changes on a regular basis. While a core of courses participate each year, there are departments that participate only when the topic is particularly relevant. This is a mechanism for drawing in a variety of less quantitative departments.

Viewing quantitative methods through the lens of policy analysis is a strong motivator for students, especially those who are "math averse," demonstrating the power of quantitative methods in a context they recognize as important.

Program History

Macalester College has no graduation requirement in mathematics. While close to 75% of our students do take some mathematics, many of the remaining students intentionally avoid any courses that are at all quantitative. Sizeable numbers of our students graduate without the basic understanding of hypothesis testing, correlation, rates of change, or discounting that would enable them to be critical readers of the popular press. For a campus that prides itself on civic engagement and the examination of political issues, this had become a matter of concern to many of the faculty.

The inability to critique quantitative arguments was recognized as a problem not just for the students who had avoided mathematics. It was clear that all our students, even mathematics and economics majors, would benefit from a program that directly addressed quantitative literacy.

During 2001–02, fifteen faculty from across the college, but representing mostly the sciences and social sciences, met every other week to create a program that would address this problem. Some of the criteria that emerged from the first meetings were that our program would have to be

- Interdisciplinary, involving many different departments,

- Well structured and focused. We were not interested in a program that only gave a "quantitative" designation to an assortment of courses,

- Built on existing courses. In a small college there is little flexibility to create permanent new courses, and what flexibility exists is jealously guarded by each department,

- Tied to Macalester's traditional emphasis on civic engagement and interest in public affairs.

It was decided that each year we would select an important issue which could be used as a source of examples of quantitative methods used in public policy debate and as a unifying theme for all participating courses.

We also sought to provide all students with a survey of the fundamental quantitative ideas that arise regularly in public debate. These were grouped into three broad categories:

- Chance: statistical hypothesis testing, sampling, experimental design, measures of correlation.

- Change: percentages and rates; marginal versus average rates; linear versus exponential growth; importance of units; estimation.

- Trade-offs: cost/benefit and cost/effectiveness analysis; other mathematical techniques for comparison.

An early proposal was to require all participating courses to spend some time on each of these topics. The problem was that we were using existing courses that already had full syllabi. There was little flexibility to add the remaining topics that were not traditional.

The solution was to create an evening time when all students from all participating courses come together. It can be thought of as a common laboratory section for all participating courses. Some of the evenings are devoted to introduction of quantitative tools in the context of the public policy issue. Other evenings provide background in the policy issue or bring in speakers who can address the issues and illustrate how quantitative tools are used to bolster their own arguments.

The first year of the program was 2002–03. The policy topic was the school voucher debate. Six departments participated: Communication Studies (introductory journalism), Economics (principles of economics), English (college writing), Geography (methods of geography), Mathematics (introductory statistics, discrete mathematics), and Political Science (empirical research methods). Some did so on a voluntary basis: encouraging but not requiring their students to attend the evening class. One hundred students enrolled in the evening class in the fall, seventy in the spring.

In the second year, 2003–04, the focus is on immigration policy. Only four departments are participating, but all now require their students to attend the evening class: Economics (principles of economics), Geography (urban geography), Mathematics (introductory statistics), and Political Science (economics and the law).

Program Goals and Learning Objectives

The purpose of this program is to give students an appreciation for the role of quantitative methods in deciding questions of public importance as well as the ability to think critically about quantitative arguments made by others. These issues are not addressed in any other courses, and so our intention is to make participation in this program a graduation requirement. No other course in mathematics or any other department would satisfy this requirement.

The evening class does not attempt to teach how to measure a correlation or calculate a net present value. When a quantitative technique is taught, that is done within the participating course. The evening class is designed to acquaint students with the concepts and vocabulary of quantitative analysis. Its purpose is to help students learn how to critique a position paper that relies on quantitative analysis.

The QM4PP program as a whole has three broad goals:

1. Introduce all students to basic methods of quantitative analysis in a context that illustrates usefulness in thinking about issues of public importance,

2. Enable students to think critically about quantitative arguments that are presented in defense of a position on an issue of public importance,

3. Assist faculty from all disciplines to understand the relevance of quantitative methods to their own scholarship, and enable them to make connections to quantitative methods in their classes.

The first goal is quantitative literacy in the broad sense. We want our students to see and appreciate its usefulness. The public policy piece is an important part of the program. It receives as much attention as the quantitative topics in terms of choosing speakers, presenting the issues, and engaging students in wrestling with the questions that arise in the policy topic. What is unique about our program is that the quantitative literacy is embedded within this policy debate.

The second goal gets to the heart of this program. We want our students to learn how to critique a statement made in a newspaper or by a proponent of a particular position. We want them to know the basic terminology, the kinds of questions to ask when judging the validity of an argument based on numbers, and where they can turn for deeper explanations. These skills are important for all students, even those in traditionally quantitative majors. It is because of the centrality of this second goal that students are not able to satisfy this requirement with any other course in mathematics or any other quantitative subject.

The third goal is unusual among quantitative literacy programs, but it is an important part of how we see QM4PP and its mission within the college. Quantitative literacy is not just a goal for the students. Appreciation for and a reasonable level of comfort with quantitative tools are aspects of quantitative literacy that we would like to pervade our campus. Our program is designed specifically to encourage and support participation by faculty who normally would not teach courses with a quantitative component. The intention is to foster community-wide appreciation of the power and pitfalls of arguments that call on numbers.

There are two important aspects of the program that were made possible by the funding from the Department of Education. The first is an annual workshop built around the policy topic for the following year designed to acquaint a broad range of faculty with how quantitative methods come into play in thinking about this issue. The second is support personnel who are available to help quantitatively literate faculty tie their courses to the policy topic, and to help non-quantitative faculty who are interested in the topic to see how they can bring quantitative ideas into their own syllabi. There are two faculty providing this support. One is a faculty member who is released from one course each year specifically for this purpose. The other is someone hired with the title of "Policy Associate." He teaches one of the participating classes each semester and the remainder of his time is devoted to supporting other faculty engaged in the program.

Student Placement into the Program

At the time this article is being written, we are in the second year (2003–04) of the piloting of the program. Ten classes are participating this year. Each requires its students to attend the Wednesday evening classes and to participate in the program. Many of these classes are part of multi-section courses. For this year, students have some choice of whether to enroll in a section that participates in the program or one that does not.

Our intention is to make enrollment in at least one participating QM4PP class a graduation requirement for all Macalester students, and one that cannot be satisfied by any other courses. We hope that this requirement will be in place by the summer of 2006. Please visit our website for the most current information.

Program Details

We are still in the pilot phase of developing the QM4PP program, so some of the program details may be changed or modified in the future. But having run it for over a year, we now have a fairly good idea of its structure. For 2003–04, the focus is on immigration policy, and the title for this year is *Policies Affecting the Immigrant Experience in Minnesota*. Because immigration policy is such a rich topic, we expect to continue to explore questions related to immigration in 2004–05. In addition to the departments that are participating this year, American Studies, Anthropology, English, History, Psychology, and Spanish, all teach courses that deal with immigrant issues. We hope to entice some of them into the second year of focus on immigration.

The Workshops

Preliminary planning for the coming academic year begins with a two-day workshop in late January. This is an opportunity to assess the progress of the current year's program and make adjustments before we run it a second time in the spring semester. It also is intended to identify faculty preferences for the questions and choice of emphasis for the following year. It is at this workshop that we seek commitments from faculty for engagement in the QM4PP program the following year. Those who are participating for the first time receive a $2500 stipend over the summer for the additional work required to adapt their class so that it takes full advantage of the program.

The primary planning workshop runs for three days and is held in early summer. We bring in potential speakers for the coming year as well as other experts in the field. The structure of these workshops has been to spend two days learning about the policy questions. The first day is devoted to establishing a broad understanding of the topic. The second day focuses on questions that have a strong quantitative component. These might include work that raises questions about experimental design and hypothesis testing or analysis of economic costs and benefits. We also bring in people who can discuss relevant databases and talk about how to access and use them.

At this stage, we are working with local experts. Our close association with the Hubert H. Humphrey Institute of Public Affairs at the University of Minnesota is particularly helpful. Their faculty have provided some of the expertise and have helped to identify others in government, academe, and the non-profit sector who can illuminate the issues and show how quantitative methods actually are used.

The third day is the real workday. This is when we sketch out the sequence of topics for the coming fall. We determine the questions that will be the primary focus of the coming year, the speakers we wish to invite, the quantitative questions that we will choose to highlight. Most of the speakers that we will ask to address our students are local experts, but we also try to identify one or two individuals who are nationally recognized for their work on the policy issue.

Our workshops have benefited from the presence of interested faculty from other colleges and universities as well as high school teachers. These have been faculty who have been interested in learning about our program and searching for ideas that they can carry back to their own institutions. Currently, while our program has federal funding, we are able to pay the costs of participation for these individuals as part of our outreach and dis-

semination. Our intention is that as our program gains in expertise and experience, the outreach and dissemination piece of these workshops will grow, possibly paying for itself or attracting additional funding.

The Evening Class

All students in all participating classes are required to register for the common evening class, held Wednesday evenings from 7:00 to 8:30 PM. Students who have previously taken the evening class are exempt from registering for it, but their instructor in the participating class may still require their attendance for particular evenings. The common evening class carries 1 credit (1/4 of a normal class's credit). Students receive a pass/fail grade for it.

One faculty member is in charge of the evening class, but there is almost always a different person who does the presentation. Often there will be a team of two faculty that presents the evening's topic. The topics are split roughly in half between those that are primarily quantitative and those that focus on the policy question.

We have thirteen Wednesday evening classes in the fall semester. The schedule for fall, 2003 is representative of how the semester was organized.

Macalester College prides itself on its small classes. Classes of over thirty students are unusual. In contrast, the common evening class is now running with close to 200, and eventually should reach over 300 students. The first part of each evening is devoted to a presentation of the

---

QM4PP syllabus for fall, 2003

September 3 Introduction to course, introduction to issues of migration

September 10 pre-test assessment, guest speaker on US immigration laws: *Gatekeeping Nation: U.S. Immigration Policy in Historical and Contemporary Perspectives*

September 17 rates of growth, average vs. marginal rates

September 24 trade-offs

October 1 guest speaker on economic impact of immigration: *Estimating the economic impact of immigration: how and why to do it*

October 8 guest speaker on reasons for more restrictive immigration policies

October 15 sampling and hypothesis testing
Give out articles for individual critiquing (major group project for course assessment).

~~October 22~~ (before fall break)

October 29 what to look for when critiquing the quantitative components of articles and opinion pieces Groups begin to build common critique of assigned article.

November 5 correlation and causation

November 12 detection

November 19 polling issues, web sites with data, information, and opinions

~~November 26~~ (before Thanksgiving)

December 3 Cost Benefit Analysis and net present value/discount rates

December 10 faculty debate

December 17 final assessment

topic, which can take as much as 45 minutes. To foster interaction among the students and to provide some sense of individualized instruction, the students then break into groups of approximately six students each. The groups are created to include students from as many different classes as possible. Here the students work on activities that allow them to explore the ideas they have just seen and to help cement their understanding of the topic from the previous week. Faculty from the participating classes circulate to answer questions. We also plan on developing a cadre of undergraduate preceptors with experience in the program who can assist and help guide the individual groups.

Each group is also given a semester-long project to complete. For the 2003–04 year, this consisted of an in-depth critique of a controversial position paper or journal article.

Program Assessment

We have retained a professional consultant for assessment. In addition, a Macalester faculty member is responsible for the actual assessment that takes place on campus.

Since the focus of our program is to be able to critique statements made by others, that is also the primary focus of our assessment. At the beginning of each semester, the students in the program are given newspaper articles, randomly assigned, which they are asked to critique. At the end of the semester, as part of their final examination, these same articles are included in a slightly larger set, and the articles are again randomly distributed. Students are asked to critique two of the articles.

In addition, focus groups and interviews with individual students are held near the end of the semester or during the following semester to gather information on student perceptions of what they learned, the value of the experience, and improvements that could be made. Our assessment also includes a piece of a larger study being conducted in preparation for our next accreditation review. Fifteen members of the class of 2007 have been selected for a longitudinal study of their development. Each semester, each student is interviewed individually. The study explores impressions of and attitudes toward the undergraduate experience, including the student's own sense of personal development.

Cross-disciplinary Commitment and Participation

The foundations of this program lie in the departments of Mathematics and Economics. This has built on a tra-

dition of strong cooperation between these departments. The faculty of both departments see the need for this program and have been willing to participate. In addition, the chairs of the departments of Geography and Political Science have supported the development of this program and have ensured that their departments participate. We have also had participation from individuals in Communication Studies (Introduction to Journalism) and English (one section of College Writing).

Other departments with an interest in the policy issues we have studied have participated in the planning workshops or assisted with evening presentations. These include the departments of Anthropology, Dramatic Arts and Dance, Education, History, Psychology, Sociology, and Spanish.

Our greatest obstacle so far has been the reluctance of many departments to require the additional component of the evening course while it is still unproven. Until the program has run long enough that it has established a reputation for being useful and interesting, departments that attract math-averse students will be reluctant to require it.

On the other hand, we have received nothing but good will from all members of the faculty. We have been careful not to convey the impression that quantitative methods are the only or the principal foundation for policy decision-making. Even those faculty members who are themselves math-averse recognize the value of what we are doing.

Outreach and Dissemination

Because our program is funded by the US Department of Education and the National Science Foundation, outreach and dissemination are important responsibilities. While it is not clear whether any other institution could import our program as it stands, we do hope that our unique approach may provide a model and inspiration that others can adapt to their individual needs, drawing on the materials that we are developing to teach quantitative literacy in the context of a focused question of national importance.

Our website contains links to Power Point slides from the evening presentations, worksheets, and other materials from the evening class.

Faculty from other colleges and universities are welcome to attend the planning workshops as either observers or participants. Until the summer of 2006, we have funding to help underwrite the cost of attending these workshops. We also have a few small subgrants to give out under our NSF-CCLI grant. These can be used to pay an individual who will spend time learning about our program, looking for how it might be shaped to fit the needs of another institution, and possibly writing a grant proposal to NSF for Adaptation and Implementation.

Another important piece of our outreach is to secondary teachers, especially secondary teachers in the social sciences. They also will be involved in the summer planning workshops, with an additional day devoted to their particular needs, showing them how they can bring an awareness of quantitative literacy and its role in understanding important public issues into their own classes.

Contact Information

The website for this project is at www.macalester.edu/qm4pp

Project director: David Bressoud, bressoud@macalester.edu

Associate director: Danny Kaplan, kaplan@macalester.edu

Policy Associate: Steve Holland, holland@macalester.edu

Evening class and assessment coordinator: Dave Ehren, ehren@macalester.edu

The Quantitative Requirement at Juniata College

John F. Bukowski
Juniata College, Huntingdon, PA

Curriculum and Program History

Juniata College is a small liberal arts institution with a strong reputation in the sciences, especially biology and chemistry. In fact, about half of each entering class intends to major in one of these two subjects. About 23 percent of Juniata students do complete a major in biology/pre-health. This context has an impact on the institutional understanding of quantitative literacy.

Before 1994, Juniata College had in its curriculum a computer literacy requirement, which was satisfied by the course "Introduction to Computing," offered by the Department of Mathematics and Computer Science (MACS). This course contained work with Minitab and some spreadsheets, along with some simple programming. In this course, the main focus was on the computer, and any mathematics that was done was driven by the computing.

In 1994, the faculty of Juniata instituted a new curriculum, which included a Quantitative Literacy requirement (the "Q"). This requirement was partly motivated by the preliminary work of the MAA's CUPM Subcommittee on Quantitative Literacy, whose final document, *"Quantitative Reasoning for College Graduates: A Complement to the Standards,"* provides many important suggestions for such programs. The college formed a four-member committee (two mathematicians, a psychologist, and a musician) to oversee the Q requirement, which is stated in the course catalog as follows: "Students must demonstrate (1) basic competence in statistics, and (2) an understanding of basic mathematical skills. To satisfy the requirement, students have three options: (1) completion of a "Q" course, which deals explicitly with both statistical and mathematical skills, or (2) completion of a statistical (QS) and a mathematical (QM) course, or (3) pass proficiency exams in math and statistics." There are only two "Q" courses at Juniata: Quantitative Methods (in the MACS department), which is the subject of Section II of this article, and Advanced Statistics for Psychology (in the Psychology department).

QS courses seek to instill basic competence in statistics, defined by the Q committee to include "sampling, data organization and representation, measures of central tendency, measures of dispersion, and elementary probability concepts." There are currently seven QS courses at Juniata:

Chemistry-Biology Lab I and II
    (Chemistry and Biology Depts.)
Biostatistics (Biology)
Statistics for Social Science (Non-departmental)

Quantitative Business Analysis II
(Acct., Business, Econ. (ABE) Dept.)
Hydrology I (Environmental Sci. and Studies)
Introduction to Probability and Statistics (MACS)
Probability and Statistics (MACS)

QM courses, according to the Q committee, offer "an understanding of mathematics includ[ing] such topics as percentages, ratios, proportionality, rates of change, linear functions and systems in two unknowns, but the true essence is a combined algebraic, graphical, and numerical approach to problem solving and an emphasis on word problems." The committee is clearly influenced here by Juniata's use since the mid-1990's of reform calculus (in particular, the books by Hughes-Hallett, et al.), which relies on the so-called "Rule of 3," the idea of solving problems using algebraic, graphical, and numerical approaches. Juniata currently offers seventeen QM courses:

Quantitative Business Analysis I (ABE)
Managerial Accounting (ABE)
Financial Management II (ABE)
Precalculus (MACS)
Linear Algebra (MACS)
Discrete Structures (MACS)
Calculus I, II, and III (MACS)
Mathematical Modeling (MACS)
Combinatorics (MACS)
Differential Equations (MACS)
Numerical Analysis (MACS)
General Physics I and II (Physics)
Introductory Physics I and II (Physics)

As evidenced by the course lists above, the Quantitative requirement is not strictly the responsibility of the mathematics department. Especially on the statistics side of the program, many students satisfy the requirement within their own departments with courses appropriate to their own subject areas. This is consistent with the CUPM suggestion that quantitative literacy is learned via "a framework of mathematics across the curriculum," with the mathematics and statistics "taught in context."

Virtually all of Juniata's students satisfy the Q requirement through coursework, that is, through either option (1) or (2) above, as the proficiency exam is very rarely taken. The Q committee tracks how Juniata students satisfy the Quantitative requirement. For the Class of 2002, which contained 276 students, 105 of them took Quantitative Methods to satisfy the Q, while two took Advanced Statistics for Psychology. The remaining 169 students took some combination of QM and QS courses. Due to Juniata's science-heavy student body, 100 mem-

bers of this class took a math or physics course, coupled with the Chemistry-Biology Lab, to satisfy the requirement. Of course, students majoring in mathematics or computer science satisfy the quantitative requirement simply by taking courses in their own department.

"Quantitative Methods" Course

As mentioned above, the mathematics course Quantitative Methods is the simplest way for a Juniata non-science student to satisfy the Q requirement. Indeed, more than one-third of Juniata students in each graduating class satisfy the requirement in this way.

Since its inception, Quantitative Methods has used a textbook written by Juniata mathematics professor Sue Esch. Over the years it has been updated and revised by Sue Esch, John Bukowski, and Jerry Kruse. Much of the philosophy of the textbook, and therefore of the course itself, is stated in the book's Preface, the highlights of which we state here with comments:

All the problems are word problems. Whenever feasible, real world data are used.

This is a very important point, as the types of quantitative problems our students will encounter in their lives are most definitely "word problems." The real world data in the book are updated in a new version each year—the federal budget, starting salaries, populations, and other such data.

The text approaches mathematics as the 'science of patterns.' It pays particular attention to the relationship between numerical patterns, algorithms, and algebraic formulas.

The text applies the Rule of 3 whenever possible. When problems can naturally be solved several ways, they are. In addition, we try to show how the algebraic, graphical, and numerical approaches complement each other—and are themselves supported and related by algorithm design. In class, and to some extent in the text, the Rule of 3 is expanded to the Rule of 4, adding writing to learn. Students are expected to document their reasoning and explain their conclusions.

This point is well-illustrated in the section on finding maximums and minimums. After figuring out how to get the function to be optimized—from a word problem, of course!—we look at finding the maximum or minimum in all three ways: graphically, by plotting and "zooming in"; numerically, by checking x-values at regular intervals, and algebraically, by completing the square, for example. It is useful and important for the student to realize that different approaches are possible and to see how these different strategies relate to each other, ultimately leading to the same result.

Writing is an important part of this course. In addition to the usual documentation and explanations on weekly assignments, students complete two projects in the course – one at the end of the statistics section, and one at the end of the mathematics section. Each project must be presented in MSWord, as an article with supporting equations, tables, and graphs embedded in the document. We do get some really nice projects from our students!

The concept of 'algorithm' is developed as a fundamental conceptual tool, not just a programming tool. ... Our emphasis on algorithms begins in the statistics sections, with the development of algorithms tailored to the form in which the data present themselves. The theme carries through the mathematics sections, presenting algebraic, graphical, and numerical algorithms for problem-solving. And finally, in the sections on personal finance, the text shows not only how repetitive tasks can be represented and implemented with simple numerical algorithms, but also how algebraic formulas can be derived by following these algorithms through algebraically instead of numerically.

One of the first times we see algorithms used in this course is in the section on data spread. When discussing standard deviation, we introduce the well-known formula, then we try to understand the formula and its notation by developing it as an algorithm. This way of thinking about the formula helps us when we are confronted with data in the form of a frequency distribution, as opposed to data in raw form. With raw data, Minitab or any similar program can quickly compute the standard deviation – not so for a frequency distribution. Now the students are forced to understand the standard deviation algorithmically, as we create a Minitab "macro" (a short program) to compute the standard deviation.

One of the central themes of the text is 'How we solve problems depends on the tools we have available.' As 21ˢᵗ century problem-solvers, we cannot ignore technology. Therefore the text integrates the 'spirit' of technology—generically discussing the use of statistics packages, calculators, computer algebra systems, etc. ... [I]t is our opinion that quantitative literacy in this day and age includes computer literacy. At Juniata, the statistics sections are implemented in Minitab. The mathematics and programming sections are implemented in Maple.

Keeping the emphasis in the course on the statistics and mathematics, as opposed to the computer, is impor-

tant. We do realize, however, that the theme mentioned here is crucial, that our approach to solving problems depends on the tools (technology!) we have available. This would have been a very different course before the advent of programs such as Minitab and Maple.

The inclusion of programming has two purposes. First, we think that a little programming can go a long way in problem-solving – and is a natural extension of numerical solutions and of algorithm design. ... Second, and equally important, is the concept of controlling and enhancing existing problem-solving tools. When a tool does not supply a command to do exactly what we want or need, it is useful to know how to create our own.

The use of the Minitab macro, as described above, is the first appearance of programming in the course. Later, during the mathematics section of the course, we introduce the fundamental ideas of program design in order to write short programs in Maple (called procedures). Writing these programs often makes numerical approaches to solving problems much simpler, as we no longer need to do many repeated or similar calculations one at a time. The ability to write (and modify) short programs comes in especially handy in the book's final chapter on Personal Finance Applications. For example, using simple, student written programs, students can produce loan payment schedules by simply executing a procedure with a few input parameters.

Quantitative Methods is a three-credit course that meets for three one-hour "lectures" per week plus a one-hour lab/help session. The three "lecture" days are partly traditional lecture, with basic theory and many examples on the board. This material, however, is enhanced by the use of problem-solving demonstrations on the computer, either using Minitab or Maple. The course is taught in a laboratory classroom, with approximately thirty PCs, so that students can work along at their seats. Time often remains at the end of the class for students to work on problems at their computers.

Homework problems are found at the end of each section of the book and are assigned each day. As stated before, these are all word problems, most of which can be solved "by hand" with the use of a calculator. Approximately weekly, computer assignments are also given, in Minitab or Maple. In all cases, students are required to document their work and to explain their results. Midterm and final projects, as described earlier, are written in Word as articles with supporting graphs and tables.

All work in the course, including exams, is done in teams of two students. A great deal of learning occurs as the students interact with each other. Additionally, working with a partner tends to have the effect of alleviating some stress for the students, most of whom are uncomfortable taking a math class in the first place.

Examples of Other Courses Used to Satisfy Quantitative Requirements

As mentioned in Section I, a majority of Juniata students satisfy the quantitative requirement by taking both a QS course and a QM course. In these courses, several of which are housed outside the mathematics department, students gain an appropriate statistical knowledge and understanding of mathematics via algebraic, graphical, and numerical approaches to problem solving. Much of the philosophy that permeates the Quantitative Methods course is present in the QS and QM courses, as well.

Because there are multiple routes to satisfying Juniata's Q requirement, not every student will emerge with exactly the same set of quantitative skills. We believe, however, that through either the Quantitative Methods course or a combination of QS and QM courses, students obtain a "habit of mind, an approach to problems that employs and enhances both statistics and mathematics," as articulated by the Quantitative Literacy Design Team (Steen, p 5).] A number of skills involved in these approaches are mentioned by the Design Team: arithmetic, data, computers, modeling, statistics, chance, and reasoning. (Steen, p 16–17) Students appear to learn these skills as they follow their own paths to the Q requirement.

The following is a collection of examples of courses that satisfy either the QS or QM requirement, which together satisfy the Q.

Chemistry-Biology Lab I and II (QS)

More than one-third of Juniata students take these two semesters of lab, both of which are needed to satisfy the QS requirement. The instructors place great emphasis on data analysis in these courses. The statistical topics used most in this sequence are average, standard deviation, confidence intervals, and t-tests. For example, in the first semester, in a module on titrating water samples for hardness, students come to understand data scatter by using a 95% confidence interval. In the same lab module, they also compare the hardness of two different water samples with a t-test.

Statistics for the Social Sciences (QS)

The syllabus describes this course as an applied statistics course, in which "emphasis will be on learning under what conditions it is appropriate to use particular tests, what those tests do, and how to interpret the results." Data used throughout the course are collected from a sample of Juniata students. Students in the class do frequent homework problems to understand the many appropriate statistical tests. These problems may or may not require the use of technology. Students also complete about five computer assignments throughout the semester, on topics such as distribution of data, t-tests, analysis of variance, correlation and regression, and chi-squared tests. They use Minitab to analyze the data, and they are required to include a written interpretation of their results.

Managerial Accounting (QM)

The catalog description states that this course "[e]mphasizes accounting concepts for the internal use of management in planning and control," and that it "focuses on spreadsheet applications to analyze management problems." Managerial Accounting is a data-driven course in which students must understand numerical relationships in data presented to them, in order to develop an Excel spreadsheet appropriate for the accounting scenario at hand. Students often use quantitative ideas such as absolute and percent change, and they present their results in numerical and graphical form. At the end of each week, students are tested with new data for their spreadsheet. They must then demonstrate their understanding of the results by writing a short memo in non-technical language to a fictional CEO.

Calculus I (QM)

As mentioned above, Juniata uses a reform style in its calculus courses, so virtually by our definition, Calculus I satisfies the QM requirement by utilizing analytical, graphical, and numerical approaches throughout. Daily homework assignments come from the textbook, which contains many word problems and very few drill problems. In addition, students complete six to eight Maple assignments throughout the semester. These assignments require the students to figure out the best way—or ways —to solve the problems (often graphically or numerically), and to document their work throughout the entire worksheet.

Assessment

Juniata has not collected much assessment data for the Quantitative requirement, but there is some information related to the Quantitative Methods course. A substantial cohort of Quantitative Methods students comes from the

Education Department, now approaching fifty students per year. All of these students are required to pass the Pre-Professional Skills Test in Mathematics (PPST:M), from the Praxis Series of the Educational Testing Service, in order to receive certification to teach in Pennsylvania. This exam has five main content categories: conceptual knowledge; procedural knowledge; representations of quantitative information; measurement and informal geometry; and formal mathematical reasoning. Many of these areas overlap with Juniata's goals for quantitative literacy.

Juniata students have done quite well on this exam, with a 99% pass rate over the past four years. The score range for the exam is 150–190, with a passing score of 173 in Pennsylvania; Juniata has a mean score of 182.

Although this data does not account for all Juniata students, it displays a certain level of quantitative success for a substantial portion of the student population.

Concluding Remarks

This college-wide framework for the quantitative requirement allows many Juniata students to achieve quantitative literacy in courses appropriate to their own fields of study. Students for whom there is no quantitative course offered in their program may take Quantitative Methods, which provides them with quantitative skills for many different applications in a broad range of areas. All Juniata students, through the completion of the Q requirement, are then able to understand and use various ideas, such as simple statistical quantities, graphs, rates of change, and algorithms. These students — tomorrow's leaders — then have the tools necessary, along with the habit of mind, to make good decisions based on quantitative information.

Acknowledgments

The author thanks his Juniata College colleagues Sue Esch, Ruth Reed, Dave Drews, Pat Weaver, Michael Byron, and Cathy Stenson for their help with this document.

References

CUPM Subcommittee on Quantitative Literacy. (1996). *Quantitative Reasoning for College Graduates: A Complement to the Standards*, Mathematical Association of America, Washington, DC.

Educational Testing Service, *The Praxis Series, Test at a Glance, PPST:Mathematics*, retrieved from http://www.ets.org/praxis/taags/prx0730.html

Esch, S. L., Bukowski, J. F., & Kruse, G. W., (Fall 2002). *Quantitative Methods*, Juniata College.

Hughes-Hallett, D., Gleason, A.M., McCallum, W. G., et al., (2002). *Calculus* (3rd ed.). Wiley, New York.

Juniata College Catalog 2002-2004.

McCallum, W. G., Hughes-Hallett, D., Gleason, A. M., et al., (2002). *Multivariable Calculus*, (3rd ed.). Wiley, New York.

Steen, L. A., ed., (2001). *Mathematics and Democracy: The Case for Quantitative Literacy*, National Council on Education and the Disciplines, Princeton, NJ.

Quantitative Literacy at Dominican University

Paul R. Coe and Sarah N. Ziesler

*Dominican University,
River Forest, IL*

Introduction

At Dominican University, in the context of a complete review of the undergraduate general education requirements, we have been able to add a Quantitative Literacy component to our curriculum. In this paper we will describe what that Qualitative Literacy component is, what it has done to departmental enrollments, our struggles with advising and placement, assessment of our program, and some outstanding problems.

Background Information

Dominican University currently consists of an undergraduate college and four graduate schools (Business, Education, Library and Information Science, and Social Work) with an enrollment of about 2,800 students (1,200 of whom are undergraduates). In 1997, the school changed its name from Rosary College and restructured its administration into a university model. Concurrent with this change was a complete review of the general education requirements of the undergraduate curriculum. The mathematics department proposed increasing the mathematics requirement for graduation from Intermediate Algebra to one course beyond Intermediate Algebra, from a specific list which follows. This list included a new course, Contemporary Mathematics, created as part of the proposal.

The proposal was based on the fact that most comparable universities in our geographical area had higher requirements, many majors already required additional mathematics courses beyond Intermediate Algebra, and a belief that graduates of Dominican University should be able to understand and use mathematics in a more meaningful way than simple algebraic manipulation. To our department's surprise, the proposal was accepted with little opposition.

The goals of the revised foundation requirement in mathematics are as follows:

The student should be able to:

- understand and use numbers and mathematical symbols,

- manipulate and understand algebraic expressions,

- think logically to solve problems,

- model real life problems using mathematics, read and understand mathematical information in the media and professional literature.

These skills may be demonstrated by placement examination or by completing with a passing grade college-level course work equivalent to College Algebra, Mathematics for Elementary Teachers, Finite Mathematics, and Contemporary Mathematics. (A student testing into pre-calculus or above is not required to take a mathematics course at Dominican, although we strongly encourage all students to do so.) We will now discuss these courses in more detail.

Curriculum Details

College Algebra (MATH 130)

This is a traditional course, which does not include trigonometry. It is the usual bridge course between intermediate algebra and pre-calculus, and its intended audience is students wanting or needing to take additional mathematics courses. Students taking college algebra are primarily majors in biology, chemistry, and the natural sciences, who need improved algebra skills before going on to a five-hour-per-week combined pre-calculus/ calculus 1 course. No major directly requires this class, except as a prerequisite for the precalculus/calculus 1 course. Consequently, the main emphasis of college algebra is to prepare students for that course. Topics covered include

- Properties of the real numbers
- Integral and rational exponents
- Radicals
- Manipulation and factoring of polynomials
- Manipulation of rational expressions
- Linear inequalities
- Complex numbers
- Quadratic equations
- Absolute value and quadratic inequalities
- Functions and inverse functions
- Exponential and logarithmic functions
- Arithmetic and geometric sequences and series
- Binomial Theorem.

While these topics do not in themselves satisify QL expectations, throughout the course there is an emphasis on applications and the modeling of real life problems, with particular attention being paid to those problems relevant to the student population. For example, when learning functions, one can discuss deforestation of rainforests, or the function describing declining cholesterol levels. Newton's law of gravity and consequences of Kepler's law can be introduced when learning direct variation. The exponential function is a rich source of applications. Possible examples include carbon-dating, radioactive half-lives, Newton's law of cooling, and the logistic growth model for the spread of a virus.

Possible texts for this course include those by Sullivan, Dugopolski and Lial, Hornsby & Schneider.

These are all texts with an optional graphing calculator component. While we have not yet required students to purchase graphing calculators for any 100-level course, many instructors in this class and finite mathematics use them for classroom presentations.

Mathematics for the Elementary School Teacher (MATH 160)

This course is only for prospective elementary school teachers. The prerequisites for this course are Intermediate Algebra and a course in geometry at the high school level. Relationship to content in the elementary classroom is stressed throughout this class and manipulatives are used as much as possible. The content is also informed by the Illinois Education Standards. Topics include

- Problem Solving
- Inductive and deductive reasoning
- Sets
- Symbolic logic
- Numeration systems
- Geometry.

We have been using a text by Miller, Heeren, and Hornsby for several years. However, in place of the material in the text on numeration systems, we use some material developed by Thomas Hungerford at Cleveland State University. It is called Fen Arithmetic and covers whole numbers and then integer arithmetic in base 5 (without calling it base 5). The intent of the material is to allow the students to experience learning how to add, subtract, multiply, and divide in this context in the same way that an elementary school student would learn these concepts in base 10. Student response to this material has always been excellent. They find it fun, unusual, and very helpful in understanding how arithmetic works and how children learn it. Thomas Hungerford's notes are available from him at no charge.

Finite Mathematics (MATH 170)

This course is designed as a service course for those majoring in computer science, business or the social sciences. It is required for students majoring in computer science, computer information systems, and computer graphics, and is strongly recommended for those majoring in accounting, business administration, economics, psychology, and environmental studies. We have had formal and informal discussions with the relevant departments to determine course content, and are careful to choose appropriate examples of applications. The inclusion of the rather unusual topics of binary and hexadecimal number systems and Boolean operators in this course is a direct consequence of discussions with our colleagues in computer science. We choose an applied text for this course. Possible texts include those by Anton, Kolman & Averbach and Mizrahi & Sullivan. Course topics include

- Number systems (binary and hexadecimal)
- Boolean operators
- Linear equations, inequalities and applications
- Matrices, linear systems and applications
- Linear Programming
- Set theory, counting techniques and probability.

Contemporary Mathematics (MATH150)

Contemporary Mathematics is a new course, created as part of the proposal to require one course beyond intermediate algebra. The target audience for this course is all students who do not need to take one of the other three options. (A discussion of enrollment figures is provided below.)

The curriculum for this course is less well defined than for the other options, and much is left to the individual instructor's preference. Some instructors also solicit student input into the selection of topics chosen. Our main aims are to demonstrate the wide range of applications of mathematics in the real world, to persuade students that mathematics can be interesting and even entertaining, and to create informed user of mathematics. Each instructor chooses different topics (although with substantial overlap). Possible topics include

- Voting theory
- Weighted voting and the Electoral College
- Apportionment
- Graph Theory (Euler circuits, the Traveling Salesman Problem, networks)
- Graph coloring
- Scheduling
- Coding theory
- Modular arithmetic and cryptography
- Fibonacci Numbers and the Golden Ratio
- Population Growth
- Statistics.

Typically, an instructor will cover at most five or six of these topics in the course.

One thing that we have noticed is that class size seriously affects both the quality of learning in this class, and also the quantity of material covered. The optimal class size for such a course is no more than 15-18, and once the size goes above 25 this is a very hard class to teach.

While the department caps most classes at 30, we now cap contemporary mathematics at 25. This course works best when students spend a considerable amount of class time working on problems. Once the class size gets too large it becomes very hard to keep all students occupied productively.

Some of our faculty assign student projects and/or papers in this course. This also works best when the class size is small, especially if one wishes to have student presentations. Many of the topics listed are very well suited to student projects/papers, and many textbooks make suggestions for such things.

There are several good options for texts for this course, including books by COMAP and Tannenbaum, and each of us in the department has different preferences for material to cover. Although we have been choosing the same text for every section in a given semester, we may discontinue that practice and let each instructor go with his/her own preference. Additional material that we have found very useful includes Donald Saari's book *Chaotic Elections* and Helen Christensen's book *Mathematical Modeling for* the Marketplace, a great source of examples for graph theory. We also usually include some material on the coding of Illinois Driver's License Numbers, since our school is in Illinois. Students find this material particularly surprising and interesting.

Advising and Placement

With our breakdown of the foundation requirement into four options, and with a very specific audience in mind for each, it is extremely important that students be placed into the correct course. We base our belief in the effectiveness of this test on success rates in the placed class (80% with a C- or better in the fall of 2004, showing that the placements are not too high) and student satisfaction surveys. (The students aren't bored or mad at taking a class in which they are already proficient, showing that the placements aren't too low.) The process for this is twofold. First, all incoming freshmen must take a mathematics placement test. This test was written some years ago by a member of the department, and has proved to consistently place students in the appropriate course. The multiple-choice test lasts one hour, and has thirty-six questions on material ranging from basic skills through college algebra. Based on the results of the placement test, in conjunction with ACT mathematics sub-score and high school mathematics classes taken, we place students in an appropriate course. The possible placements are

- Basic Skills in Mathematics (MATH090)

- Intermediate Algebra (MATH120)
- One of the four college algebra equivalents discussed in this paper: College Algebra (MATH130), Contemporary Mathematics (MATH150), Mathematics for the Elementary School Teacher (MATH160), and Finite Mathematics (MATH170)
- Mathematical Functions and Calculus I: our combined precalculus/calculus class
- Calculus 1.

The second part of the process is the advising component. Having received the placement MATH 130/150/160/170, students need to make the appropriate choice. The audiences for college algebra, finite mathematics and mathematics for the elementary teacher are well defined and we have rarely (if ever) had a problem with students who need to be in one of those classes mistakenly enrolling in contemporary mathematics. There have been occasions when students have chosen to take contemporary mathematics and have later decided to go into education, computer science or business. In this case they have had to take a second mathematics class. This seems unavoidable.

The most significant problem has been to ensure that the students for whom contemporary mathematics is designed, which are the majority of our students, do not mistakenly enroll in one of the other options. Historically, the main reasons for this happening have been poor advising and scheduling conflicts. In order to ensure that students enroll in the appropriate course both advisors and students need to be well informed. When the quantitative literacy component was introduced, our first step was to distribute written information to all advisors describing possible placements, course descriptions, and most importantly, intended audiences. Another part of the process has been to ensure that at least one of the mathematics faculty attend the annual advisors meeting to present the same information, both orally and in writing, and to give advisors the opportunity to ask questions. Although this is an important forum for ensuring that advisors have up-to-date information, these meetings are not mandatory, and many advisors do not attend. Consequently, we also present the same information to the freshman advisors at the (mandatory) meetings that they hold every year. We also ensure that mathematics faculty are available for questions throughout the biannual advising periods.

Ensuring that students are well informed has been more straightforward. To ensure that students who place into intermediate algebra make the appropriate choice of which course to take next, a full-time faculty member visits each intermediate algebra class in the fall before the spring advising period. We have not done this in the spring; however, we may consider doing so in the future. We also make a point of discussing the various placement options on the first day of all MATH 130/150/160/170 classes.

Word of mouth has also been instrumental in getting students to select the appropriate course. The response to contemporary mathematics has been overwhelmingly positive, and consequently many students tell their friends to take the class.

Program Assessment

Over the last few years our departmental assessment development has focused on creating, implementing, and refining goals, objectives and assessment tools for our major. We are now at the beginning of a similar process for our quantitative literacy requirement. The goals are as stated earlier; we are now working on the assessment component. All of our courses are assessed both numerically, using the SIR II forms, and qualitatively, using a common locally-created form for all undergraduate courses. This form solicits written answers to a variety of questions. Some of these are routine questions concerning issues such as organization, fairness, and overall quality of teaching, however there are also questions concerning the stimulation of intellectual curiosity, and the development of critical thinking. Some typical responses to these latter questions are presented at the end of this section.

Our program assessment involves both assessing each course individually, and also assessing the extent to which students are enrolled in the appropriate classes.

Tables 1 and 2 show the enrollments in each of our four alternatives over the years 1993–2003. The years 93–97 have been grouped together and the average taken over that period. When looking at these tables, it helps to note that Dominican University has experienced consid-

Table 1. Enrollment figures 1993–2002

Academic Year	Fall FTE	Math 130	Math 160	Math 170	Math 150
93–97	739	15	16	19	
97–98	778	55	17	46	10
98–99	860	42	18	71	39
99–00	919	46	19	79	62
00–01	930	32	14	75	47
01–02	1008	45	14	83	66
02–03	1010	43	12	61	87

Table 2. Percentage of college algebra level students in each of MATH 130/150/160/170

Academic Year	Math 130	Math 160	Math 170	Math 150
93–97	29.59	32.65	37.76	0
97–98	42.97	13.28	35.94	7.81
98–99	24.71	10.59	41.76	22.94
99–00	22.33	9.22	38.35	30.10
00–01	19.05	8.33	44.64	27.98
01–02	21.63	6.73	39.90	31.73
02–03	21.18	5.91	30.05	42.86

erable growth over the period under consideration, with a change from 739 FTE's prior to 1997, to our current 1010 FTE's. Consequently the numbers must be interpreted in the context of substantial institutional growth.

The percentage of students enrolling in finite mathematics (MATH 170) has remained essentially steady, falling in 2002, with the number of computer science and business majors, in reaction to the national economy. Satisfaction levels seem to be steady over time.

The number of students enrolling in mathematics for the elementary teacher (MATH 160) has been steady. The percentage decrease is because the growth in student numbers has not been matched by an increase in the number of pre-service elementary teachers. However, student satisfaction with the course has increased with the greater focus on the elementary curriculum.

One can see that by far the most dramatic changes have been the enrollments in contemporary mathematics and college algebra. The first year that contemporary mathematics was offered only 10 students (8% of college algebra level students) enrolled, and there was a surge in the number of (unhappy) students enrolled in college algebra (43% of college algebra level students).

There are several possible reasons for this. First, there is anecdotal evidence that students and advisors mistakenly assumed that Math 130 must be the easiest course, as it had the lowest number. Second, contemporary mathematics was an unknown, and, therefore, students may have been reluctant to enroll in it. Third, students may have been poorly advised by advisors who were not aware of the changes in our program.

However, in the next two years, one sees the impact of our promulgation efforts, with a big increase in the percentage of students in our contemporary mathematics classes, and a corresponding decrease in our college algebra classes.

In terms of student satisfaction, contemporary mathematics may be our most successful course. A selection of student comments from our qualitative assessment tool is given below.

- This class is fun!
- I think that it helped me a lot to think in a critical way.
- I really dislike math in general but this class has helped me to understand it, and look at it from a different perspective.
- Since the material in this particular course applied to everyday situations and problems, I found it very interesting.
- It challenged me unlike any other class I have ever had.
- This course opened up a new world of possibilities and fine-tuned my critical thinking.
- A few things we did I found myself doing on my own time. A first for me math-wise.
- This was the first math course that I truly was intrigued by.
- I am not a person who enjoys math but I have found that this class is actually my favorite class this semester! I like seeing how math is applied to everyday life and situations.

The percentage of college algebra students has settled to around 20%. Now that the audience in college algebra is primarily students who need to take further mathematics, the satisfaction levels in this class are back to their pre-1997 levels.

Outstanding Issues

Advising

In spite of all our efforts, we still cannot be sure that we are reaching all advisors. Although we can be fairly sure that incoming freshmen are advised correctly, many mathematics averse students delay taking their mathematics requirement, often until their senior year, and we cannot be so confident that their major advisors are well informed. However, seniors who started at Dominican as freshmen will usually have learned the appropriate choice by word of mouth from their peers. Because of the value of the content of the Quantitative Literacy courses to courses in their major fields, we believe that all students should take these courses in their first or second year at Dominican. We strongly encourage advisors to follow this policy, but we have no way to enforce it.

Transfer Students

Placement of transfer students is less straightforward. While formal times are set up for incoming freshman to take the placement test, transfer students are handled on a case-by-case basis. Transfer students who have credit for a math class at the college level are not currently required to take the placement test at all. Once at Dominican, these students only see advisors in their major fields, who are not the best equipped to handle math placements. A solution to this problem may be to require all transfer students to take the placement test and meet with an advisor in the math department to determine their placement. A solution would have to be developed to address students who placed at or below the level of a course for which they already had college credit.

Another problem for transfer students (and some seniors) is that they often have more restrictions in terms of scheduling, and so may be unable to choose the appropriate course. One partial solution to this would be to offer an evening section of contemporary mathematics, and we may do this in the future. (See below for a discussion of evening classes).

Articulation

The State of Illinois has an articulation agreement requiring acceptance of community college general education courses such as intermediate algebra, college algebra, finite mathematics and mathematics for the elementary school teacher, so these courses transfer in (and out) without difficulty. Unfortunately, we have no way of ensuring that transferred courses meet the goals that we have established for quantitative literacy.

Transfer in and out of credit for contemporary mathematics is not straightforward, and at this point is reviewed on a case-by-case basis by us and, we believe, by other schools as well.

Evening Classes

Currently only finite mathematics and college algebra are offered in the evening, so part-time students taking evening classes are restricted in their options. Historically, evening classes have been taught by adjunct faculty, who may not have the background to teach either of the other options. The number of elementary education majors does not justify adding an extra evening section; however, as mentioned above, we may add an evening section of contemporary mathematics. An appropriate instructor for the latter course would have to be secured, perhaps from the full time mathematics faculty.

Conclusions

In 1997, in conjunction with a complete revision of the general education requirements, the newly-renamed Dominican University increased its undergraduate graduation requirement in mathematics to include a Quantitative Literacy component and created a new course, contemporary mathematics, as one of four courses to fulfill it. We believe the addition has been a success. After several years of struggling with advising and proper placements of students, word of mouth and increasingly well-trained advisors now place most students in courses in which they are interested. If the students in math courses at this level leave the class more interested in and less anxious about mathematics than when they entered, we consider this a success. Our qualitative evaluations attest to the fact that this is happening. In addition, in these courses students are engaged in mathematics that is applicable outside of these courses and at a level that they can understand.

Our challenge now is to develop and implement effective assessment tools for our quantitative literacy goals.

References

Anton, H., Kolman, B. & Averbach, B. (1992). *Applied Finite Mathematics*, (5th ed.). Saunders College Publishing.

Christensen, H. (1995). *Mathematical Modeling for the Marketplace* (2nd ed.). Kendall/Hunt.

COMAP, (2003). *For All Practical Purposes* (6th ed.). W.H.Freeman and Co.

Dugopolski, M. (1998). *College Algebra* (2nd ed.). Addison Wesley Longman.

Lial, M.,.Hornsby, J., & Schneider, D. (2001). *College Algebra* (8th ed.). Addison Wesley Longman.

Miller, C. , Heeren, V., & Hornsby, J. (2001). *Mathematical Ideas* (9th ed.). Addison Wesley.

Mizrahi, A., & Sullivan, M. (2000). *Finite Mathematics: an Applied Approach* (8th ed.). John Wiley and Sons.

Saari, D. (2001). *Chaotic Elections*, American Mathematical Society.

Sullivan, M. (2002). *College Algebra, A Contemporary Approach* (6th ed.).

Tannenbaum, (2004). *Excursions in Modern Mathematics* (5th ed.). Prentice Hall.

The Quantitative Reasoning Program at Hollins University*

Caren Diefenderfer, Ruth Doan and
Christina Salowey
Hollins University, Roanoke, VA

Introduction

An intelligent citizen reads a newspaper account of an outbreak of disease in a small community. How can she tell if the number of those afflicted looms out of proportion to the expected incidence of disease? A parent must choose whether or not his child will receive a smallpox vaccine. How can he evaluate the benefits and the risks of such an inoculation? An employer asks an employee to develop a profile of the local population to provide a foundation for a marketing campaign. How can the employee assess the significance of distributions of age, race, gender, or other categories in the population? In order to become effective citizens, workers, parents, advocates, indeed in order to perform a great variety of roles, students must become competent in using and reading quantitative data, in understanding quantitative evidence and in applying basic quantitative and mathematical skills so that they can solve real life problems. Lynn Steen, past president of the Mathematical Association of America (MAA) notes, "Quantitatively literate citizens need to know more than formulas and equations. They need a predisposition to look at the world through mathematical eyes, to see the benefits (and risks) of thinking quantitatively about commonplace issues, and to approach complex problems with confidence in the value of careful reasoning. Quantitative literacy empowers people by giving them tools to think for themselves, to ask intelligent questions of experts, and to confront authority confidently. These are skills required to thrive in the modern world."

Quantitative understanding, also called numeracy, is traditionally taught through work in mathematics and statistics courses, but it can often be learned more effectively through work in courses within the student's own major or minor discipline or in the context of courses of interest to the student. "To be useful for the student, numeracy needs to be learned and used in multiple contexts, in history and geography, in economics and biology, in agriculture and culinary arts. Numeracy is not just one among many subjects but an integral part of all subjects." (Steen, 2001)

A program that involves quantitative reasoning across the disciplines gives students an opportunity to learn the broad significance and applicability of quantitative reasoning and mathematical skills in the particular subjects that are meaningful, important, and interesting to them. In this sense, quantitative reasoning across the curriculum becomes a partner with writing across the cur-

---

* This essay is extracted from the longer monograph written by the authors listed in the references above.

41

riculum. College teachers have too long heard the complaint, "This is not an English course, why should grammar and style count?" The writing across the curriculum movement has sought to address that misunderstanding on the part of students by demonstrating that writing is a skill necessary across disciplines and across jobs, responsibilities, and social roles. Similarly, too many students believe that quantitative reasoning comes into play only in mathematics courses, and that once one fulfills a math requirement, those pesky numbers will disappear. Scholars know better; quantitative reasoning enters into work in fields as diverse as English and biology, history and physics, theatre and statistics.

If those who teach know that students need to become competent in quantitative reasoning, students must gain the motivation to achieve that competence. Offering a student the opportunity to analyze and apply quantitative techniques in the process of studying a subject that the student cares about sparks such motivation. The student has the opportunity to see that her understanding of a question which engages her will be deepened by applying quantitative techniques or that her ability to persuade others to accept her point of view will be strengthened by the use of quantitative evidence carefully presented.

Hollins' General Education Program

In the fall of 1998, the Hollins faculty began to work on a major overhaul of general education requirements.

Under the leadership of the Vice President for Academic Affairs and the Academic Affairs Council, the central curricular body of the university, the Hollins community worked together to develop a new framework to define the intellectual perspectives students should engage during their course of study at Hollins, as well as various skills students should acquire. In particular, our new general education requirements, Education through Skills and Perspectives (ESP), allow for foundational work in the skills areas (writing, oral communication, quantitative reasoning and information technology) as needed, and then encourages the melding of skills acquisition within courses designed to introduce students to various perspectives. (For more details visit our website, given in the references.) ESP requires that students complete four semester credits in each of seven perspectives: Aesthetic Analysis, Creative Expression, Ancient and/or Medieval Worlds, Modern and/or Contemporary Worlds, Scientific Inquiry, Social and Cultural Diversities, and Global Systems. In addition, there is a language requirement. The Hollins' faculty approved the ESP program in

the spring of 2001, and all students entering Hollins since the fall of 2001 are following this program.

The QR Requirements

Quantitative Reasoning is one of the skill areas in this new general education program. We have two requirements in this area.

The QR Basic Skills Requirement. The QR Basic Skills Requirement is designed to help students gain an understanding of fundamental mathematical skills that are required for success in quantitative reasoning. The basic skills requirement can be satisfied by achieving a satisfactory score on the Quantitative Reasoning Assessment (given to new students each fall) or by successful completion of Mathematics 100: An Introduction to Quantitative Reasoning. A student who has satisfied the QR basic skills requirement will demonstrate a baseline understanding of such topics as algebra, graphing, geometry, data analysis, and linearity.

The goals of the QR Basic Skills Requirement are

- To understand mathematical and statistical reasoning.
- To use appropriate mathematical and/or statistical tools in summarizing data, making predictions, and establishing cause-and-effect relationships.

In addition to covering what may be considered to be traditional topics in the mathematics curriculum, our introductory QR course has a computer lab every week. Students learn how to use Excel in a variety of ways – to graph data, to analyze data, to explore and model growth, and to learn about loans and financial planning.

The QR Applied Skills Requirement. The QR applied skills requirement is designed to provide students with the opportunity to apply quantitative skills as they solve problems in fields of study in which they have an interest. The applied skill requirement can be satisfied by passing a course designated as a QR applied course.

The goals of the QR Applied Skills Requirement are:

- To give students the opportunity to apply mathematical and statistical reasoning in a chosen discipline.
- To involve students in the application of quantitative skills to problems that arise naturally in the discipline in a way that advances the goals of the course and is not merely a rote application of a procedure.

Each QR applied course must include at least two QR projects. A project might, for example include data collection, discussion of the data, collaborative work on finding appropriate uses of the data, and use of appropriate technology in presentation and writing. The end result of each QR project should be a written assignment that includes a statement of the problem, an explanation of the methods used, and a summary of the results. When appropriate, the written assignment should discuss any limitations encountered and possible improvements to the procedure and/or results.

In the first two years of the program, Hollins had thirty-seven QR applied skills courses from a variety of disciplines, including history, philosophy, theatre, classics, sociology, political science, economics, humanities (French), biology, chemistry, physics, mathematics, statistics, and computer science. The Hollins program was cited as one of nine exemplary programs in the nation in *Mathematics and Democracy*.

Faculty Development

A major boost to the quantitative reasoning program came when Professors Diefenderfer and Hammer applied for and received an NSF Grant for "A Faculty Development Program for Quantitative Reasoning Across the Curriculum." This grant (NSF/DUE Project 9952807) brought four visiting scholars (Jerry Johnson from the University of Nevada at Reno, Dorothy Wallace from Dartmouth College, Helen Lang from Trinity College in Connecticut, and Lou Gross from the University of Tennessee at Knoxville) to the Hollins campus during 2000-2001. Each scholar gave an evening lecture to the University community and led a faculty workshop to explain how they approached quantitative methods in a variety of disciplines at their institution.

Professors Diefenderfer and Hammer led two series of four day workshops where faculty members discussed the recently published *Mathematics and Democracy* (Stein 2001), investigated topics in Hollins' basic QR course (An Introduction to Quantitative Reasoning), shared and critiqued one another's QR project ideas, and presented their QR work-in-progress. Thus, instructors had the opportunity to test out their assignments on a willing audience and to receive feedback on their proposed projects. Twenty faculty members participated in the NSF funded workshops and their work resulted in twenty-seven QR applied skills courses.

We were happy with both the number of participants and the variety of disciplines represented. Anita Solow, Vice-President of Academic Affairs at Randolph Macon Woman's College from 1998 to 2003, prepared an evaluation of the program and wrote, "The faculty unanimously found the project to have value to them. Although many of the comments were expected, I was impressed by the number of faculty members who explicitly talked about the faculty development benefits to them and their sense of empowerment when it came to quantitative reasoning." As an important side benefit, the workshops provided an opportunity to establish cross-disciplinary connections on the campus and to increase discussion of teaching beyond issues related to quantitative reasoning.

After the NSF workshops, faculty members were invited to submit their courses for approval as QR applied skills courses. The application form is fairly simple and requires instructors to describe the two QR projects so that the reviewers can ascertain that the proposed projects fit the guidelines. From 2001 to 2003, Professors Diefenderfer and Hammer served as the screening committee for these applications. They reviewed the applications, made their recommendations (and occasionally asked faculty members to clarify and/or revise certain ideas), and sent the applications to the Academic Policy committee for final approval. Currently, Professor Diefenderfer works with our director of quantitative reasoning, Professor Phyllis Mellinger (hired in fall 2003), on this review. We hope to establish a QR Advisory Board to serve as the screening committee to work with the QR director in the future. This would insure broader input from the faculty members teaching QR applied courses and promote less dependence on the mathematics department for program leadership.

Five faculty members who did not participate in the NSF funded workshops are responsible for teaching twelve of the thirty-seven approved QR applied skills courses. This indicates another side benefit of the grant. It generated enthusiasm for the program that has encouraged additional faculty members to participate, and thus, the grant lives on.

Participation in the workshops, and indeed in the QR applied program in general, is entirely voluntary for faculty. Professors who find themselves working on too many initiatives already, those who question their own competence to teach quantitative techniques, and those who may have doubts about the validity of teaching QR across the curriculum simply choose not to sign on. On the other hand, a number of those who did not understand what quantitative reasoning might mean or who had doubts about the program have had the chance to learn about QR and have become enthusiastic supporters of the requirement and of the educational process involved.

Six Applied QR Projects

The creativity of the quantitative projects that are now embedded in our curriculum is the major success of the Quantitative Reasoning program at Hollins. Here we highlight six projects to demonstrate both the variety of disciplines and the meaningful applications that characterize our program. Individual professors developed these six projects during on-campus NSF funded workshops in January, April, and May, 2001.

American Social History (Professor Ruth Doan): Census of Families in Bristol, Rhode Island, in 1689. In American Social History, we focus on themes related to family, work, and community. Assignments on Puritan New England come at the very beginning of the semester. These assignments introduce students to a number of concepts, skills, and approaches that we draw upon throughout the semester. Goals of the QR project in particular include:

- To encourage students to think about aspects of family life that change over time: structure, function, relationships within the family. This project focuses especially on structure.

- To learn vocabulary used in distinguishing types of families (nuclear, blended, and augmented, for example).

- To expose students to the varieties of data that historians might use and to encourage them to see both how rich and how limited such data might be.

- To exercise certain skills in quantitative reasoning, including finding the mean, median, and mode of a data set, and creating meaningful tables or graphs.

We begin this unit of study by reading and discussing both primary and secondary sources on Puritan New England. The readings do not center on families or on family structure, but rather provide a context for the Bristol census. Thus, for example, students read about and discuss Puritan behavioral norms, the physical shape of a Puritan town, and Puritan spirituality. We then turn to a series of handouts: vocabulary of family structures, the Bristol census itself, and specific questions about the Bristol census.

Quantitative exercises are divided between those done in class and those done as homework. In-class work includes counting how many households of each size and finding the mean, median, and mode of household sizes. Homework includes counting the number of children per household and determining the mean, median, and mode of the data. Thus we practice together the same kind of work that students are sent off to do individually. In class, we discuss representations of the data. Does a pie chart work for the data? A histogram? Why or why not?

The final product of this project is a five-page paper. Students write about what they have discovered in their mining of the Bristol census. They represent their data

in tables or graphs and refer to those representations of the data in their texts. They are also asked to consider issues that might be implied rather than proven by the census. Finally, they discuss the limitations of the data. What questions remain that cannot be answered by the available information?

The students expressed a great deal of enthusiasm for this assignment, somewhat to my surprise. Ten out of eleven in the first class I taught worked willingly and enthusiastically. One stated that she was not good at math and that she had math anxiety, and she showed some inclination to withdraw from group participation. (One student confessed after the fact that she was terrified but had chosen not to show it.) All, including the self-professed victim of math anxiety, did more than adequate work in the end.

Ancient Art (Professor Christina Salowey): Quantitative Analysis of Doric Temples. Students in Ancient Art learn the basic elements of Greek architecture by studying both primary source texts and archaeological data. The goals of this specific project are to introduce the textual and material evidence for the Doric temple, to introduce quantitative skills necessary for deeper understanding of ancient Greek architecture and to show an application of these skills that a working archaeologist would use in the field.

During the first weeks of class, students learn precise and detailed vocabulary necessary to describe specific features of Greek architecture. Vitruvius' *de architectura* defines in great detail, the mathematical relationships between, and the proportions of the elements, of an ideal Doric temple. However, as we look at various temples from 600-250 BCE we discover that Vitruvius' ideals are not always met. In fact, when we use the existing data and graph the ratio of column height to column diameter during this time period, we discover that the ratio varies a great deal. The graph of these ratios encourages students to raise many questions and also shows that there are significant gaps in the data, an indication that beckons students and professionals to complete future field work in temple analysis.

As students become familiar with the ideal proportions of Vitruvius, we observe and measure a terracotta triglyph from Cosa (a temple from sometime between the first century BCE to the first century CE) and reconstruct a temple plan based on this small fragment. Students follow a hexastyle prostyle floor plan and are able to calculate the actual temple dimensions. We then draw a detailed scale diagram that includes the exact number of columns, column width, column height, and distance between columns. In creating this scale diagram we tried to convert all measurements to meters and had each square grid on our graph paper represent one square meter. However, our calculations involved fractions of meters that were cumbersome to deal with and difficult to draw accurately. We quickly discovered that it is much easier to use a module system and assume that each square grid on the graph paper is a square module. The amazing thing about this discovery is that it became clear to us that the ancient Greeks knew and understood this concept. Using the module system makes our drawing process much easier and our result more accurate. It was exciting to experience this intellectual moment of discovery and understanding with my students.

Calculus I (Professor Trish Hammer): The McDonald's Coffee Lawsuit — AKA Newton's Law of Cooling. Students in traditional Calculus I classes spend most of their time with formulas and algebraic manipulations. Calculus reform of the 1990s emphasizes concepts and applications. I strongly believe that students understand the concepts of calculus by seeing how they apply to real world problems. The goal of this project is to show students an interesting application of mathematics in a field that most people would describe as non-quantitative — law. The McDonald's Coffee Lawsuit is a case that most students have heard about. In fact, most have developed a non-mathematical opinion about the case, which is very different than approaching a problem with no background or context. This project allows students to view and analyze a newsworthy problem in a mathematical way. The idea for this project comes from "Coffee to Go," published in Saunders College Publishing's *Instructor's Resource Manual for Calculus.*

In class, we discuss several basic differential equations and their solutions. In addition, we have studied Newton's Law of Cooling and have completed some easy examples that deal with cooling objects and Newton's Law of Cooling. The problems we work in class consider only one environment. As students complete this project, they take the coffee from one environment (the person's hands) and move it to another environment (the cupholder).

Students work together during non-class times, in groups of two or three, to complete the assignment. I require students to present both the mathematical work and a verbal argument that gives their verdict as to whether or not McDonald's is liable for damages.

In Calculus I, I was very pleased with students' work. Students really get into this project, possibly because many of them have a strong opinion on the case

beforehand. One group submitted a letter on law firm stationary, stating their opinions. Another group submitted a very elegant mathematical solution, where they used a single formula to give the temperature of the coffee after so many minutes in the first environment and so many minutes in the second environment. The best solutions always involve some discussion about "if the plaintiff was off by x seconds, then the coffee was above (or below) the industry standard."

Since I have used this assignment for several years, I have learned that I need to stress how I want students to write up their solutions. I tell students that they should think of this as a technical report, that includes writing and mathematical calculations. I am pleased that students feel that they have solved a real world problem when they complete this project.

One of the great things about this project is that even after students complete the mathematics, there is plenty of room for interpretation. What if the coffee is above (or below) the industry standard by 0.3 degrees? Should we round up, round down, or round at all? Is 0.3 degrees worth a million dollars? Is the possibility of being off by 30 seconds a big deal? I get many different and correct interpretations that are based on the same mathematical calculations. It is very interesting to see how students use their mathematical work to support their opinions.

Ecology (Professor Renee Godard): Demography Life Tables, Survivorship Curves, and Patterns of Fecundity. Population biology covers a myriad of subjects: longevity, mortality, sex ratios, fecundity, and so on. The numbers may seem daunting to students, and it is difficult to collect meaningful data in a time period as short as one semester. The purpose of this project is to introduce students to concepts associated with understanding the dynamics of a population in a way that grabs their attention. Focusing on the grave markers of our own species avoids some of the usual pitfalls of population biology.

To prepare for the project, we read the textbook material relevant to population biology. Students also read the materials handed out for the lab, and those materials, also, include background information. By the time this project comes along, the students are fairly comfortable with working with data in Excel, so that part of the project does not have to be introduced. Before we proceed to the project itself, we talk about questions raised by the readings in class and we also talk about what we are going to do when we head out to the graveyard.

Working in pairs, the students collect data in the graveyard. In fact, because two lab sections carry out this project during the same semester, we can gather data from two graveyards. Within each lab, the pairs collect their data, and then the whole group comes together, still in the graveyard, to hear summaries of the data. After the collection of data, I pull it all together and hand it back to the students to work with. The summarized data that they receive are essentially the beginnings of life tables for the two sexes in the two cohorts. In class, we discuss how the students should complete the life tables (essentially what the variables mean), how to draw survivorship curves (including discussion of the value of semilog graphs), and how they might approach the questions asked.

Of course, the ideal approach to population biology, would be to follow a population from birth to death, but most of the inherently interesting species have life-spans that far exceed a semester. However, our October graveyard walks are memorable to the students, and examinations of life-history patterns of our own species makes the material come alive.

This was also a positive experience from a faculty perspective. It gave me the opportunity to bring in current fecundity data and apply it to the survivorship patterns of the earlier group. The project illuminates how patterns of survivorship as well as birth rates and age at first reproduction influence patterns of population. Thus a number of significant points arise out of this project and dramatize important concepts.

France Since the Revolution (Professor Andre Spies): A Quantitative Analysis of Napoleon's March to Moscow. Students of history know that Napoleon's march to Moscow, and the retreat of his forces, took place under cold and brutal conditions. In this project students work with a nineteenth century document that brings the disastrous historical event to life. As they consider such questions as what proportion of those ordered to Moscow survived the march to that city, how many soldiers died per day on each stretch of the march, and, on average, how many yards lay between corpses, students discover and experience the conditions of Napoleon's march and retreat in vivid terms. Students do not need advance preparation for this assignment; rather, they work through the material together in class. I distribute copies of the map of Napoleon's march and retreat along with copies of questions to be addressed. Students take turns standing at the board to record the estimates and conclusions of the group. Some students measure distances on the map. Other students wield their calculators to translate numbers and distances into answers to the questions. An essential piece of this group work is that I'm a participant and not an expert. I work through the material with the students rather than preparing it ahead of time, and students see me as a colleague in search of interpretations.

After the group works through the questions in class, students write papers individually. Their papers must include an explanation of the mathematical processes. Conclusions must be presented both in numerical form and in prose. Students not only analyze the results but also discuss what they have learned through the project. They are asked to include adjectives that they would use to describe Napoleon's march.

Students did very good work on this project. Seven out of eight in the first class to tackle the problem worked enthusiastically on it. Even students who said that they had math phobias succeeded, and sometimes did the best work.

The benefits of the QR component, and of this project, are many. The in-class work loosened up the class, and contributed to improved class dynamics throughout the semester. I became reacquainted with quantitative methods to the point that I am now studying regression analysis, a skill that I hope to use in my own research. For both students and myself, this project proved broadening in the way that the liberal arts are supposed to be.

The QR project changes the way that students see the study of history. This approach demonstrates to students that historians have a variety of interests and skills, that they take interdisciplinary work seriously, and that history professors are not afraid to try some different approaches and different ways of examining material. Similarly, the QR project exemplifies some of the key virtues of the general education program: it shows that many disciplines draw and depend on a number of different skills—even historians can do quantitative work! —and QR provides a model of how the teaching of skills across the curriculum works well.

Lighting Design (Professor Laurie Powell): Creating Even Washes of Light on a Theatrical Stage. In Lighting Design class students examine the potentials and problems of theatrical lighting through lab exploration with standard industry equipment. Students work with script-based design projects and develop the technical support information that is necessary to produce a stage design. One of the QR projects is designed to allow students to use specific lighting equipment in the Hollins theatre to produce even washes of light on the stage. The specific goals of the project are:

- To create a light plot that includes three washes for a bare stage
- To choose correct instrumentation
- To determine the best placement of instruments for continuity of angle of light.

Students begin by breaking down the stage space (via a ground plan) into sized areas. These sized areas are circles, each of which represents the circular area on the stage that can be illuminated by an individual light. We have a group lab session become familiar with the instruments and the quality of light that they produce. In addition, I work with students to develop vocabulary, introduce the ground plans and section views that we'll be completing, and understand how to use scale measurements.

The assignment requires students to prepare three different washes of light. We complete the first wash together as a group. Students then complete the second and third wash on their own, using the group work as their model. Classes consist of ten students due to limited lab space. This size makes it easy and fun to work as a group on the technical paperwork.

I was pleased with the students' work on this project. At first, many were overwhelmed with the number of steps involved in making decisions. However, part of the exercise is learning how to focus on one step at a time, even though the task seems chaotic. By the end of the project, students were comfortable with the process.

The first time I used this project, I introduced it as our QR project and noticed that many of the students tensed up for a full class period before they relaxed and realized that they were able to understand and complete the task. The next time I teach this class, I will simply introduce this as a lighting project and hope that approach will create less anxiety. In addition, when I assign this project again, I will use a smaller stage space and include a smaller number of lighting areas in order to reduce the frustrations that students experience at the beginning of the task. I will also have the class work on the project in the lighting lab in order to have a three-dimensional reference instead of relying on the two-dimensional paper representation. I plan to continue to use the entire sequence of three assignments, because this was effective and allowed students to master one component at a time as they build on the previous assignment.

While completing this project, my students became aware of the many steps involved in creating a lighting design for stage. They now appreciate the systematic and structured nature of lighting design in the early phases, a process that must occur before the "artsy" work in the theatre space. This project destroys the myth that all lighting instruments are the same and that any one will work fine if you just point it in the right direction. My students have discovered that a theatre design class is not an easy A or a filler course, but one that is intellectually challenging and

artistic at the same time. I am pleased that my students now believe that applied QR is not necessarily evil.

This class worked so well that I have recently created QR projects for my Scene Painting course and it has been approved as one of the Applied QR classes. I continue to examine my other design courses and am discovering that quantitative methods are inherent in everything that I teach.

Pedagogy

A change in the general education requirements at any institution affects both students and professors, sometimes in unexpected ways. A reconsideration of general education requirements should cause each professor to reflect on the material contained in a given course topic, how it is presented to the students, and what the students are expected to gain from the educational experience. The implementation of an applied quantitative reasoning requirement in the general education program at Hollins encouraged professors from many different disciplines to recognize that quantitative reasoning was a skill necessary for the mastery of material in courses they were already teaching. Faculty who teach quantitative reasoning material in their courses observe a variety of benefits both to their development as more active, engaged, and creative teachers and to the enhancement of their students' classroom experience.

The NSF-funded seminars were a productive first step for many professors. The introductory readings and interactions with the organizers, Professors Diefenderfer and Hammer, gave the participants ideas about changing their own classes to include quantitative reasoning assignments. The seminars also provided a template for writing a quantitative reasoning assignment. For faculty who teach in fields other than mathematics and the sciences, the creation of an exercise that guides the students step-by-step through a problem solving process may not be a regular part of their classroom preparation. The peer review of the quantitative reasoning assignments proved instructive for all participants and added to their pedagogical repertoire. The gathering of faculty from several different disciplines had the additional benefit of increasing collegiality among those faculty, generating interest in the goals of courses taught outside of their own disciplines, and raising the level of respect they had for each other's intellect, scholarly ability, and pedagogical technique. The seminars thus expanded the pedagogical horizons of the faculty involved and created a mini-community of exploration and learning that bolsters the educational mission of the university.

Many faculty noted that the techniques they used to present the quantitative reasoning assignments created new classroom dynamics. A number of the assignments were multi-step procedures involving data collection, calculation, presentation of the results, and interpretation. The step-by-step nature of the assignments alleviated student anxiety about the quantitative component, made the assignments accessible, and had a natural fit in the course material. Group work, especially for data collection, was a common feature, and faculty found that students enjoyed working with each other. Students discovered that they each had different strengths which contributed to solving a complex problem. Student collaboration added a strong element of fun and excitement to the task thus removing any stigma that the quantitative reasoning course label might have carried. Instead of being daunted by the in-depth problem solving they were being asked to do, students became engrossed in the work, drawn in by the practical nature, and proud of the results they were able to produce.

The quantitative reasoning exercises developed by many faculty members have the added benefit of coming from real-life examples and data. In Professor Doan's history class, students wrestle with how to deal with the individuals listed in the Bristol census who do not fit into neat family units. In Professor Salowey's classics class, the measurements of extant Doric temples raise many open-ended questions about temples from antiquity: Was Vitruvius' ratio actually the standard, or was it only his imagined ideal? In addition, Professor Salowey's project on the ratio of column height to column diameter shows clearly that professionals need to find and analyze more data from the time period of Vitruvius. In Professor Spies' history class, as students investigate the extraordinary document that records quantitative information about Napoleon's march to Moscow, their analysis conveys a seriousness and weight that make this historic event become real, present and disastrous. In each of these settings, academic material comes to life when dealing with the messy, complicated, sometimes incomplete real-life data. We have discovered a powerful principle: using data from real situations invites students to explore and even struggle to understand the material so that they own the process of interpretation. Contrived textbook examples are simple and easy, but do little to build confidence or promote deep understanding.

The quantitative reasoning requirement at Hollins serves as a cornerstone of the skills aspect of the new general education program and has proved to be a model for inspiring more effective teaching and learning. The assignments encourage many faculty to move in new pedagogical directions, providing benefits for their students not only in general education but also in the mastery of knowledge and skills essential to their specific fields. The quantitative reasoning program invites students to use all the resources of the academic community, an important hallmark of a successful liberal arts education. Barriers between disciplines begin to fade when a student in a history class thinks about the meaning of numbers reported in statistical documents or when a student in a calculus class notes the importance of the interpretation of a liquid cooling curve in a multi-million dollar lawsuit. Students will leave this academic environment not only knowing how to read texts and images, but how to read the very important language of numbers and be critical of their interpretations.

Assessment

We have used several assessment instruments to measure the effectiveness of the Hollins program since we introduced our basic skills quantitative reasoning requirement in the fall of 1998. One measure of effectiveness is to consider final course grades. Of the 363 students who enrolled in Mathematics 100 during the past five years, 85.1% passed the course. Of those who completed the course, 88.5% passed. (Fourteen students withdrew from the course within the approved drop/add period.) The 302 students who enrolled in this course and received a grade, earned an average of 2.18 quality points. (On the Hollins scale, a C receives 2 quality points and a C+ would receive 2.3 quality points.)

All entering students complete a quantitative reasoning assessment and students enrolled in the basic skills quantitative reasoning class retake the assessment at the end of the semester. A comparison of these two scores gives us another measure of their progress. Our data from this five-year period shows that on average, students improve 13% on the assessment after completing the course. (The assessment is based on 50 points and the average score improvement is 6.5 points.) Both of these numerical measures indicate that students who enroll in the course become stronger in analyzing quantitative information.

We also have collected qualitative data. During 2001–02, a campus assessment committee devised student perception surveys to assess the new general education requirements. The data for students in the basic skills quantitative reasoning class shows a very high self-assessment of improvement. The percent changes range from +93.9 percent to +140.7 percent on four survey items. Data for students in the applied skills quantitative reasoning classes also shows positive student self-assessment, with percent changes of 51 percent to 52 percent.

Hollins has been selected to be a pilot site for an NSF grant, "The Development of Assessment Instruments for the Study of Quantitative Literacy", under the direction of Susan Ganter at Clemson and Jack Bookman at Duke. The purpose of this grant is to develop appropriate assessment instruments for quantitative literacy and to train a small group of professionals to conduct the assessment. Hollins faculty members will help to write the assessment instruments and then test the instruments on campus.

Conclusions

There are many practical reasons for including courses in quantitative reasoning in an undergraduate curriculum. The skills learned in these courses will help students in both their future academic work and the job market. Prospective employers are often impressed with candidates who have strong quantitative skills. Informed citizens need to know how to make arguments and interpret data that they see and hear in the news. Learning how to make appropriate choices when faced with complex issues is an important life skill.

In addition, there are strong academic reasons for preparing students to think quantitatively. Techniques learned in our basic and applied courses give students the confidence to solve problems in new situations. The proj-

ect-oriented nature of the applied quantitative reasoning assignments encourages students to approach discovery and interpretation as professionals. Students are getting more practice in solving real-life, open-ended problems.

Providing all students with the knowledge, ability and confidence to solve and understand quantitative issues was the original goal of the Hollins quantitative reasoning program. In designing projects to give students these skills, faculty members have become more conscious and deliberate about creating assignments in all their classes. We have discovered that quantitative perspectives can be found everywhere, in many disciplines and in many classes, not just in the classes that now satisfy our applied quantitative reasoning requirement. Our collective efforts to create projects and assignments that will strengthen the quantitative reasoning abilities of our students, are leading us to discover a great deal about interdisciplinary work. The journey continues to be enlightening for us and for our students.

References

Interdisciplinary Quantitative Reasoning, Hollins University, 2004.

Instructor's Resource Manual for Calculus from Graphical, Numerical, and Symbolic Points of View, Volume I, Saunders College publishing, 1995.

Steen, L., et al. (2001). *Mathematics and Democracy: The Case for Quantitative Literacy,* National Council on Education and the Disciplines.

A Decade of Quantitative Reasoning at Kalamazoo College

John B. Fink and Eric D. Nordmoe
Kalamazoo College,
Kalamazoo, MI

Program History

In 1996 Kalamazoo College revised its General Education Program. Until this reform the science requirement could be satisfied by taking any three courses from the Division of Natural Sciences, as long as not all were from the Department of Mathematics. There was no specific mathematics or quantitative reasoning requirement. Among the reforms of 1996 was a reduction of the number of courses in the Division of Natural Sciences from three to two, and the introduction of a new Quantitative Reasoning (QR) requirement.

One of the reasons for introducing this new requirement was the ubiquity of quantitative information in contemporary society. The faculty wanted to be confident that each graduate of Kalamazoo College had mastered certain fundamental quantitative skills.

In keeping with this rationale it was decided that the quantitative reasoning requirement would not be confined to the mathematics department, but could be satisfied through any course meeting the goals of the requirement. An *ad hoc* Quantitative Reasoning Committee was named to define these goals. Its members were drawn from the Departments of Sociology, Economics, Psychology, Chemistry, and Mathematics. A biologist chaired the committee. One of the chief documents to inform the work of this task force was the MAA Report, *Quantitative Reasoning for College Graduates: A Complement to the Standards*. Several members of the committee also attended a Quantitative Reasoning Workshop organized by Project Kaleidoscope in Santa Fe, New Mexico, during the summer of 1996; other members visited successful quantitative reasoning programs at Mount Holyoke, Saint Olaf, and Macalester colleges.

Program Goals and Objectives

In its final report to the faculty, the committee recommended a Quantitative Reasoning Program "across the curriculum." Courses identified as satisfying the quantitative reasoning requirement would provide students with repeated practice and coaching in a variety of environments, help them strengthen their analytical abilities, and cultivate a more confident understanding of the meanings (and uses) of numbers and their presentation.

QR Courses, as these came to be called, would fall into two categories: Courses whose major focus is skill development, but which do this in the context of real-world applications; and courses in which existing quantitative reasoning skills are used to explore more fully various topics in the discipline in which the course is taught.

Some people call these "little q" and "big Q" courses, respectively.

The Task Force recommended that each student be required to take a course in one of these categories. Students with sufficient background could enroll in "Q" courses. The others could develop the necessary skills in one of the "q" courses and would be strongly encouraged to further develop these skills in a "Q" course. This would ensure that each graduate would be exposed to at least a few of the most fundamental aspects of quantitative reasoning. In the larger context of the new distribution requirements, to require *two* QR courses for the least-prepared students would have been unworkable. Ultimately, the distinctions between these two kinds of courses were dropped. The unifying activity in all of them was to be engagement with data-rich topics that provide many opportunities for analysis, interpretation, and construction of persuasive arguments.

"There are many reasons for wanting students to develop confidence in their quantitative competence," the committee wrote in its final report to the faculty (LaPlante et al, 1996). Borrowing language from Project Kaleidoscope materials, they continued: "The reason to be literate in science and mathematics is the same as to be literate in history, literature, philosophy, or art. Ignorance causes lives to be lived superficially…Innumerate workers cannot do back-of-the-envelope calculations that yield odds on events, economic preferences, and basic insight about the plausibility of claims. They are more fearful, more subject to the predations of charlatans and the whims of fortune. Adults who are incapable of reasoning quantitatively are less effective citizens."

Descriptors of Quantitative Reasoning Courses

Because Quantitative Reasoning courses would be taught across the curriculum, it was necessary to specify the elements that would be necessary if a course was to satisfy this requirement. The guidelines and descriptions listed below were adopted. (It is interesting to note that the first three of these are mostly concerned with communication skills.)

A course will satisfy the Quantitative Reasoning requirement if students in the course develop their ability in all of the first three areas, and three of the last four following areas:

Organize Ideas Effectively. This includes using quantitative language and mathematical symbols to clarify ideas and using sketches, diagrams, graphs, tables, and other mathematical models to analyze situations.

Communicate Ideas and Information Clearly. This includes writing and speaking about quantitative ideas clearly in words, using mathematical notation correctly, presenting relevant data effectively, and using graphs and tables when appropriate.

Construct and Defend an Argument Using Evidence Persuasively. This includes reasoning deductively, using statistics appropriately, and using estimates and error analysis correctly.

Interpret and Create Graphs and Tables. This includes understanding Cartesian coordinates, converting information given by a formula, graph, or table to another format, understanding the significance of the slope and concavity of a graph, and understanding histograms and other ways to present data. It also includes using a software package such as Excel, Cricket Graph, Derive Maple, Mathematica, or MATLAB, to work with data presentation.

Use Various Measurement Scales to Interpret Data. This includes converting between scales, converting units, and using appropriate scaling in graphs and tables.

Apply Simple Mathematical Models. This includes using various functions as mathematical models, and using algebra to make predictions from mathematical models.

Interpret Statistics. This includes the understanding of mean, standard deviation, correlation coefficient, and regression lines, and using software packages such as Fastat, Minitab, and SPSS.

Curriculum Details

The only assessment that we do of the mathematical skills of our incoming students is for the purpose of placing them into the appropriate level of calculus. Therefore, which course a student will use in satisfying the Quantitative Reasoning requirement is left entirely up to the student and the advisor.

For many students, the requirement can be satisfied through a required course in their major. For students in Sociology and Anthropology, a new course was created. But for some—English majors, for example, or Theatre majors—there was no "natural" way to satisfy this requirement.

To accommodate the needs of these students, the Department of Mathematics introduced a new course called Quantitative Reasoning and Statistical Analysis.

"An introduction to some of the quantitative techniques used to clarify ordinary experience," began the catalogue description, "and to some of the statistical ideas used to shape public policy and human sciences, with emphasis on the concepts involved in producing, organizing, and drawing conclusions from data."

Since its inception, we have used a number of different textbooks for this course but the most successful one seems to be David Moore's *Concepts and Controversies*. It is data-driven, requires little explicit mathematical skill, yet cultivates a sophisticated and confident approach to most of the elements specified in the goals of our Quantitative Reasoning Program.

In addition to these two new courses, there are twenty others in eight different departments that meet the goals of the Quantitative Reasoning requirement. These are:

Chemistry: Introductory Chemistry II

Computer Science: Introduction to Programming with Lab

Economics: Quantitative Methods I; Quantitative Methods II

Interdisciplinary: Dynamic Models in Social Science

Mathematics: Mathematical Reasoning Through Problem Solving; Calculus With Review; Intermediate Calculus; Calculus I, II, III; Linear Algebra; Applied Statistics I; Applied Statistics II

Physics: Astronomy; Energy and Environment; Musical Acoustics; Introductory Physics with Lab I and II

Psychology: Experimental Methods

Program Assessment

Several years after the new General Education requirements were adopted, a committee was formed to assess the Program. One of its tasks was to determine the extent to which the goals of the Quantitative Reasoning requirement were being met, to identify strengths and weaknesses of the program, and to identify course-specific issues and patterns across the courses.

The work of the committee is ongoing, and its approaches are still being revised. The committee has piloted two different assessment tools: 1) Pre-post testing, and 2) self-reported competencies, attitudes and beliefs. Samples of each of these tools are included in the appendix to this article.

In the Pre-post testing, two equivalent twenty-question multiple-choice exams were developed to test performance against the general QR skills list. These were administered on the first and last days of the term in selected QR classes in the spring of 2001.

The strengths of a tool like this are that it offers the possibility of measuring skill gains objectively, and is relatively easy to administer and track. Its weaknesses are that it is difficult to develop valid and reliable instruments in multiple versions. Moreover, the actual skills gained might be content-specific and not suited to measurement by a single QR exam administered across the program.

The Self-Reported Assessment of skills, attitudes, and beliefs consisted of two parts: A forced-choice QR skill rating, and an open-end response on attitudes toward the course and QR activities. This pilot was administered in selected QR classes in the spring of 2002, and the results were discussed with the instructors.

The strengths of a tool like this are that it produces "quantifiable" perceived gains in understanding and competence, and it gives sensible results. The weaknesses are that perceived and actual competencies may differ greatly.

The Assessment Committee is rethinking strategies for assessment of general education. It recommends that the ongoing assessment of QR should emphasize learning outcomes, and is currently considering the possibility of developing pre-post tests for specific courses or course clusters.

Cross-disciplinary Commitment and Participation: What has Worked and What Hasn't

Most of the twenty-two courses in our QR Program are part of the major in the department in which they are taught. For these courses, there is little intentional connection to the QR Program: The necessary skills are covered naturally as the course unfolds.

Outside of those teaching these courses, it is not clear how widespread awareness of the goals of the QR Program are among the rest of the faculty. Indeed, now that the program has been in existence for nearly a decade, some of the younger faculty teaching QR courses have expressed surprise when told that their course satisfies the requirement.

Once the faculty had adopted their recommendations, the work of the Ad Hoc Quantitative Reasoning Committee was technically finished. The group continued to meet occasionally for the next several years in order to monitor the progress of its ideas, but has not evolved into a standing committee of the faculty.

In retrospect, we believe it would have been a good idea to institutionalize a group like this as a subcommittee of our Educational Policies Committee (the committee charged with oversight of the curriculum at Kalamazoo College). This would be a natural group to heighten the awareness of the goals of the QR program among the rest of the faculty. Without a body charged with the oversight of this program, there is no natural way to counter the prejudices and misunderstandings that faculty continue to hold about the quantitative instincts the program seeks to cultivate.

We also believe that the problem of "transfer" has not been sufficiently addressed by this program. The original rationale for this requirement was "the ubiquity of quantitative information in contemporary society." This suggests that the same quantitative metaphors—exponential growth or decay, for example—have application in a variety of contexts. But transferring skills from one domain to another is notoriously difficult for students. It would improve the likelihood of success if, when a QR topic is developed in Chemistry, for example, its relevance to Economics or Biology would be emphasized at the same time.

All good programs need to be re-examined after they have had a chance to take hold. Our QR Program is no different. We are now approaching the end of our first decade of this program, and will be able to incorporate some of what we have learned into the next chapter of its existence.

References

LaPlante, M., P. Sotherland, and L. Supnick, (1996) *Education at Kalamazoo College: Renewing the K-plan.*

Sons, L.R., (Ed.) (1996) *Quantitative Reasoning for College Graduates: A Complement to the Standards.* MAA.

Moore, D. D., (2000). *Concepts and Controversies* (5th ed.). Freeman.

Interconnected Quantitative Learning at Farmingdale State

Sheldon Gordon and Jack Winn
Farmingdale State University of New York, Farmingdale NY

Introduction

In recent years, the economy of the Long Island region has been completely transformed. What had been, since the late 1940s, a base of a handful of large defense contractors such as the Grumman Corporation has changed to a large number of relatively small to medium sized high-technology corporations. Simultaneously, Farmingdale State University of New York has itself undergone a total change in its mission and the underlying academic culture. The college has evolved from a two-year agricultural and technical college to a four- year university college of technology with eighteen baccalaureate programs and twelve associate degree programs. Most of these programs are in the areas of applied sciences and technologies relevant to the current Long Island economy. Farmingdale State is located on Route 110 on the Nassau/Suffolk County border in NY, about 25 miles east of New York City. The area is a hub of high-tech industries on Long Island known as the "Route 110 Corridor." The college is the home of the Broad Hollow Bioscience Park, which is viewed as the centerpiece for the many high-tech facilities found within the Route 110 Corridor.

As a four-year College of Technology within SUNY, one of the official goals at Farmingdale State is "to provide students with a broad academic foundation which includes an appreciation of the interrelationships among the applied sciences, technologies and society." Although the College's focus is on the applied sciences, we also have programs such as liberal arts, business, nursing, and dental hygiene, among others, which require us to serve a wide range of students. From the perspective of the mathematics department, this requires us to provide a meaningful mathematical experience to all students, regardless of major, which relates mathematics to the real world in a way that resonates with and draws upon the interests of the students. To this end, in all courses we include student projects and assignments that go beyond symbol manipulation and template problems. We present topics within the context of an intellectually stimulating problem, model, or analytical challenge.

In order to succeed at its new mission in a changing regional economy, Farmingdale State had to undergo a major restructuring which included a fundamental change in the campus culture. As we faced this challenge of totally redesigning our academic programs, we were invited by Alan Tucker of SUNY Stony Brook to join a consortium he was organizing in response to the NSF *Mathematical Sciences and their Applications Throughout the Curriculum* initiative. The project, the

Long Island Consortium for Interconnected Learning in the Quantitative Disciplines (LICIL), was intended to promote both a greater degree of realistic applications in mathematics offerings and a greater degree of mathematical sophistication in the offerings of the client disciplines ranging from the traditional areas in the physical sciences to the life sciences, the social sciences, business, technology, and even the humanities. The nine specific goals of LICIL were:

- To increase connections between mathematics and other quantitative disciplines
- To change modes of instruction and learning
- To encourage the use of educational technology
- To encourage development of new interdisciplinary courses
- To encourage calculus reform activities
- To encourage precalculus reform activities
- To unify courses, such as statistics, that are taught in different departments
- To increase the number of students from underrepresented groups entering quantitative fields
- To improve training for K–12 teachers.

This project provided a framework under which we could completely revitalize and refocus Farmingdale State's quantitative programs, since virtually every one of these areas is something that is important to the institution's mission.

The primary tenet in the LICIL project is that mathematics is a discipline that connects to most other academic areas. Our experiences have verified this. We began our revitalization activities a decade ago with changes that eventually involved the entire mathematics curriculum and then, in conjunction with faculty from most other quantitative disciplines, developed ways in which mathematics and quantitative literacy have been incorporated into courses in most other areas of the college's academic programs. We will describe many of these changes below. We will also discuss the impact on the students, the faculty, and the institution. Finally, we will discuss how our experiences at Farmingdale State can be used by other institutions to implement large-scale changes in quantitative literacy in their own curricula.

Changes in the Mathematics Curriculum

The revitalization of Farmingdale State's programs entailed the creation of an academic culture that fosters interdisciplinary cooperation and innovative instruction in all quantitative disciplines. In particular, these innovations include a restructuring of all mathematics courses to "reform curricula" in developmental mathematics, college algebra, precalculus, calculus, and post calculus courses, and involves all members of the mathematics department, including adjunct faculty. The overriding emphases in all our mathematics courses are to stress conceptual understanding and to apply the mathematics in realistic contexts via modeling. A special focus is use of real-world data, both as a source of mathematical problems and as a motivation for the mathematical developments. We have found that these philosophies have transformed the courses, and the entire mathematics program, into something that directly supports the mathematical needs of our other departments. In turn, it provides the other disciplines with the quantitative foundation on which to build the use of mathematics in their courses. This is quite unlike the traditional, skills-oriented mathematics courses we used to give that never seemed to connect to the other disciplines in students' minds. Specifically:

- Our developmental mathematics sequence is based on the text *Mathematics In Action,* that was developed by the NSF-supported collaboration *Consortium for Foundation Mathematics.* Arlene Kleinstein, one of our math faculty, is a member of that project team.
- Our precalculus offerings are based on *Functioning in the Real World: A Precalculus Experience*, which was developed by the NSF-supported Math Modeling/ PreCalculus Reform project. Sheldon Gordon, who headed that project and is principal author of the text, has since joined Farmingdale State's faculty.
- Our calculus offerings are all based on texts that were developed by the NSF-supported Calculus Consortium based at Harvard, including *Calculus* both in our university calculus track and in our alternate track for non-majors, and *Multivariable Calculus* in our Calculus III course.
- Our differential equations course now incorporates *Interactive Differential Equations* (workbook and CD-Rom) by West, Strogaty, et al, that complements the emphases on a qualitative approach to the subject and the modeling of real-world phenomena.
- Technology has been integrated into all math offerings. All students in developmental math, precalculus, calculus, and above are required to have and use graphing calculators. Students in multivariable calculus, differential equations and linear algebra utilize computer software packages such as Multigraph, Derive, Mathematica, MPP, and Matlab. Students in statistics are required to use a statistical calculator and

the software package Minitab. Students in finite mathematics use spreadsheets and special software packages for matrix algebra and the Simplex Method.

- The math department has received several grants to examine the implications of hand-held computer algebra systems on the entire math curriculum from introductory algebra up through upper division offerings. The math faculty are working with faculty from all the other quantitative disciplines to develop a comprehensive strategy for either implementing the use of such technology or adjusting the content of all courses to reflect the ready availability of such technology even if it is not actually used by the students in particular courses.

- Writing and communication skills are another important dimension of many of these mathematics courses. Students are expected to conduct and write up individual and/or small group projects and to make presentations based on their projects, something which takes place in courses at all levels from precalculus and introductory statistics up through advanced offerings for the majors.

Another important dimension of revitalization in mathematics is our new B.S. program in Applied Mathematics. This program is designed for students with an interest in the mathematical sciences who may not have achieved their full potential in high school or who have never thought of mathematics as a potential career. We specifically recruit students in precalculus and first-year liberal arts math courses by giving them meaningful mathematical experiences that they can excel at and by demonstrating to them that the *practice* of mathematics is very different from the type of mathematical education most have previously received, which is typically designed to prepare students for subsequent courses. In particular, our goal is to build a new type of math major with highly portable skills (e.g., analytical thinking, problem solving, and communication ability) as well as contextual skills (e.g., computer programming), all based on a strong foundation in applying the mathematics to other disciplines. In the process, our emphasis provides the mathematical experience the other disciplines want, so that they can build upon it.

LICIL Curriculum Projects at Farmingdale State

On a larger scale, the entire institution has recognized the need for both a multidisciplinary approach to education and a greater level of emphasis on quantitative reasoning. This reflects a new focus on and sensitivity to the need for multidisciplinary education in today's workplace, particularly the high-tech workplace here on Long Island. Employees need quantitative skills, though not necessarily traditional algebra skills. They need to see the mathematical component in a situation (be it a set of data or a graph or a quantitative description of a process), to understand the mathematical ideas that arise and how those ideas naturally lead to mathematical problems that require solutions, be comfortable with a variety of mathematical tools (pencil-and-paper, calculators, software packages, etc) and, be able to communicate their findings to others. If they are to do this on the job, they need to develop these same skills in their coursework in all disciplines. Fortunately, our reform efforts in mathematics set the stage to carry over these same philosophies to the other disciplines.

The LICIL project provided the framework for involving large numbers of faculty in the development and implementation of many curricula changes in this spirit. Much of this was accomplished through small summer grants, on the order of $700-$1000 per person, primarily to faculty working in interdisciplinary teams. The curriculum projects that were developed range across activities involving many disciplines we originally never envisioned as being part of the project. What is especially significant is that the spirit of these curriculum reform activities have far outlived the duration of the LICIL project. Over the years, our projects have included:

- In one of our statistics classes, the students work jointly with students in a manufacturing engineering class. Teams of manufacturing engineering students design and manufacture a machine tool to produce models of airplanes. The statistics students come into the lab to perform an analysis to see which tool best meets the design specification, thus emulating a real world manufacturing environment.

- We developed several student workshops such as the *Interdisciplinary Workshop in Mathematics, Physics, and Technology*, which is designed to facilitate the transfer of concepts from the mathematics classroom to the physics classroom. This is but one of a variety of collaborative efforts involving faculty from several departments who are working in concert to achieve common educational goals.

- In another student workshop, students taking Ordinary Differential Equations (ODE) visit a physics laboratory to conduct a variety of physical experiments to obtain empirical data with which to verify the analytical results obtained in the ODE classroom.

- Our Urban Sociology course now includes a sequence of quantitative modules created with LICIL funding so that the students work with real world census data taken from a CD-Rom and the World Wide Web. The goals of these modules include increasing the students' ability and comfort level with quantitative work, the integration of critical thinking, and the reinforcement of clear communication skills and teamwork.

- The Department of Construction/ Architectural Engineering Technology has restructured several of its courses to directly link with mathematics and physics. An environment is being created that fosters peer tutoring and support groups, active and cooperative learning, critical thinking, and student self-assessment. In addition, the department incorporates capstone student projects and makes extensive use of the World Wide Web for instructional purposes.

- Faculty members from mathematics and physics have developed a joint course in Fourier series, Fourier transforms, and vector calculus.

- One of our math faculty has developed an interdisciplinary course in mathematical modeling in the biological sciences in conjunction with faculty from biology and biomedical technology. The course features a variety of student projects ranging from activities in which applied math majors are teamed with students from biology and biomedical technology so that the math students can bring their more sophisticated mathematical knowledge to bear while the other students will bring their more detailed knowledge of the biological processes and systems.

- As a direct consequence of the math department's adoption of graphing calculators in its courses, the chemistry department redesigned its laboratories around the same calculator and the use of the CBL for data acquisition. For instance, in the titration experiment, the students collect data, plot it on the calculator and locate the point of inflection of the titration curve, thus showing a nice connection between chemistry and mathematics. Since making these innovations, there has been significant improvement in the students' laboratory results, a clear decrease in math anxiety, and an increasing awareness of the role of mathematics in chemistry.

- The biology department has incorporated two lab modules into anatomy and physiology that introduce the students to the statistical analysis of experimental data. The department also uses a computer based data acquisition system that allows students to record and store measurements in the laboratory. Using this software, teams of students analyze results from graphical representations of the data, something that is a major focus in many of the mathematics courses.

- We created a new course on mathematical methods in linguistics, which is designed primarily for liberal arts and computer science students. Using basic algebra and statistics, the students investigate areas such as the rank and frequencies of words in languages and how the core vocabulary is retained or lost in a language. Cluster analysis is used to study the closeness of languages in the same family. The mathematical techniques needed are taught before the corresponding linguistics application is studied.

- A group of faculty from electrical technology and mathematics collaborated to develop a pair of modules to link several courses in electrical technology to precalculus through the study of sinusoidal functions that are used to model audio amplifiers. In the process, the faculty discovered some subtle, yet important, differences in how the word frequency is used in the two fields. Clarifying this discrepancy for students should contribute greatly to easing their transition between the two courses.

- An interdisciplinary workshop was created for students in Precalculus and Electric Circuits I. The students work on a series of technical problems involving basic mathematics skills. The graphing calculator is used in this optional workshop.

Although many of the activities started under LICIL are still in effect, by far the most significant legacy of the project are the fundamental changes in approach and attitudes toward teaching. The exact activities change over time (they come and go depending on who is teaching which course and other factors); but the attitudes of the faculty and the administration and the new student-centered and multidisciplinary-centered attitudes toward teaching have changed fundamentally. Philosophically and intellectually, the faculty is now prepared to undertake interdisciplinary work, something that would have seemed awkward and would not likely have been well received a few years ago. For instance, prior to the project, there were no interdisciplinary courses or programs; now they are fully accepted as part of the standard offerings at the college. Thus, it is not just the students, but also faculty and administrators who are the beneficiaries of our efforts at quantitative literacy and interconnected learning across the disciplines.

Connections With Business, Industry and Government

Farmingdale State has also made substantial progress in creating connections with business, industry, and government. At a regional conference hosted by the college and attended by 41 local companies, one representative from local industry stated "...*the large size companies that can afford hiring specialized engineers and technologists have almost disappeared from Long Island... the remaining small size companies can only afford hiring a limited number of professionals who possess a wide knowledge base*" and another stated ... "*once a task is completed and the engineer is unable to work efficiently in a different area, his/her service will be terminated.*" These remarks, together with subsequent surveys, indicate that to maintain our students' long-term employability, broad multi-disciplinary programs that emphasize flexibility in thinking are essential to prepare the future workforce. A fundamental component of such training must be quantitative reasoning.

The mathematics department's *Center for Applied Mathematics* is also very active in the *Route 110 Redevelopment Corporation,* a non-profit organization dedicated to enhancing the development of the Route 110 corridor in multifaceted ways. Our involvement enables us to learn about the needs of local industry through networking activities and also provides us with a source of real world student projects.

Farmingdale State has also developed a collaborative relationship with the Cold Spring Harbor Laboratory in the areas of bioscience, bio-informatics, and automation technology. New York State committed over $25 million of state funds to the development of a 100,000 square foot bioscience research facility at the college to be run jointly by Farmingdale State and Cold Spring Harbor Laboratory. This venture has been so successful that a second building is now being added to the on-campus complex. As part of the agreement, our students will be able to use laboratory space. The joint relationship brings start-up companies spun out of Cold Spring Harbor research projects to the campus and provides the opportunity to develop curricula tailor-made to the needs of these new bioscience firms. This also provides opportunities for student internships, senior level projects, and faculty consultations. Our new course in *Mathematical Modeling for the Biological Sciences* is intended as the math department's first step in this direction.

The geographical region surrounding the campus is undergoing a transformation from a commercial shopping area to one that is a major center of biotechnology research and development, and the college is central to this development. The types of industry that will be attracted to the new Route 110 corridor will increasingly need employees at all levels who have a significant degree of quantitative skills. It will be the responsibility of the college to produce and maintain this workforce and this is not something that can be achieved exclusively through mathematics courses. Rather, it requires our maintaining and expanding a broad program in developing quantitative literacy for all students in all academic areas.

New Directions

One of the strong messages that has come from our relationship with the Route 110 Redevelopment Project is the essential need for students going into the biosciences to have a stronger quantitative background, one that is different from the traditional mathematical program that was originally created to support the physical sciences. In response to this challenge, we have begun (with support from the NSF) to develop a new curriculum geared to the mathematical needs of the biosciences. Virtually all of the existing models for mathematics and biology start at either the calculus or the differential equations level. However, here at Farmingdale State (and likely at most other institutions), students going into biology typically start their program at the precalculus (if not the college algebra) level.

Our first step in creating a mathematics curriculum to serve the biosciences is to develop an alternative to our regular modeling-oriented precalculus course. The focus here will be almost exclusively on mathematical models that arise in the life sciences. In addition, we are working with our biology faculty to develop an accompanying one-credit lab course that will be taught in the biology department. In this lab, students will conduct a weekly experiment in which they will collect a set of data and analyze it using the mathematical topic (typically having to do with one of the families of functions that are the focus of the math course). In this way, the students will gain a much deeper appreciation of the value of the mathematics they are learning by actually using it. In turn, the quantitative ideas and methods will be something that can easily be built upon in subsequent lab courses in the biosciences, so that the quantitative level of all courses given by biology will be able to increase significantly.

Simultaneously, we have begun looking for ways in which we can extend these ideas to subsequent mathematics offerings to make the biosciences a significant aspect of our entire program. We have already begun re-thinking both our ordinary and partial differential equations courses to reflect this, as well as the senior projects course. The next step will be to create a more appropriate calculus-level course for the bioscience students, one that will likely also include a joint lab component to be run by the biology department.

Interestingly, once the news about this project has gotten out across the campus, the math department has been approached by several other departments about the possibility of developing comparable collaborations with a math course and an associated discipline lab. For instance, the technology department wants to use this as a model for a new statistics offering in Statistical Process Control where we would teach the course and they would offer an associated lab course in which the technology students would conduct experiments tied directly to the statistics topic of the week.

Another important theme evolving at Farmingdale State is that no science, mathematics, engineering technology (STEM) course should stand alone - all STEM courses should have links in subject matter, active learning, contextual learning and realistic applications. In order to develop this theme, our vision includes the establishment of a program in which every STEM student will be provided with an applied learning experience in conjunction with corporations and government agencies that submit research projects to be investigated by teams of students under faculty supervision. We foresee that many of these projects will produce "spin-off" mini-projects that will be appropriate for introductory courses, thus introducing beginning students to real world industrial applications early on in their education. This would address the need expressed by most of our students to see how their classroom work is relevant to the real world. We have already involved students from our introductory statistics course in performing analyses of traffic studies of the Route 110 corridor conducted on behalf of several local and regional governmental agencies.

Impact on Students

All students majoring in the quantitative disciplines at Farmingdale State have experienced the effects of the methods described above and many "non-quantitative" majors have experienced these approaches while meeting their general education mathematics requirement. For instance, many introductory statistics students work on real world projects using minitab or another statistical package. Example projects include a traffic flow survey con-

ducted for the Route 110 Redevelopment Corporation, an analysis for a major car rental company, and an analysis of the utilization of ATM's for a local financial institution. Also, it is a college requirement that all students in our baccalaureate programs engage in a substantial real world learning experience such as a project suggested by local industry, a civic association, or a faculty member. In Applied Mathematics, this requirement is met through the required senior Applied Mathematics Seminar Course.

At the end of every semester, we have presentations of student projects. Many of the presentations are of professional quality. In fact, some of our students from courses as "low" as college algebra, precalculus, and introductory statistics have presented their work at local, at state-wide, and even at national conferences and have matured tremendously in the process. In one case, a student presenting his work at a local LICIL conference on a project in his precalculus class was actively recruited by a physics professor at Stony Brook to apply to their graduate physics program. We have seen students start as weak students at Farmingdale State and end up as successful students in graduate programs at major universities. In site visit reports and in reports from the LICIL external evaluator, reviewers noted our ability to successfully work with students encompassing a wide range of preparation.

Four of our former Farmingdale Applied Mathematics students, who went on to earn graduate degrees at a major university, are currently working as adjunct faculty members in our department. When asked about his education in an interview, one of these students stated "Every field of applied science and technology needs a basic tool to operate and that tool is mathematics. An Applied Math major is exposed to the sciences, computer technology, business and industry in his or her studies. The Applied Math major has the flexibility to enter almost any field and apply the knowledge gained in his or her studies in the real world. That flexibility is a very valuable tool." This quote exemplifies some of the values instilled in our students through our departmental philosophy and approach. Other Applied Mathematics students are now successfully working in teaching, computer science, business, and finance as well as attending graduate school. We believe that this is an indication that our pedagogical methods are working.

Faculty from the other quantitative disciplines at Farmingdale State also appear to be happier with the students who come through our courses than in the past. Certainly, there are still complaints that students are not as good as they were years ago, but there also seems to be a general perception that the students are learning more mathematics that is useful for courses in the partner disciplines.

At the same time, the majority of the students seem very appreciative of the changes that we have made. We no longer hear the old complaints about "why are we learning this" or "when will we ever use this"; the students see the immediate applications of the mathematics in contexts that are real and interesting to them. In turn, as mentioned previously, we now recruit our Applied Math majors in courses such as precalculus; if these courses didn't capture the imaginations of the students, there is no way that they would be willing to switch their majors.

Lessons to be Learned

Colleagues who have visited Farmingdale State as external evaluators for departmental reviews or grant on-site visits have very graciously made quite complimentary comments regarding our accomplishments. In reflecting on this, we would like to share some of our thoughts regarding our progress including some lessons we have learned. Some of these lessons were taken from [Tucker, 2002].

- The change in institutional designation from a two year school to a four year school with a very specific mission to serve the changing regional economy with a high technological focus forced us to rethink all of our programs. Moreover, the fact that the new institutional focus was on technology made quantitative literacy an essential dimension for all students.

- An institutional program such as LICIL can result in a new spirit of interdisciplinary cooperation and instructional reform that prevails over a long period of time. But it does require a strong institutional commitment, both financially and academically.

- It helps if the project leaders have many professional connections on and off campus and have a good working relationship with the campus administration.

- The mini-grants provided under the LICIL grant were enormously effective, both at Farmingdale State and at the other LICIL institutions, in encouraging large numbers of faculty to become involved in curriculum renewal efforts. It was certainly not the money ($700-$1000 per person) that was the impetus to get so many people to work on these projects; rather the mini-grants provided the opportunity and encouragement that recognized and gave visibility to people's activities.

- We have always been very fortunate at Farmingdale State that through several administrations, the college's administrators – the president, the provost, and the deans – went well beyond being supportive of our projects, but strongly encouraged faculty to become deeply involved. The administration here dramatically recognized project-related activities by awarding merit salary increases to faculty who were especially active in the project and counted such involvement heavily in tenure and promotion decisions. This strong administrative support continues, as the college moves to implement its new mission of serving not just its students, but also the needs of business and industry in the region.

- Many of the Farmingdale State administrators have themselves come from academic positions in the sciences and other technological areas; and so have a thorough understanding of the importance of mathematics as the central link in all quantitative disciplines.

- The State University of New York and the faculty union, United University Professionals, have a faculty grant program that is administered independently at each SUNY campus. At Farmingdale State, almost all of the faculty who received awards from LICIL also received funding under this program to provide either matching funds for released time or further funding for released time to assist them in implementing their project development work.

- Project leaders should help coordinate project activities and act as cheerleaders for the collective undertaking, not run such a project. Good ideas can come equally from all participants and are far more likely to be implemented if they come from the grass-roots level. In this regard, faculty should feel free to participate in the project on their own terms.

- It is essential to respect competing alternative approaches to instruction rather than to attempt to inflict a single approach on all.

- It is important to learn what your colleagues are already doing, especially in the other disciplines and see how it can be incorporated into the project's agenda.

- Faculty should come to view new instructional approaches as a natural intellectual process similar to the questions and new approaches that go on in research.

- Curriculum renewal should be viewed as an on-going process, not as something that is established once and then allowed to exist indefinitely. Changes are taking place too rapidly in every discipline today and, as the need for collaboration grows, the need to rethink and redevelop the corresponding curricula becomes ever more compelling.

- When individual faculty members come together, they have a more visible, persuasive impact on administrators, on other faculty, and on each other. This dynamic provides the force needed for a large scale project to succeed.

- The LICIL project at Farmingdale State developed a structure with on-going meetings, roughly twice a semester, involving all faculty involved in project activities. This motivated the faculty involved to maintain a high level of project activity. At the same time, the frequent meetings contribute to a high level of enthusiasm among the individuals involved, which tends to infect other faculty and draw them into the project.

- The frequent project meetings are part of an institutional culture that encourages numerous meetings at the departmental, college, and institution-wide level. In turn, this leads to a high degree of interdisciplinary contact, which makes it easier to build the interdisciplinary activities.

- The college and the faculty take the challenge to provide the students with the best possible education very seriously. In turn, this means that the faculty are very willing to put their students first, even if it means working harder to improve student education.

References

Consortium for Foundation Mathematics. (2001). *Mathematics In Action: An Introduction to Algebraic, Graphical, and Numerical Problem Solving*, Addison-Wesley, Boston, MA.

Gordon, S. P., F. S. Gordon, et al. (2004). *Functioning in the Real World: A Precalculus Experience* (2nd ed.) Addison-Wesley, Boston, MA.

Hughes-Hallett, D., A. Gleason, et al. (2003). *Calculus* (3rd ed.) John Wiley & Sons, NY.

McCallum, W., D. Hughes-Hallett, et al. (2003). *Multivariate Calculus*, John Wiley & Sons, NY.

Tucker, Alan, Playbook of the Long Island Consortium for Interconnected Learning, *PRIMUS* vol. XII, no. 3., 2002, pp. 193–208.

West, B., S. Strogaty, et al. (2000). *Interactive Differential Equations*, Addison-Wesley, Boston, MA.

Quantitative Reasoning Across the Curriculum

Beth Haines and Joy Jordan
Lawrence University, Appleton, WI

Program History

Lawrence University (LU), with an enrollment of 1350 students, is a selective undergraduate college of liberal arts and sciences with a conservatory of music. Following a 15-year hiatus, LU reviewed its general education requirements (GERs) and in 2000 adopted new multidimensional GERs. These include three components: competency requirements (in foreign language, quantitative reasoning, speaking, and writing), distribution requirements, and diversity requirements. The GERs went into effect in fall 2001 so the class of 2005 was the first to graduate under the new requirements. In this article, we discuss Lawrence's successes and challenges in implementing its new quantitative reasoning requirement. We also reflect on how an across-the-curriculum approach to fostering quantitative reasoning skills contributes to the development of quantitative literacy in college students.

Lawrence's quantitative requirement, called the "Mathematical Reasoning or Quantitative Analysis Requirement," evolved out of discussions with faculty, students, and alumni, as well as transcript analysis and study of curricula at other schools. It reflects the belief that our college could and should do more to explicitly foster abilities, like critical thinking and quantitative reasoning, associated with a liberal arts education. Explicit identification of those aspects of the curriculum that develop quantitative reasoning skills does not reflect a lack of confidence in the liberal arts education, but rather provides an opportunity to define quantitative literacy goals in higher education and assess the college's success in meeting them. Lawrence's quantitative requirement is based on an across-the-curriculum approach in which particular courses in a wide variety of disciplines are designated as meeting the requirement. Students are required to take one designated course. In addition to the designated quantitative courses, and following the well-established writing-across-the-curriculum pedagogy, faculty are encouraged to demonstrate, explain, and provide practice in the application of quantitative reasoning in other courses throughout the curriculum.

In order to support faculty and student needs, LU built a new Center for Teaching and Learning (CTL), with a well-equipped quantitative lab. Lawrence also appointed a faculty member (Haines) to serve half-time as the director of the general education program, and hired a quantitative consultant to staff the CTL. An advisory board was established to implement the quantitative requirement and support faculty development initiatives in this area.

Program Goals and Learning Objectives

The LU faculty approved a set of criteria for courses designated as meeting the quantitative requirement. The criteria specify that: 1) at least 50% of the final grade be based on evaluated quantitative exercises, 2) students do a substantial amount of quantitative work distributed over the course of the 10-week term, and 3) teachers provide explicit instruction in quantitative methods and quantitative reasoning. During the implementation year, faculty submitted course proposals explaining how their courses would meet the criteria. The advisory board for the quantitative requirement worked to operationalize the criteria, provide faculty with feedback, and address any concerns, resulting in the approval of courses in 12 departments by the Committee on Instruction (COI). Courses in traditionally quantitative disciplines were approved (e.g., chemistry, economics, physics) as well as a few courses in other disciplines (e.g., anthropology, psychology). The COI also approved the mathematics and computer science department request that all of its courses meet the requirement. In addition, some departments developed quantitative reasoning courses for non-majors (e.g., Physics of Music, Topics in Astronomy).

The implementation process helped to identify several challenges for LU's quantitative reasoning program. First, as the quantitative advisory board and COI transformed the criteria into operational goals, it became clear that despite extensive faculty discussions, there was not agreement on particular learning objectives associated with the quantitative requirement. For example, there was debate regarding whether teaching of abstract mathematical concepts, like those in a calculus course, develops students' understanding of quantitative reasoning. On the flip side, there was debate about whether using measurement and statistics in biological anthropology provides understanding of quantitative analysis at a sophisticated enough level. It became clear that LU need to define particular learning objectives and the level of quantitative expertise expected of its graduates, and we have initiated faculty discussions of these issues.

A second and related programmatic challenge concerns the relationship between LU's criteria for quantitative courses and the broad goal of cultivating quantitative literacy in its students. That is, in order to be more explicit in promoting quantitative literacy, LU might want to further delineate the criteria to specify the types of quantitative reasoning and methods that promote QL. Conceptual work on quantitative literacy emphasizes breadth of application of quantitative reasoning skills and recognizes the importance of repeated practice in a wide variety of contexts. This work suggests that foundational mathematical skills are an important contributor to QL, but the abilities to critically apply foundational skills and interpret quantitative reasoning on diverse real world problems are necessary as well (Steen, 2001). Steen and colleagues also point out that instruction in advanced mathematics promotes highly abstract reasoning, whereas advanced quantitative literacy moves toward breadth of application rather than increasing abstraction. Consequently, some LU faculty are concerned that the criteria do not put enough emphasis on application of reasoning and are too broad in allowing all mathematics courses to satisfy the requirement. Our assessment plan (described below) will examine how specific types of training relate to students' level of QL. The plan also recognizes the importance of assessing whether the single-course requirement in combination with the across-the-curriculum approach, is sufficient in achieving our QL goals. For example, the statistics education reform movement emphasizes broad application of skills and suggests therefore that a statistics course would be a useful component of a QL curriculum (Scheaffer, 2001). At LU many departments require statistical training, however, our current curriculum could not accommodate a requirement that all students take an elementary statistics course.

Thus, a third challenge involves balancing practical curricular constraints with our vision of the optimal QL curriculum. Lawrence's previous GERs required a course in mathematics. One motivation behind the new quantitative requirement was to alleviate the burden on faculty in mathematics of teaching introductory courses. Consequently, although the substantial interest in elementary statistics can be viewed in a positive light when considering QL goals, it recreates the burden on the mathematics department to offer many sections of introductory statistics. Another QL goal is to spread quantitative courses across the curriculum, allowing students to practice skills in a variety of domains. However, creating quantitative courses in the humanities and fine arts often requires interdisciplinary co-teaching, which even when faculty interest is high, is costly for the university. Practical constraints do not always mesh with learning objectives based on QL standards, which only highlights the importance of assessing the most efficient ways to promote the development of QL.

A final challenge concerns student placement into the quantitative program. Lawrence does not use a placement test, however, students may "place out" of the quantitative requirement with appropriate advanced placement credit.

Unlike the policy that students take a writing-intensive course at LU regardless of Advanced Placement (AP) credit, AP credit in mathematics or statistics is allowed to satisfy the quantitative requirement. Some faculty are concerned that AP credit does not signify that a student has sufficiently developed quantitative *reasoning* skills. The policy difference reflects, in part, curricular pressures to provide sufficient seats in quantitative-intensive courses. In addition, students are allowed to enter the calculus sequence at a more advanced level. Consequently, students with advanced mathematics skills could satisfy the quantitative reasoning requirement with an advanced calculus course. Part of our assessment plan involves examining the extent to which various types of disciplinary training are associated with QL skills.

Cross-Disciplinary Curricular Approach and Courses

As noted above, LU takes an across-the-curriculum approach to developing QL through its quantitative reasoning GER and the incorporation of opportunities to practice quantitative reasoning throughout the curriculum. That is, a critical component of the across-the-curriculum approach lies in encouraging all faculty to explain the quantitative reasoning employed in their disciplines when opportunities arise in courses. The vast literature on transfer of learning (e.g., Barnett & Ceci, 2002; Detterman, 1993), shows that transfer of concepts and skills is most likely to occur if teachers point out how quantitative concepts they teach relate to quantitative applications in other disciplines. In an effort to establish these important curricular practices, we have held luncheons and a workshop to begin conversations about QL goals and discuss the types of quantitative reasoning taught in various disciplines.

For our first quantitative workshop, we invited three speakers who helped LU develop its cross-disciplinary approach to fostering QL. Joan Garfield from the University of Minnesota helped us to consider the importance of statistical reasoning to QL. John Schlotterbeck talked about his experience teaching a quantitative-intensive history course at DePauw University and providing faculty support for an across-the-curriculum program. Dorothy Wallace talked about the Mathematics Across the Curriculum program at Dartmouth, and helped us to identify curricular needs for our program. The workshop participants concluded that LU could use two or three additional quantitative intensive courses aimed at students majoring in the humanities or fine arts. This conclusion

is consistent with research showing that students are better able to master sophisticated problem solving skills in contexts that are familiar to them (e.g., Kuhn, 1990). Although a chemist, a mathematician, and an artist were excited about the possibility of developing a course in art and mathematics, they simultaneously recognized the difficulty of carving a place for one more course in their teaching schedules. On a more positive note, a theatre professor and a historian are considering developing quantitative courses in their disciplines.

Given that LU is now in the third year of its new quantitative curriculum, we are able to evaluate our progress to date. As supported by our initial assessment results below, LU has successfully offered courses satisfying the quantitative requirement in 12 departments. Those courses with a connection to the social sciences, humanities, or fine arts, like Biological Anthropology, Physics of Music, and Symbolic Logic, are popular among students majoring in the humanities or arts. Nevertheless, we recognize that the addition of two or three quantitative-intensive courses in the humanities or arts would strengthen our quantitative curriculum. Lawrence has also seen increasing pressure on its statistics curriculum from two sources. First, more departments now require a statistics course for their majors. Second, students seem to flock to the statistics course as a way to fulfill the quantitative requirement. Although the interest in statistics is encouraging from the perspective of achieving QL goals, it also creates a significant staffing challenge for the mathematics department. A final challenge lies in promoting cross-disciplinary discussions of QL goals and in encouraging faculty in all disciplines to agree to teaching quantitative reasoning with the same commitment and enthusiasm they bring to teaching writing across the curriculum. We believe that the greatest QL challenge lies in promoting transfer of skills to new contexts. Reinforcement of concepts and opportunities to practice solving quantitative reasoning throughout the curriculum is necessary to build students' repertoire of QL skills.

Program Assessment

As an initial assessment step, Lawrence designed and implemented a quantitative-intensive course evaluation form. At the completion of all quantitative-intensive courses, students are asked to report on the types of quantitative work they did in the course, evaluate the opportunities to develop quantitative reasoning and the usefulness of feedback on quantitative work, and provide self-reports of changes in their quantitative reasoning skills. The evaluation form also asks students to identify concepts and skills they learned that have practical applications. These student perception data have been collected for seven terms, beginning in the first year the new requirement went into place.

Data from the first term illustrate some interesting points. These data include responses from 335 students in 21 courses representing 7 disciplines. Students rated (on a 10-point scale) opportunities to develop quantitative reasoning quite highly in both the lower-level courses (mean = 7.4) and upper-level courses (mean = 7.9). Introductory statistics (mean = 8.3), symbolic logic (mean = 9.5), and introductory computer science (mean = 8.4) stood out as particularly strong in this area. In terms of applications to other courses or practical applications, the overall means for lower- and upper-level courses were also encouraging (means for all items were 7 or above on a 10-point scale). For example, statistics courses were rated highly (mean = 8.1) in terms of practical applicability. In terms of applications to other courses, upper-level statistics (mean = 8.8) was rated significantly higher than the upper-level mathematics courses (mean = 6.8). This finding is consistent with the argument that advanced math is increasingly abstract, whereas statistics emphasizes conceptual application, which contributes to QL (Steen, 2001).

With regard to pedagogy, students reported that feedback on their quantitative work and explicit instruction on quantitative skills were particularly useful (means for all items above 7). Students also indicated that they were asked to explain the reasoning behind their work more often in upper-level courses (mean = 8.3) than in lower-level courses (mean = 7.4). This difference may be accounted for by the smaller class sizes in upper-level courses. Nevertheless, if the goal is to improve QL, this result suggests that an area for possible improvement is encouraging students to explain their reasoning at all course levels.

After collecting this baseline perception data, we incorporated a few questions from this more extensive form into every course evaluation (we anticipate that the extensive form will be used as a part of the regular evaluation cycle for the quantitative GER). Hence, the student perceptions will always be a part of Lawrence's general education assessment plan.

Besides measuring student opinions, we plan to assess actual quantitative skills. The proposed plan requires a more thorough assessment of the quantitative requirement every five years. Instructors of quantitative courses will be asked to incorporate the assessment instrument as part of their course requirements and additional evaluative

data will be collected from outgoing seniors. Although this is a very difficult task, assessing quantitative competence is a necessary part of a comprehensive assessment plan. We proposed an assessment instrument that would measure (1) foundational mathematical and statistical skills; (2) quantitative reasoning skills, both general and discipline-specific; and (3) attitudes and beliefs about mathematics and quantitative literacy. Use of discipline-specific measures of quantitative reasoning in conjunction with a general QL instrument will allow exploration of important questions about the transfer of quantitative skills across different contexts, and the contribution of discipline-specific training to overall QL. Because Lawrence takes an across-the-curriculum approach to developing QL, students take discipline-specific courses rather than a general course focused exclusively on QL. Thus, it is essential to determine whether discipline-specific training successfully meets Lawrence's QL goals. In a similar vein, Lehman and Nisbett (1990) demonstrated that particular types of disciplinary training were related to improvement in specific types of quantitative reasoning. For example, students majoring in the social sciences showed substantial improvements in statistical reasoning, whereas majors in the humanities and natural sciences showed smaller gains in this area. Furthermore, students majoring in the natural sciences or humanities showed improved understanding of conditional logic, though majors in the social sciences did not. Disciplinary analyses will help us to uncover strengths and weaknesses of various types of training, and thereby identify areas where students may need additional experiences to have well-rounded QL skills.

We think it is also important to measure students' developmental progression in acquiring QL. To this end, we plan to include assessment questions that measure students' ability to *identify* sound quantitative reasoning, as well as questions that measure students' ability to *generate* sound quantitative reasoning. Research in statistics education indicates that students may be able to identify strong statistical reasoning prior to their ability to generate it on their own (Garfield, 1998). Identifying a sound quantitative argument is an important skill in everyday problem solving (e.g., making sense of a political argument about tax cuts).

Another element of QL is a "confidence with mathematics" (Steen, 2001, p. 8). Therefore, we also plan to measure student attitudes about mathematics and quantitative literacy. The Dartmouth College Mathematics Across the Curriculum Survey (Korey, 2000) provides a good starting point. As a first step, we administered to an introductory statistics class ($n = 33$) pre- and post-course attitudinal assessments based on the Dartmouth survey. The attitudinal survey contained 51 items, 35 from the Dartmouth study that focuses on mathematics and 16 items reworded to focus on statistics. The items generally cover three areas: anxiety and concern about mathematical or statistical competency, level of interest in pursuing further study in mathematics or statistics, and perception of the practical utility of mathematical or statistical concepts.

Overall, we found reduced post-course student anxiety about mathematical and statistical competency. For example, in the post-test, students reported significantly lower anxiety about learning statistics. Also, we were delighted to find that 84% of the students thought statistics helped them to understand the world; unfortunately we also found that only 23% of the students wanted to study more statistics. That is, even when students became convinced of the applicability of statistics in other areas, they were reluctant to pursue further study. Garfield and Ahlgren (1994) found similar results in their evaluation of the nationwide Quantitative Literacy Project. This reluctance may reflect a variety of concerns. For example, students may recognize that it is challenging to transfer skills to new contexts and may be reluctant to take on this challenge. Hesitancy to pursue further study may also reflect students' lack of confidence in their quantitative skills, coupled with their comfort in relying on intuitive, experiential reasoning.

Interestingly, it is not simply student attitudes that can be improved. An additional challenge is to boost faculty members' comfort level with quantitative methods and reasoning. At our quantitative workshop and luncheon, some faculty members expressed concerns about their expertise in teaching quantitative concepts and whether the kinds of quantitative applications they taught were sophisticated enough to meet the requirement. Lawrence's goal of an across-the-curriculum quantitative program can only be achieved if faculty from all disciplines embrace the importance of quantitative reasoning and feel confident in their ability to include quantitative elements in their courses.

Conclusions and Future Directions

In reflecting on the success of our new quantitative GER in fostering quantitative literacy, we have mentioned several positives about the program as well as several steps LU could take to strengthen the program. We see the fact that LU has adopted an across-the-curriculum approach to fostering QL as a strength consistent with the available research on transfer of learning and QL. Sophisticated quantitative literacy is more likely to develop in an environment where students have opportunities to practice quantitative reasoning skills in a wide variety of contexts. However, the success of this across-the-curriculum approach requires cross-disciplinary commitment to providing these opportunities, in courses designated as quantitative-intensive and in as many other courses as possible. That is, we need a structure for teaching quantitative reasoning that parallels the approach taken for writing-across-the curriculum and speaking-across-the curriculum courses. Just as all faculty expect to model and teach good writing and speaking skills, faculty should be aware of and comfortable with modeling and teaching quantitative reasoning. We realize that increasing faculty comfort with teaching QL may be a significant faculty development challenge.

Given our society's propensity towards math anxiety and view of mathematical ability as a fixed inherent trait, we anticipate a need for at least two types of faculty development initiatives. First, it is important to have multidisciplinary discussions of appropriate QL goals and to create a shared language for talking about specific quantitative concepts. We have noticed, for example, disciplinary differences in the way that faculty talk about and use statistical concepts such as significance testing and measurement error. It is no surprise then that students may not see how concepts are parallel or related if the surface presentation is different across courses. Faculty often seem to fear appearing unknowledgeable when opportunities arise to analyze or even ask about an unfamiliar quantitative application. For example, in our cross-disciplinary Freshman Studies course, faculty generally feel comfortable analyzing and asking questions about works of literature, yet they are sometimes reluctant to engage with quantitative works and even dismiss the works as incomprehensible. In order to create student enthusiasm about quantitative reasoning, faculty need to model a willingness to engage with complicated quantitative questions. Identifying specific quantitative learning goals and creating a shared language for discussing quantitative concepts would help to build faculty confidence and simultaneously model good quantitative reasoning skills. We anticipate that cross-disciplinary commitment to promoting QL will increase as faculty confidence increases.

Second, establishment of a strong QL curriculum will require leadership from faculty members who are comfortable with teaching quantitative reasoning. Chemists, mathematicians, physicists, statisticians, and social scientists are among the faculty who might serve as models of how to ask good quantitative questions and apply quantitative concepts to solve academic and everyday problems. Effective models will make their reasoning explicit and will also demonstrate how they stumbled and worked through a challenge. That is, they will model what psychologists term metacognitive problem-solving skills: skills in monitoring one's own cognition. This type of modeling clarifies the reasoning process and can be used to teach people how to avoid reasoning biases, an important element of QL.

Obviously, these types of faculty development initiatives require time and resources. Using funding from an Andrew W. Mellon grant, LU provides course development grants to faculty interested in creating quantitative-intensive courses. Lawrence also supports co-teaching, making it possible for cross-disciplinary teams to co-teach quantitative-intensive courses in, for example, quantitative concepts in art. However, it is challenging to find room in teaching schedules to meet all of the curricular demands on faculty time. At a small college, it is difficult to juggle the need to teach courses required for disciplinary majors with the desire to offer quantitative-intensive courses aimed at a general audience. Nevertheless, given the demands of our sophisticated technologically-based society and the abundant examples of poor quantitative reasoning available in any newspaper, colleges like ours should take on the challenge of creating strong QL curriculums for their students.

References

Barnett, S.M. and S. J. Ceci, (2002). "When and Where Do We Apply What We Learn? A Taxonomy for Far Transfer." *Psychological Bulletin*, 128 (4), 612–637.

Detterman, D. K. (1993). "The Case for the Prosecution: Transfer as an Epiphenomenon," in *Transfer on Trial: Intelligence, Cognition, and Instruction*, D.K. Detterman, and R.J. Sternberg, (Eds.) Norwood, NJ: Ablex Publishing, 1–24.

Garfield, J. B. and A. Ahlgren, (1994). "Student Reactions to Learning About Probability and Statistics: Evaluating the Quantitative Literacy Project." *School Science & Mathematics*, 94 (2), 89–95.

Garfield, J.B. (1998). "Challenges in Assessing Statistical Reasoning", presented at the symposium: Innovative Assessment Strategies for Improving the Teaching and Learning of Statistics.

Korey, J. (2000). "Dartmouth College of Mathematics Across the Curriculum Evaluation Summary: Mathematics and Humanities Courses," *Mathematics Across the Curriculum at Dartmouth College.* http://www.math.dartmouth.edu/~matc/Evaluation/humeval.pdf.

Kuhn, D. (Ed.). (1990). *Developmental Perspectives on Teaching and Learning Thinking Skills*, Karger, Switzerland.

Darrin R., D. R. Lehman, & R.E. Nisbett, (1990). "A Longitudinal Study of the Effects of Undergraduate Training on Reasoning." *Developmental Psychology*, 26 (6), 952–960.

Scheaffer, R. (2001). "Quantitative Literacy and Statistics." *Amstat News*, 293, 2–3.

Steen, L. (Ed.) (2001). *Mathematics and Democracy: The Case for Quantitative Literacy*, Princeton, New Jersey: The National Council.

Mathematics Across the Curriculum

Rebecca Hartzler and Deann Leoni
*Edmonds Community College,
Lynnwood, WA*

Program History

The Mathematics Across the Curriculum Project (MAC) hosted by Edmonds Community College in Lynnwood, Washington, began in 1999. The project was initially created to support the Quantitative Skills College Wide Ability, identified by the faculty of the college in the early 1990s as one of four key learning outcomes for students graduating with a two-year transfer degree. In the summer of 1999, Rebecca Hartzler, a physics instructor and one of the two current project coordinators, was asked by the college to perform a literature survey on quantitative reasoning/literacy projects and practices across the country. The survey revealed two projects, one at Alverno College and the other at Dartmouth College, that integrated mathematics or quantitative reasoning across the disciplines and whose goals fit well with the learning environment at Edmonds. The principal investigators of these National Science Foundation-funded projects, Dr. Susan Pustejovsky (Alverno College) and Dr. Dorothy Wallace (Dartmouth College), were contacted and graciously agreed to assist Edmonds Community College in adapting their programs. In the fall of 1999, Deann Leoni from the Mathematics Department at Edmonds Community College joined the project.

The original scope of the project was to focus on effecting curricular reform at Edmonds Community College. To stimulate student and faculty discussions on the importance of quantitative literacy in their lives and in students' education, a speaker series was created bringing nationally recognized personalities such as John Paulos, Sheila Tobias and Albert Bartlett to speak to the college community. Throughout that year, Leoni and Hartzler also began working with faculty on how to include or deepen mathematics in their courses.

In the summer of 2000, Edmonds Community College, Edmonds Community College Foundation and the Washington State Board for Community and Technical Colleges funded the first MAC Summer Institute. At this first 3-day institute in Woodway, forty-five faculty from around Washington state attended. While half of the participants were from Edmonds Community College, the institute had been advertised in the spring at two statewide educational meetings which brought in faculty from seven other institutions of higher learning. The response to this first institute from other schools was so positive that the scope of the project was expanded to include other institutions from across the state of Washington, and grants were written to obtain funding to continue the project. In the following academic year, Edmonds Community College was awarded a National Science Foundation Course

Curriculum and Laboratory Improvement, Adaptation and Implementation Grant. This grant, matched by funds from Edmonds Community College, its Foundation, the Edmonds Articulation Council, the Washington State Board for Community and Technical Colleges and the Puget Sound Center for Teaching and Learning, has funded the Mathematics Across the Curriculum (MAC) Project in Washington State since 2001.

At the time of this writing, over 1500 students in Washington State had taken courses that have been directly affected by the MAC project. Approximately 80 faculty representing over 26 different disciplines from 18 different institutions had attended the MAC Summer Institutes. The range of disciplines is varied and exciting. The 26 disciplines include not just those more naturally tied with mathematics such as physics, biology, chemistry, and economics, but also include those with more obscure connections to math such as art, gerontology, saddle making, animation, and writing. Information and drafts of implemented curriculum are available on the MAC Web site, given in the references.

Summer Institutes

The MAC Summer Institutes are the core of the MAC project. These four-day, three-night workshops provide the time and resources for participants to adapt or create projects and/or courses incorporating mathematics into their curricula. Participants come primarily from two-year colleges but also from high schools and baccalaureate institutions. Faculty are encouraged to attend the institutes in interdisciplinary teams from their schools in order to develop local and on-going support networks. Often, the teams include one "math mentor," who helps the team incorporate and/or teach effective and correct mathematical content. At the institute, participants are offered sessions on subjects such as statistics, ethnomathematics, Excel graphing, establishing learning communities, and quantitative assessment. There is also ample time for participants to create, plan, and reflect on their work. Consultants from Alverno and Dartmouth Colleges also attend and are available for the participants. A reference library of books and materials supporting interdisciplinary teaching in mathematics are available to use. Also, networked computers are provided to participants for word-processing and internet research in support of their projects.

Program Goals and Learning Objectives

The goals of the MAC project have been adapted from both Alverno's and Dartmouth's projects. The goals of

Edmonds Community College's MAC project are as follows.

1. Support faculty in creating projects and/or courses that make the mathematical dimensions of their disciplines more explicit.

2. Support faculty in choosing the degree to which they want to infuse math into their curricula.

3. Provide students with experiences that demonstrate the utility, beauty and value of mathematics in their studies and everyday lives.

4. Make mathematics welcome and indispensable across the entire curriculum.

5. Make the methods and materials designed to further the above goals available, accessible, and friendly to the broad national audience of faculty in undergraduate institutions.

6. Collaborate with other projects or initiatives in Washington State concerned with promoting mathematics across the curriculum and improving quantitative or symbolic reasoning or numeracy.

Curriculum Details

The MAC project has supported faculty from across Washington state to reform their curricula to whatever extent and in whatever manner suits them personally and/or the culture of their home institutions. The result of this is that the curricula emanating from the project are diverse in depth, scope and implementation.

Initially many faculty found integrating mathematics into non-traditional subject areas challenging. Some participants found it difficult and a bit intimidating to leave the comfort of being an expert in their fields to do this collaborative and creative work in another discipline. Often faculty participants have not worked with mathematics for decades. This challenge of leaving the comfort zone applies to both non-math faculty learning about math and math mentors learning about a non-math discipline. As daunting as it is, many of the faculty participants have found their work in MAC exceedingly rewarding.

MAC curricular projects have been small and large endeavors. Many MAC projects have been simply a single assignment within a traditional curriculum. These have been implemented with or without the help of a math instructor. Larger commitments have been made to create small- and large-scale coordinated studies courses. Schools in Washington State have much experience with coordinated studies courses. Consequently, the administrative structure for combining two entire courses with two teachers in the classroom at once was easily available for this type of infusion of mathematics into different disciplines.

MAC Project: Single Assignment

A small MAC project can affect as little as a single class or single assignment. An example of this occurred in a Business Writing class at Edmonds Community College in which a "math mentor" gave a one-hour guest lecture on graphical ethics to the students. The students then used these criteria for graphical ethics in a writing assignment involving the use of graphs as evidence. In another example, a lecture on regular polygons and tessellations was given by a "math mentor" in a Two-Dimensional Design course. The students applied this geometry content to a block printing assignment emphasizing geometric shapes and tessellations. The concepts of geometric structure, repetition, and pattern were then threaded throughout the quarter by the art instructor to assist the students with future design compositions. Other small projects have been implemented in political science, computer information systems, health, and chemistry courses.

MAC Project: One- and Two- Credits of Math Support

Another form of a MAC small project has been to add one or two credits of math to a traditional non-math course to support student learning of the mathematical outcome of the course. In this model, a math instructor teaches the appropriate mathematics either alongside the content instructor in a coordinated studies manner or alone during a corresponding time period to students desiring the math assistance. For example, an art history course was combined with two credits of "Topics in Math." In this course, the math instructor worked alongside the art historian, to teach any math that arose in the art history curriculum. The students learned about such topics as the Golden Ratio, Fibonacci Numbers, Magic Squares, perspective, ratios, and geometric constructions with straightedge and compass. In another instance the one-credit "Topics in Math" course was used to support English for Academic Purposes. This combination was designed to serve ESL students, whose math skills are typically stronger then their writing skills. The math and EAP instructors worked together to design one essay assignment on a mathematical topic. The math topics for the essays have included exponential growth and analysis of the use of statistics. Other examples of courses that have been combined with one or two credits of math are biology and political science.

MAC Project: Large Scale

Many participants have taken on larger projects where they have created entirely new courses or created coordinated studies of ten or more credits. An example where an entirely new course was created was *Statistical Methods for Sociology,* in which one instructor taught statistics in the context of sociology. More commonly, faculty have chosen to work together in a learning community. Over the past three years the MAC project has supported curriculum development for several coordinated studies courses. One such example was *Math the Write Way,* which combined intermediate algebra and essay writing. The faculty members planned the entire course in coordination, using the writing to reinforce the mathematical concepts and using mathematics as a topic of journal and essay assignments. Another example was *Algebra, Reality and the Rollercoaster*, which combined physics and intermediate algebra. In this course traditional algebra topics were supported by application to the analysis or design of rollercoasters. Other examples of coordinated or linked courses include physics and art history, physics and animation, political science and statistics, biology and anthropology, and environmental science and math.

Case in Point

Dr. Robin Datta teaches political science at Edmonds Community College. He has been involved with the MAC project since 1999. He has integrated mathematics into his freshman level American government course using several of the models listed above. The first year he tried integrating quantitative reasoning throughout the course unaccompanied. He required his students to buy a workbook entitled *Critical Thinking and American Government* as a supplement to their textbook. The workbook provided assignments but no worked examples. The content of the mathematics was pre-algebra, and mostly included calculating change, percentages and percentage change. Dr. Datta did not find this first attempt to be successful for several reasons. He commented,

> American government is a natural fit; however, it was exceedingly difficult to add the math component into an already stuffed curriculum. Also the students didn't have the math basics. The students had different levels of competence and phobias about math and this got in the way. The students needed much more preparation than I wanted to spend time on in class. Also I am not a math teacher and the students who were capable were not math

teachers either. On the whole it was not successful. The students found it burdensome and were more confused.

The next year Datta regrouped and had Leoni, one of the MAC coordinators, join him in class for one week to work with his students on a specific project involving public opinion polls. The purpose of the project was to have the students collect and analyze survey data. Datta designed a survey around "news awareness about military spending" and his students collected data from students on campus. The data was analyzed in class using Excel. From the project the students gained awareness of survey design/bias, issues of sample size and demographics. Leoni was present to teach the students the mathematics underlying the analysis, such as calculating and interpreting margin of error. This experience was much more positive for Datta and his students. He commented

> The students really, really liked it. They began to think more critically about public polls and got some experience using some analytical tools. It still took too much time. The students needed more than one week so they could do more. I would have liked the students to use Excel, do the data merging and the graphing. But I still see it as an extra. I would have to sacrifice it if time got too low for other content.

This positive experience led Datta to his third experiment, which was a 12-credit coordinated studies he taught this past year entitled *Pop Goes the Government*. This course coordinated a 5-credit American government course with a 5-credit English composition course and included a 2-credit optional math support course in which 80% of the students enrolled. The course was an experiment in many ways including that it was an online "hybrid" course, meaning that students met in class only two days each week with the rest of the work done online. The course explored the nexus between politics and popular culture with the mathematics support focusing on statistics and its use in politics. This time the students constructed their own surveys, administered, analyzed, and reported on them both in writing and in an oral presentation. While the students were more involved, Datta found a few more issues to be worked out.

> It did get confusing for students because the math wasn't truly integrated. Because of the hybrid model, it was more like tag-team teaching. There needed to be more than a 2-credit add on course.

Trying again to find a better solution, Datta planned to teach in fall 2004 another coordinated studies course, this time integrating an American government course with a 5-credit Statistics course. Statistics has a mathematics prerequisite of intermediate algebra so the students in the class have stronger math skills than in his past experience. The course was called *Your Vote Counts*, and Datta's aim was to give students the opportunity to learn to find their way through political spin. He felt it was a perfect time for the course as the country went through the 2004 presidential election.

Why does Datta persist to integrate mathematics into his American government course? For him the answer is obvious:

> People need to know how to use math to evaluate the political world — how to evaluate public opinion polls, statistical claims about government activities, campaign claims, demographic issues … we need a numerate citizenship.

Program Assessment

The MAC project is being evaluated in three ways: facts and figures on involvement, student attitudinal surveys, and faculty surveys. Data is being collected on the number of faculty participants, approximate numbers of students affected, the disciplines represented, the courses that have been enhanced, the institutions which have participated and the extent of their participation.

Student Attitudes Towards Mathematics

During the 2002–2003 academic year, students in MAC courses around the state were surveyed for changes in their attitudes about mathematics and their ability to learn mathematics. The attitudinal survey was created by Dartmouth College as a part of the assessment of their MATC program. The front page has 35 statements reflecting research documented issues on students' attitudes about the personal and professional relevance of mathematics, their confidence in learning mathematics, their enjoyment of mathematics, etc. Students are asked to rank their agreement with the statements on a five point Likert scale. The back of the survey requests demographic and tracking information. The survey is administered at the beginning and end of the academic quarter to monitor changes in student attitudes.

Survey Results

At the time of this writing 487 pre- and post- survey data sets have been analyzed. Fifty-five percent of the students surveyed were women and forty-five percent were men. Seventy-one percent were Caucasian, twenty-five percent from under-represented groups (African-American/Black, Asian/Pacific Islander, Latino/Hispanic, or Native American) and four percent did not indicate race/ethnicity.

Below is a list of the survey statements that currently show a small effect size for all students in the sample. The Likert scale on the survey ranged from 1 = Strongly Agree to 5 = Strongly Disagree. An average shifting to a lower value means that the students agree more with the statement.

S. 1. To understand math I sometimes think about my personal experiences.

pre = 3.19   post = 3.02 $(p < .001)$

S. 2. I am good at math.

pre = 2.65   post = 2.55 $(p < .01)$

S. 10. Math helps me understand the world around me.

pre = 2.85   post = 2.73 $(p < .01)$

S. 11. Mathematics has been an important tool to help me learn other subjects.

pre = 2.71   post = 2.60 $(p < .05)$

S. 12. I have taken some math course in high school and college that were taught in a very interesting way.

pre = 2.80   post = 2.64 $(p < .01)$

S. 24. Writing about mathematics makes it easier to learn.

pre = 3.34   post = 3.21 $(p < .001)$

S. 32. Mathematical thinking helps me make intelligent decisions about my life.

pre = 3.05   post = 2.93 $(p < .05)$

S. 35. I don't need a good understanding of mathematics to achieve my career goals.

pre = 3.62   post = 3.48 $(p < .05)$ (note: change is in the "undesirable" direction)

With the exception of statement #35, these changes in student attitude are all considered as movement in the positive direction. While we cannot establish causation, the data seems to support the statement that participation in MAC courses seems to improve students' confidence in math and their opinions that math is helpful in other subjects and in their worlds at large. The data also seems to suggest that students perceive that MAC courses are taught in a more interesting way than previous math courses.

Gender Differences

The data also was analyzed for gender differences in shifts in attitudes. For men and women respectively there were some statements that showed a statistically significant shift between the pre- and post-survey.

For **men** the results are as follows.

S. 1. To understand math I sometimes think about my personal experiences.

pre = 3.25   post = 2.97 $(p < .001)$

S. 12. I have taken some math courses in high school and college that were taught in a very interesting way.

pre = 2.74   post = 2.51 $(p < .01)$

S 14. I like exploring problems using real data and computers.

pre = 2.76   post = 2.61 $(p < .05)$

S. 32. Mathematical thinking helps me make intelligent decisions about my life.

pre = 3.05   post = 2.93 $(p < .05)$

S. 4. Most subjects interest me more than math.

pre = 2.46   post = 2.31 $(p < .05)$ (note: change is in the "undesirable" direction)

For **women** the results are as follows.

S. 2. I am good at math..

pre = 2.79   post = 2.67 $(p < .01)$

S. 4. Most subjects interest me more than math.

pre = 2.18   post = 3.14 $(p < .01)$

S. 5. Mathematics is essentially an accumulation of facts, rules and formulas to be memorized and used.

pre = 2.37   post = 2.53 $(p < .05)$

S. 10. Math helps me understand the world around me.

pre = 2.97   post = 2.81 $(p < .01)$

S. 11. Mathematics has been an important tool to help me learn other subjects.

pre = 2.76   post = 2.59 $(p < .05)$

S. 24. Writing about mathematics makes it easier to learn.

pre = 3.32   post = 3.18 $(p < .01)$

S. 26. After I've forgotten all the formulas, I'll still be able to use the ideas I've learned in math.

pre = 2.62   post = 2.50 $(p < .05)$

S. 29. Learning mathematics makes me nervous.

pre = 2.89   post = 3.03 $(p < .05)$

We find it interesting that the women in the sample seem to have made more significant changes in attitudes than the men. We find it satisfying that at the time of the post-test, the women are agreeing more with the statement "I am good at math" and agreeing less with the statement "Learning math makes me nervous" since confidence and anxiety about learning math can be obstacles for some women to be successful in math courses.

Faculty Development

Our third program assessment method is to gather information about the project's impact on faculty development. Dr. Rob Cole of the Evergreen State College is currently in the process of obtaining qualitative data from faculty participants. He is assessing the effect that creating MAC curricula has had on faculty's teaching both in their MAC courses and in general.

Conclusion

The MAC project completed its final year of funding from the National Science Foundation. While flexibility in scope, content, and level of implementation of MAC projects has made it possible for many faculty from varied institutions to participate in the project, this same feature has made assessment of impact on student learning difficult. Through interactions with the students, the faculty participants believe that their curricular changes have made a positive impact on students' learning. The participants also have acknowledged that the opportunity for interdisciplinary teaching and increasing their mathematical knowledge of their disciplines has been highly worthwhile.

The most rewarding outcome of MAC has been the network of faculty and institutions across Washington State who are committed to curricular reform. This network of faculty and their history of success in the project provide a foundation for the broader institutionalization of infusing quantitative literacy at schools across the nation. In order to support and sustain this increase in scope the established MAC network is collaborating with similar initiatives such as the National Numeracy Network and Dartmouth College's Center for Mathematics and Quantitative Education. Further, the project directors of MAC are partnering with the American Mathematical Association of Two-Year Colleges (AMATYC) to be able to transition the MAC conferences into a permanent part of the summer institute and traveling workshop offerings from AMATYC.

The Math Across the Curriculum Project, which started as an assessment initiative at Edmonds Community College, continues to expand to an increasing number of students, faculty and institutions. While sustainability and institutionalization are still challenges for the MAC movement, the collaboration with AMATYC puts forth the vision that in the future the presence of mathematics throughout the curriculum will seem natural and commonplace rather than a curriculum reform project. Only after this level of integration is achieved will all students view math as something applicable and necessary for all.

References:

Edmonds Community College, Mathematics Across the Curriculum Project. http://mac.edcc.edu

Dartmouth College, Electronic Bookshelf. http://www.math.dartmouth.edu/~matc/eBookshelf/index.html

Brudney, K., J. Culver, M. Weber (1999). *Critical Thinking and American Government*. Wadsworth Publishing.

The Washington Center for Improving the Quality of Undergraduate Education, Quantitative Literacy Across the Curriculum Project. http://www.evergreen.edu/washcenter/events.htm

Math Across the Curriculum at UNR

Jerry Johnson
University of Nevada, Reno, NV

Introduction

Math Across the Curriculum, conceived at the University of Nevada, Reno in 1993, aims to improve students' quantitative skills and appreciation of mathematics by integrating quantitative components into a variety of courses in the university's core curriculum.

Math Across the Curriculum was modeled on UNR's *Writing Across the Curriculum* program, whose goal was to make the learning of good writing a "shared responsibility" across disciplines. In the same way, Math Across the Curriculum seeks to improve students' quantitative skills and their attitudes toward mathematics by making quantitative learning a shared responsibility.

As the name indicates, the original concept was **math** across the curriculum, and we were aiming at a level above what one would today call Quantitative Literacy. As time went on, we learned that this was a mistake because it was much too ambitious. It would have been better to have called it *QL Across the Curriculum*. (It actually evolved into that as we went along.)

Therefore, in this essay, "math" may mean anything from quantitative literacy through basic college algebra, statistics, or perhaps calculus, depending on the context. Accomplishing the goal of the project required enhancing the quantitative content of courses where it existed and introducing it where it did not, thereby increasing students' exposure to applications of math in a variety of courses. Obviously this requires the close cooperation of faculty in other disciplines, and accomplishing this was the most challenging part of the project. NSF support and the University's commitment to the goals of a "Core Curriculum" provided incentives for this cooperation.

The Core Curriculum and The Math Center

The Core Curriculum was established about twenty years ago and consists of selected courses in key areas. From these, all students are required to take one math, one fine arts, two social science, two natural science, two English, and three humanities courses. Outside the one math course, students may not have to take any other courses with significant quantitative content. The Core courses are intended to promote critical thinking, quantitative reasoning and good writing, among other virtues. The university's strong commitment to the Core is one of the reasons it made resources available for both Math and Writing Across the Curriculum.

This author was hired to implement Math Across the Curriculum and to establish a Math Center that would support it. The Math Center has the customary computer lab and student staff, but what makes it unusual is its original mission, which was primarily to support the integration of math into courses across disciplines. This involves not only helping students, but also working with faculty to accomplish this goal.

Overview of the Issues

A very large number of students in the targeted courses were majoring in non-technical areas, and many of them had weak math backgrounds and poor attitudes toward math. By promoting their exposure to mathematics in a wide range of courses, we hoped to improve this state of affairs.

The strategy for incorporating mathematical content into courses varies. Some elementary courses, such as Physics and Chemistry, should naturally use a fair amount of math, but we found that instructors sometimes avoided it.

For example, several years ago the most elementary Physics course we offered was taught in a largely descriptive way without much math. It had evolved to this state in response to students' weak math skills. By decreasing the emphasis on math, the instructor was able to increase the class grade average and decrease the withdrawal rate. In such courses, our hope was to restore and enhance the central role of math without harming student success.

In other courses, such as Music or Art appreciation, it is challenging to find accessible applications of mathematics that an instructor feels comfortable with and is willing to include in the course. There are also courses that fall between the extremes (exemplified by Physics and Music) such as Sociology and Psychology. Here statistics is a natural vehicle, but we are still faced with students whose math preparation may be very weak. It should be noted that we are talking about freshman courses in which students may have weak math backgrounds and be afflicted with "math phobia."

It is also important to emphasize that there are two separate goals one may aspire to: improving skill and improving attitude. One can reasonably expect that a student's algebra skills may improve during a Physics course if the instructor uses it regularly. However, it may not be reasonable to expect this to happen in an art class. If one can hope in some way to convince an art professor to do something "mathematical" it will probably not involve anything like solving quadratic equations. What we might hope for in an art class is something that improves a student's attitude towards math. Therefore, our goal in one course may be skill improvement while in another

course it may be improvement in attitude.

By exposing students to natural applications of math in a variety of settings our hope is to illustrate that math is not just an isolated subject of no value.

One thing that surprised me is that students may not realize they are seeing an application of math unless it is called to their attention. Here at UNR we do "exit interviews" in which graduating seniors are asked about their college experience. In one such interview a senior was asked, "Did you use math very much?" He responded, "I used statistics, but not math." In another case, students in Psychology 101 used a computer algebra system to generate regression lines and answer questions about data. When asked about their experience, several of them said they used computers, but not math.

One message from these examples is that students, like most people, think of mathematics as either arithmetic or the pointless manipulation of formulas. One small contribution of this project may simply be the raising of "math awareness" among students and teachers.

Eventually the project touched at least one course in each of these disciplines: Agricultural Economics, Anthropology, Art, Biology, Chemistry, Economics, English, Environmental Studies, Geography, Geology, Mathematics Core Courses, Nutrition, Physics Political Science, Psychology, Sociology, and Core Humanities (formerly known as "Western Traditions").

Following is an example that was used in an art class and a brief summary of a few others. For details, one should visit the UNR Math Center Web Site, given in the references.

An Example in Art

As a practical matter, injecting math into certain courses is not easy. You have to find a faculty member in the department willing to do it, and you have to find a reasonable example that the instructor is comfortable with and that is accessible to the students. (In the case of art we could have gone for one of the standard examples such as perspective or the golden rectangle, but I wanted to do something more original and with a more modern flavor.)

In 1994 a new assistant professor in the art department, agreed to discuss fractals from a visual and artistic point of view in his section of ART100, which is an introductory course called *Visual Foundations*.

As part of the assignment, students were shown one of Michael Barnsley's ferns, which is generated by something called an iterated function system. They were then shown the mathematical formulas that generate it, and finally actually asked to do some computations by hand to understand how the computer implements it. (The fern can be implemented with the public domain program FRACTINT.)

Part of the assignment sheet discusses the artist's view, and part gives the mathematical view including a mention of the practical application to image compression. The following is an excerpt from the artist's point of view:

"As we have discussed earlier, the development and utilization of the science of visual perspective during the Renaissance was a unique convergence of art and science, which continues to significantly inform our perception of the world. The discovery of fractal geometry and chaos theory continues to intrigue, engage and challenge us to expand our collective vision. Once again, we are seeing mathematically based phenomena that are radically altering our perception of our reality."

A portion of the actual worksheet follows:

Recall that a point is determined by two coordinates, x and y. The point $(2, 3)$ has x-coordinate 2 and y-coordinate 3.

Exercise: Plot $(1, 2)$, $(0, -1)$ and $(-1, 3)$

Stored in the computer are four sets of equations:

newx = 0
newy = 0.16 y (Probability 0.01)

newx = 0.85 x + 0.04 y
newy = -0.04 x + 0.85 y + 1.6 (Probability 0.85)

newx = 0.2 x + 0.26 y
newy = 0.23 x + 0.22 y + 1.6 (Probability 0.07)

newx = 0.15 x + 0.28 y
newy = 0.26 x + 0.24 y + 0.44 (Probability 0.07)

1. The computer lets $x = 0$ and $y = 0$.

2. The computer chooses one of these four sets of equations by a random method according to the assigned probabilities.

3. It "plugs in" the x and y values in step 1.

4. It plots the point generated: (newx, newy)

5. The computer goes to step 1, but this time it takes x = newx and y = newy.

The computer then continues this process over and over again. Each time a new point is generated and plotted. This happens very fast, so you see the fern "grow."

Exercise: You be the computer for a while. Execute the procedure we described to generate and plot three points.

[Remark: The question is: how do you decide which set of equations to choose? Instead of doing it stochasti-

cally, the class was divided into four groups and told to do it in the orders shown.]

Group 1 use 2,2,4   Group 2 use 2,2,3
Group 3 use 2,3,4   Group 4 use 3,2,2.

The art professor felt that this was an interesting assignment and that it fit into his curriculum in a natural way. Furthermore, student comments revealed that they enjoyed it.

Brief Summary of Other Examples

In Psychology 101 and Geography 103 students used the Math Center computers to plot data and regression lines. The purpose was to give them some intuition about data correlation and some experience using computers to analyze a problem.

As mentioned earlier, much of the quantitative substance had been removed from Physics 100 by a previous instructor because the students had weak math skills. We restored it, gave students math competency tests to prepare them, and provided tutors for students who needed assistance through the Math Center.

MATH120: This is the core course at UNR with the highest enrollment. It is what many commonly refer to as "math for liberal arts." We currently use *Mathematics, A Practical Odyssey* by David Johnson and Timothy Mowrey, along with a supplement. The course is taken by non-technical majors and is generally considered to be the minimal way to satisfy the core math requirement. Our concern is to make the course as relevant and interesting as possible, but many students never anticipate using the math we show them, and may not be impressed by applications just because we think they are interesting. One of the things that does catch a student's attention is the realization that the math you're showing them is actually used in a class they plan to take.

We collected specific examples where math is used in some of the core courses and put them in a booklet with cross-references for instructors. The courses were actually listed by number, like "Geology 101," so as to be recognizable to students. Of course, in several cases there was little if any math in many of those courses until the Math Across the Curriculum project put it there. Thus, when I taught linear regression in MATH120 several years ago, I could stop and say, "If any of you are planning to take Geography 103, you will see this material applied there, and there are other core courses where you will see it, like Psychology 101 and Biology 192." Incidentally, we encouraged the geography instructor, in this case, to recall for her students that they should have seen linear regression in MATH120 and that this is now a payoff, an application of the math in another course.

By carefully integrating this information into the MATH120 syllabus and encouraging instructors to use it as often as possible, we can make that connection between the math content and the rest of their college experience.

Gateway Competency Exams

In the paper (Bauman & Martin, 1995) the authors discuss a testing procedure at the University of Wisconsin, Madison, in which diagnostic tests are designed in consultation with faculty in certain non-math courses to measure the math skills necessary for success in those courses. We developed a program of math competency testing in selected non-math courses similar to this but with some important differences which we will discuss shortly.

Each math competency exam is developed by an instructor specifically for his or her class in consultation with the Math Center. As in the Wisconsin model, the test is not a "wish list," but should cover only the necessary skills the student will be required to have in the course. We felt it was very important for the topics on the competency test to actually be encountered by the students in exams, labs, or other assignments in the course. If the skills tested are never used, the students will see the exam as pointless and of no real value—the way many of them see math.

The exams involved no more than the basic math that students should reasonably be expected to have already learned. They were not intended to push students beyond the prerequisites, and they were supposed to be not so long or difficult as to seem onerous. The exams were intended to diagnose and remediate, not to punish or discourage.

Our testing program had a significant feature missing from the model described by Bauman & Martin. The test is remedial as well as diagnostic. There is a passing score set by the instructor, usually something approaching mastery, for example, 80% or higher. However, students may seek help in the Math Center and re-take different forms of the test several times until they have passed. In some cases a student must pass the test by a certain date in order to complete the course, thus the term "gateway." In other cases the student may get bonus points for completing it in a timely fashion. All this is up to the instructor. It was important to encourage students to pass early, since the rationale for the test is to ensure that students have the math skills necessary for the course.

Ideally, the exam is given in class during the first week, and graded and returned by the next class meet-ing. Re-testing is normally done on a drop-in basis in the Math Center by its staff. They are also available to help grade the papers and record the scores. It is important for the first test to occur in class so students will see it as an integral part of the course, but further testing would take up valuable class time and the grading could become onerous for the teacher. It is very important to avoid both of these things, because class time is precious and instructors may be more willing to buy into the idea if they are convinced that it is not too taxing.

Another reason for re-testing in the Math Center is to help the student learn. When students come in to re-test, they can sit down with a Math Center staff person who will go over the test and help them correct their mistakes. Thus, it becomes a real learning process, not just a diagnostic with no follow-up. Of course large numbers of students could overwhelm the Math Center, but in most cases a majority of them pass the first time and do not have to come in. Others pass on the second try and do not need consultation. Therefore, the numbers have so far remained manageable.

Unfortunately, our experience is that many students will not take initiative to correct their deficiencies unless there is an incentive, such as something that affects their grade. Just showing them that they made a poor score on a diagnostic and warning them that they may be at risk usually does no good.

Several instructors reported that they have usually felt it necessary to take time in their lectures to explain a math concept that students should already know. By implementing the competency test they find that the students are up to speed and this time is saved.

So far we have experimented with this competency testing strategy in Geology 101, Agricultural Economics 202, Economics 101, 102, Physics 151, Chemistry 101, 102.

Where Things Are

As one might expect, a program like this requires a great deal of work to initiate and just as much to sustain. The director of the Math Center has primary responsibility for the program and there have been two changes in the directorship since I left the post. Some of the competency testing is continuing and it is still a stated objective of the core curriculum to have quantitative components for core courses. However, several of the individual efforts have faded away because the committed instructors went on to teach other courses or because departments changed the course formats. Also, when funding runs out it becomes more difficult to create new initiatives.

Nevertheless, the project did cause a heightened awareness among faculty that quantitative literacy is important and that it needs to be a "shared responsibility" across campus.

Resources on the Web Site

A Math Across the Curriculum Web site has been established that will allow users to download documents and resources and get information about Math Across the Curriculum. (See references for the URL.) Among the resources available are examples of competency exams, assignments, accounts of instructor experiences, and links to other sites.

Two free videos that show applications of elementary mathematics were produced with support from NSF and may be ordered on the Web site. The first one features Dr. Jim Trexler of the Geology Department explaining how trigonometry is used by geologists to measure strata thickness. The second video was shot at a local company called International Game Technologies. It is the world's largest maker of gaming devices, such as video poker and slot machines. It employs numerous mathematicians and engineers.

References

These items are provided as a possible resource for those seeking relationships between mathematics and other fields as well as information on competency testing.

Bahna, J. T. (1991). The relationship between mathematics and music: Secondary School Student Perspectives, *J. of Negro Education*. Summer, v60, n3, p. 477.

Barnsley, M. (1996). *Notices of the AMS*.

Bauman, S. & Martin, W. (1995). Assessing the quantitative skills of college juniors, *Coll. Math. J.*, v26, n3, p. 214.

Bickley-Green, C. A. (1995). Math and art curriculum integration: a post-modern foundation, *Studies in Art Education*, v37, n1, p. 6.

Chapnick, P. (1993). The music of reason and the dynamics of ambiguity, *The Mathematica J.*, v3, n3, p. 14.

Coombs, C. H. (1983). *Psychology and mathematics: an essay on theory*. Ann Arbor, University of Michigan Press.

Di Prisco, C. A. (1995). Mathematics and music: the delights of performing mathematics, *Interciencia*, v20, n2, p.66.

Disher, F. (1995). Activities: Graphing art, *Math. Teacher*, v88, n2, p. 124.

Dowd, F. (1990). Geography in children's literature, math, science, art and a whole world of activities, *J. of Geography*, v89, n2, p. 68.

Dugas, L. S. (1988). The Problematics of Political Polls: Mathematics Curriculum for Social Understanding, *Bulletin of Science Technology & Society*, v8, n6, p. 601.

Fishman, J. (1993). Analyzing energy and resource problems: an interdisciplinary approach with mathematical modeling, *Math. Teacher*, v86, n8, p.628.

Goldberg, S. (Ed.) (1990). *The New Liberal Arts Program*; A 1990 Report Alfred P. Sloan Foundation, New York, NY.

Gracyk, T. S. (1992) A. On competency testing and critical thinking, *Informal Logic*, v14, n2/3 p, 165.

Grandy, D. (1993). The musical roots of western mathematics, *Journal of Interdisciplinary Studies*, v5, n1/2, p. 3.

Haack, J. K. (1991). Clapping music — a combinatorial problem, *Coll. Math. J.*, v22, n3, p. 224.

Huynh, H. (1990). Error rates in competency testing when test retaking is permitted, *J. of Educ. Stat.*, v15, n1, p. 39.

Johnson, D. & Mowrey, T., 2001, *Mathematics, A Practical Odyssey*, 4th ed, Brooks Cole.

Lee, T. (1990). Fun with music and coding theory, *J. Rec. Math.*, v22, n1, p. 7.

Liebermann, P., & Liebermann, R. (1990). Symmetry in question and answer sequences in music, *Computers & Mathematics with Applications*, v19, n7, p. 59.

Messick, D. M. (1968). *Mathematical thinking in behavioral sciences; readings from Scientific American with introductions*. San Francisco, W. H. Freeman .

Nisbet, S.(1991). Mathematics and music, *The Australian Mathematics Teacher*, v47, n4, p. 4.

Ridgway, J., & Passey, D. (1995). When basic mathematics skills predict nothing: implications for education and training, *Educational psychology*, v15, n1, p. 35.

Robinson, J., & Wronkovich, M. (1991) Proficiency testing in Ohio, *American Secondary Education*. v20, n2, p. 10.

Rogers, G. E., & Steinhoff, C. R. (1991). Florida community colleges meet the challenge: preparing students for minimum competency testing, *Community College Review*, v18, n4, p. 33.

Schwartzman, J. (1989). Square-dance numbers, *Math. Teacher*, v82, n5, p. 380.

Sterling, B. (1989). Interrelating art and math...and Picasso, *School Arts*, v88, n7, p. 22.

UNR Math Across the Curriculum. www.unr.edu/mathcenter/mac

Walton, K. (1994). Albrecht Durer's renaissance connections between mathematics and art, *Math. Teacher*, v87, n4, p. 278.

Wongbundhit, Y. (1996). Administration of standardized competency tests: does the testing environment make a difference? Spectrum: *J. of School Research and Information*, v14, n2, p. 3.

Zeidner, M. (1991). Statistics and mathematics anxiety in social science students: some interesting parallels, *The British J. of Educational Psychology*, v61, p. 319.

The Quantitative Literacy Program at Hamilton College

Robert Kantrowitz and
Mary B. O'Neill
Hamilton College, Clinton NY

Quantitative Literacy at Hamilton — Historical Background

Hamilton College is a small, residential, private liberal arts college with an enrollment of approximately 1700 undergraduate students, most of whom live on campus. The College is in the process of implementing a new academic curriculum, beginning with the class of 2005. Distribution requirements have been eliminated. Through a strengthened relationship with their advisors, students are encouraged to assume more responsibility for constructing their own course schedule based on their plans, goals, and interests. Apart from completing a concentration, or major, the new curriculum features only a sophomore seminar requirement, three writing-intensive courses, and the quantitative literacy and physical education requirements. The Quantitative Literacy Program at Hamilton consists of two components: the Quantitative Literacy Center and the Quantitative Literacy Requirement.

It was in the late 1970s that concerned faculty members, specifically in the economics department, noticed that some students were deficient in the quantitative skills needed to be successful in their courses. A committee was formed to gather more information from faculty members about their students' quantitative abilities and to seek a grant to study the problem. In 1979, Hamilton College received an IBM grant for a study of quantitative literacy among our students, specifically to investigate possible deficiencies in quantitative skills and to make recommendations about how the College might remedy any such deficiencies. In 1984, the Quantitative Literacy Committee designed a written examination to be given to all incoming students. The purpose of the exam was to measure students' mastery of some elementary quantitative skills. The exam questions include topics in algebra, geometry, probability, and basic consumer mathematics. The results of this exam would be used as an advising tool. Typically, fewer than 25% of the students taking the exam do not pass.

After its investigation and development of the Quantitative Skills Exam, the Committee recommended that the College establish a Quantitative Literacy Center. Students scoring below a designated cutoff on the Quantitative Skills Exam would be advised to seek tutoring at the Center to improve their quantitative skills. Qualified student tutors, with majors in such areas as Biology, Chemistry, Economics, Geology, Mathematics, Philosophy, Physics, and Psychology, would staff the Center. Peer tutoring would be available on a drop-in basis to all students—self-identified and referred—taking courses with a quantitative component.

In 1996, the faculty agreed to increase the rigor of the program by making quantitative literacy a graduation requirement. Previously, students could avoid taking a course with a mathematical component, even though their advisors recommended it. By making quantitative literacy a graduation requirement, the faculty ensured that students could no longer avoid quantitative work. The Quantitative Skills Exam would be used to identify students with quantitative deficiencies, who would then be given the option of enrolling in one of several designated quantitative courses, or taking a non-credit tutorial offered through the Quantitative Literacy Center. The goal of the tutorial would be to help students develop the skills that enable them to be better prepared for college-level courses with a quantitative component. The peer tutors at the Quantitative Literacy Center would serve as mentors for the non-credit tutorial.

The Quantitative Literacy Requirement

The Quantitative Literacy Requirement, as described in the Hamilton College catalogue, states that students must demonstrate basic quantitative literacy by passing a quantitative skills examination given to all first-year students and transfers during Orientation, by passing a designated quantitative course, or by completing a non-credit tutorial. This requirement should be completed by the end of the first year. Before first-year students and transfers register for their fall semester courses, they meet their advisors to discuss the results of the Quantitative Skills Exam and to plan how to fulfill the requirement. Following is a list of courses that may be used to satisfy the Quantitative Literacy Requirement. Offerings typically change from year to year.

Archeology 106	Principles of Archeology
Biology 110	Principles of Biology: Organismal
Chemistry 107	Environment, Technology and Chemistry
Chemistry 120	Principles of Chemistry
Economics 265	Economic Statistics
Economics 275	Microeconomic Theory
Economics 285	Macroeconomic Theory
Geology 209	Hydrology
Government 230	Data Analysis
Mathematics 100	Statistical Reasoning and Data Analysis
Mathematics 103	Explorations in Mathematics
Mathematics 107	Mathematics of Finance
Mathematics 108	Transformation Geometry

Mathematics 113	Calculus I
Mathematics 123	Discrete Mathematics
Philosophy 240	Symbolic Logic
Physics 120	Survey of Physics
Physics 130	Physics of Architecture
Physics 140	Light and Laser
Physics 150	Astronomy
Physics 190	The Particular Universe
Psychology 280	Statistical Psychological Research
Soph. Seminar 210	Physics of Musical Sound

As mentioned above, tutors at the Quantitative Literacy Center are available to assist any student taking a course with a quantitative component.

The Non-Credit Tutorial

The non-credit tutorial was created by the Committee in the summer of 1996 and instituted that fall, with the introduction of the Quantitative Literacy Requirement. The tutorial is a self-paced, tutor-based mini-course, available to students through the Quantitative Literacy Center. The course serves well the student who will commit to sharpening his or her quantitative skills by working for no course credit, with the support of competent, well-trained, carefully supervised, committed student tutors, in a grade-free setting. This option also works well for students who are inclined to avoid mathematics and quantitative courses. Alternatively, students could devote their efforts to a regular course (see the list of offerings above), receive quantitative accreditation, course credit, and fulfill a graduation requirement as well. And the Quantitative Literacy Center is available for support as needed.

It is hoped that students who choose to fulfill the Requirement via the non-credit tutorial acquire "life skills"— skills that can be applied to day-to-day activities, including nutritional analysis, banking, finance, and exercise analysis. Hopefully, the math skills learned in the tutorial are also transferable to work in courses containing a quantitative component. With these broad goals in mind, the committee finally decided on a tutorial consisting of the following four main modules:

   I. Basic Computation

  II. Algebraic Expressions

 III. Graphs and Charts

 IV. Proportional & Functional Reasoning.

The committee wanted the modules to be relevant and challenging, while, at the same time accessible to students who might describe themselves as "math phobic."

Clearly, not all quantitative topics could be included. For example, counting and probability is not represented in the modules.

Tutorials are offered in the Quantitative Literacy Center at various times Sunday through Thursday and run for about ten weeks. Students are encouraged to attend regular tutorial sessions and to make up missed sessions. The Director of the Quantitative Literacy Center administers the program, resolves scheduling problems, and tracks and monitors students' progress towards completion of the Quantitative Literacy Requirement. During a given year, the number of students who choose to take the tutorial to fulfill the requirement ranges from twenty-five to thirty-five.

In the past, students re-took the Quantitative Skills Exam upon completion of their study of the modules. The Quantitative Literacy Committee recently created a new exam that is tailored specifically to the tutorial modules. The new exam is more consistent with the material studied in the tutorial and better measures students' mastery of that material.

Outline of the Tutorial Modules for the Non-Credit Tutorial:

I. Module I - Basic Computation
Lesson 1 - Nutrition Problems
percentages, decimals, multiplication, addition, subtraction, and problem solving

Lesson 2 - Personal Finance
interest calculations, percentages, fractions, spreadsheet use, and problem solving

Lesson 3 - Geometry
perimeter, area, volume, circumference, and the Pythagorean theorem

II. Module II - Algebra
Lesson 1 - Algebraic Expressions
use of variables to represent unknown quantities and problem solving

Lesson 2 - Averages
averages, weighted averages, and average velocity problems

Lesson 3 - Linear Equations
Fahrenheit/Celsius conversion formula, slope, slope-intercept form of equation of a line, finding the equation of a line through two points or given one point and the slope

Lesson 4 - Work Problems
classical problem of computing the time required for workers to complete a job together, given the time it takes each of them to complete the job individually; practice with fractions

Lesson 5 - Rational Numbers
representation of rational numbers as terminating or repeating decimals and as quotients of integers

Lesson 6 - Arithmetic and Geometric Sums
introduction to these two types of sums

III. Module III - Graphs and Charts - Applications to Economics
Lesson 1 - Time-Series Graphs
time line graphs, bar graphs, percentages

Lesson 2 - Graphing Two-Variables
more line graphs

Lesson 3 - Slope of a Line
concept of slope as a rate of change

Lesson 4 - Slope of a curve at a point concept of tangent lines, more conceptual exploration of slope

IV. Module IV - Proportional and Functional Reasoning
Lesson 1 - Simple Proportions and Proportional Relations
Lesson 2 - Applications in Geometry
Lesson 3 - Lengths, Areas, and Volumes
Lesson 4 - Inverse Proportions and More General Functions

Functions of the Quantitative Literacy Center

The main function of the Quantitative Literacy Center is to offer academic support to students in courses with a quantitative component. The Center is staffed as a drop-in clinic by student tutors 7:00–9:00 p.m. Sunday through Thursday, 2:00–4:00 p.m. Sunday, and 4:00–6:00 p.m. Tuesday and Thursday. The Center usually employs fourteen to sixteen tutors. Every effort is made to be sure that most disciplines are represented when the Center is open.

The Center is a classroom located adjacent to the Director's office. It is used for classes daily until 4:00 p.m., then as the Quantitative Literacy Center. Overflow tutoring is done in neighboring classrooms. Some faculty set up exercises and problem sets on the college network, so a computer is available for student use.

Undergraduate tutors are chosen from among nominees submitted by the faculty. New tutors meet as a group in the beginning of the year for training, which includes: discussing learning styles, tutoring strategies, tutoring in a multi-cultural setting, and how to communicate effectively. Staff meetings are held throughout the semester, and at least once each semester, tutors meet with the Quantitative Literacy Committee.

An important aspect of the Program is communication with professors of classes that the Center supports, as well as communication with advisors of students who may need to use the Center. To this end, frequent e-mails, memoranda, and flyers are sent to community members about the Center. At the beginning of each term, tutors visit the quantitative classes to hand out flyers and to give information about the tutoring program.

At the beginning of the fall semester, the Director of the Quantitative Literacy Center holds meetings for groups from various departments. For instance, the introductory physics professors meet with the physics tutors during lunch to talk about the professors' expectations of the tutorial process. Instructors advise the tutors about how to work on the problem-solving process with students, not just on arriving at an answer.

A typical evening of tutoring will find a group of first-term calculus students working on their homework, stopping from time to time to ask a question of the tutor. In the corner, two chemistry students might be working with a tutor on a lab report. At the board, a physics tutor demonstrates a solution to a problem. Nearby, a Quantitative Literacy Tutorial tutor works with students on module exercises.

The tutorial services for quantitative courses are intended to supplement the help that instructors provide to their students during office hours. The peer-tutoring environment is less threatening for some students since tutors are not the ones giving course grades. Tutors can help fill in the gaps that sometimes occur between class and homework.

The use of the Center is carefully tracked by asking students to sign in. On an average day, ten to fourteen students come to the Center. Sometimes the number has reached as high as twenty-eight. Tutors are asked to write a detailed report of their work at the Center. They list the names of students with whom they worked, the course that they tutored, and some of the problems that they worked on. They are also asked to provide an assessment of how helpful they think they were. This information is helpful to the director if instructors or advisors inquire about a student's problems.

A questionnaire is distributed every semester to students who have used the resources of the Quantitative Literacy Center. Students are asked how they found out about the Center, how often they have used the Center,

how the tutors were helpful, if they would use the Center again, and if they would recommend the Center to another student. Results of the questionnaire sent to students at the end of spring term 2003 were varied. Students who came in often found the Center to be a kind of "home base," a place to sit and do homework and ask the occasional question of tutors. Some students preferred working exclusively with one particular tutor. Students liked getting other strategies and ways to solve problems. They appreciated the evening and afternoon hours that were more convenient than professors' office hours. One student said that he didn't need help, but coming to the Center motivated him to do the homework. Some students felt that the Center was too busy, that they had to wait too long to get a tutor's attention. Students often get frustrated when tutors don't give them the answers. Some students won't come back to the Center if the tutor can't help them with a problem.

Use of the Center is higher during the fall semester than the spring. Visits to the Center do seem to diminish as the semester progresses. Spikes in a given discipline at a given time depend on individual courses and instructors' requirements. While the Center supports many disciplines on campus, it is most visible to students in mathematics courses since it is housed in the same building as the Mathematics Department. Other factors to which Center visits are sensitive include the extent to which individual instructors encourage and advertise its use. Although many instructors support the program enthusiastically, some faculty seem reluctant to imply that students should visit the Center rather than meet with them. Others do not want to send the signal that success in their courses will require outside tutoring.

Assessment of the Current Status of the Quantitative Literacy Program

The Quantitative Literacy Program at Hamilton College, as it is currently construed, has realized some positive results. Regrettably (and ironically) most of reportable results are qualitative and anecdotal. For one thing, there has been a growing awareness on the part of the faculty and administration of the need for a minimum standard of quantitative literacy. As we mentioned in the opening section above, the Quantitative Literacy requirement survived the college-wide, comprehensive curricular review and reform that resulted in the elimination of distribution requirements starting with the class of 2005. But while the college is committed to quantitative literacy, the Quantitative Literacy requirement is the least demanding of the academic requirements. One way in which students can satisfy the Quantitative Literacy requirement is by scoring 50% on the Quantitative Skills Exam that is administered during first-year orientation. Typically, about 75% of incoming classes satisfy the requirement in this way. But the exam is comprised of high school level mathematics questions, and the Quantitative Literacy Committee has always been concerned about students' demonstrating quantitative competency by correctly responding to only 14 out of these 28 multiple-choice problems. (Example: If T tons of snow fall in 1 minute, how many tons of snow fall in Q hours?)

The Quantitative Skills Exam also purports to serve a diagnostic purpose. Students' scores on the exam are included in their academic advising folders so that faculty advisors can assist students with course selection. In particular, advisors can use the test results to help determine which courses with a quantitative component might be most appropriate and also to help students anticipate any difficulties they might encounter in quantitative courses.

A careful assessment of the correlation between scores on the Quantitative Skills Exam and grades in Hamilton's quantitative courses has never been undertaken. Therefore, the extent to which a poor score on the Quantitative Skills Exam predicts difficulty and the need for extra help or intervention in specific courses is unclear. Even though the original purpose of the Quantitative Literacy Center was to support students taking the introductory quantitative courses, students who perform poorly on the Quantitative Skills Exam are not required to come for tutoring. Moreover, the reported results of the Exam are not itemized, so they do not inform students and their advisors about which skills appear to not have been mastered.

There is an inherent "chicken-and-egg" problem with the current requirement. Which comes first: demonstrated quantitative proficiency by passing the Quantitative Skills Exam—or—taking a course with a quantitative component? That is, should students be required to demonstrate proficiency before being admitted to quantitatively demanding courses like chemistry, calculus, economics and physics, or should students who display a lack of proficiency be required to take such courses so that they become proficient?

Finally, as we mentioned in the preceding section, the end-of-semester questionnaires indicate that students who participate in the tutorial generally have a positive experience. The substantial tutoring support for students taking quantitative courses is appreciated and well received. The student tutors also report that they benefit from participating in the program. They gain tutoring experience and also have an opportunity to review topics that they learned some time ago. It is clear, however, that a more systematic, comprehensive assessment of the Quantitative Literacy Program is overdue.

Faculty Commitment and Participation

From the start, faculty participation in the program has been varied. Some instructors are reluctant to certify that their courses have enough quantitative content. Others do not want their courses on the list of those that may be applied towards fulfilling the requirement because of their reluctance to have disinterested students taking their courses for the sake of fulfilling a requirement. The content of some courses depends largely on who is teaching them, so that it becomes difficult for the Committee to label a course "quantitative-intensive" when its coverage is not uniform each semester. In a given semester, there are usually few courses that may be used to satisfy the requirement. Apart from mathematics courses, the other offerings may vary from semester to semester, and there is always the need to revisit the question of which courses should be on the list. So, while many agree that quantitative literacy should extend across the curriculum, the list of courses with a significant quantitative component is consistently dominated by mathematics courses. Beyond the tutoring support that is offered by the Quantitative Literacy Center, many faculty members do not see an advantage in having their courses listed.

Finally, there is the issue of stronger regulation of the requirement. The Director of the Center spends time tracking down students who have failed the exam and who have not made progress towards fulfilling the requirement. Even though the new curriculum features enhanced communication between students and their advisors, completion of the Quantitative Literacy Requirement is often overlooked. If the Quantitative Skills Exam were a pre-requisite for taking courses in which the skills are necessary, more attention might be paid to the results of the exam.

What can be done to increase faculty commitment to the program?

1. Find ways to increase faculty understanding of the requirement.

2. Enlighten students of their responsibilities regarding the requirement.

3. Work on the advising system to enable faculty and students to think more clearly about how their quantitative ability fits into their college careers.

4. Using the Writing Across the Curriculum model, hold workshops on using quantitative literacy in the classroom, and offer stipends to faculty who attend.

The Quantitative Literacy Program's tutoring Center is very successful, but the future of the Quantitative Literacy Requirement at Hamilton College is in a state of flux. The Quantitative Literacy Requirement is an important component of the curriculum at Hamilton College, but it still needs strengthening. If we can find ways of increasing the commitment of faculty across the curriculum, it can be made better still, but even in its current form it maintains a presence that can't be ignored.

Quantitative Reasoning at the University of Massachusetts Boston

Maura Mast and Mark Pawlak

University of Massachusetts Boston, Boston, MA

After years of watching students graduate from the University without taking a math course or having failed a math course when they did attempt one, a group of faculty at the University of Massachusetts Boston recently began to seriously address the following problems: How could they teach meaningful mathematics to students who do not like mathematics and who think that mathematics has no place in their lives? How could they better prepare students for the work they will do at the University? How could they help students to be better members of their communities, able to process and analyze the vast amount of information that is part of our complex society? The answer was to develop a Mathematics/Quantitative Reasoning requirement and new courses designed specifically for that requirement. All students, both incoming freshmen and transfer, would have to satisfy the requirement by taking a newly designed Quantitative Reasoning course or Mathematics course from an approved list, or by showing proficiency in Mathematics at the PreCalculus level or above. Since the introduction of the requirement, the results have been encouraging and astounding, particularly for students who take a Quantitative Reasoning course and for the faculty who teach it. One student's reflection captures the experience of many: "this course has changed the way I have looked at Math almost my entire life. Despite the fact that I do like Math, I was often discouraged by my inability to find a connection between what I was learning in class and things going on in real life…. In this course I have learned how to apply mathematical concepts to real life issues."

The Development of the Mathematics Quantitative Reasoning Requirement

The University of Massachusetts Boston's traditional mission is to offer access to an excellent education at an affordable price to the people of the greater Boston area. Situated near downtown Boston, this urban, commuter campus is the only public university in the city. As such, it attracts large numbers of non-traditional students.

The majority of UMass Boston students are older: 42% are ages 22–29, 37% are ages 30 or older. One-third are members of minority groups traditionally underrepresented in higher education, and the majority of undergraduate students are low-income and first-generation college attending students. In addition, more than two-thirds of the undergraduate students started college at another institution and transferred to UMass Boston to complete their degrees.

In the mid-1990s faculty at the University began developing a new General Education program that would better meet the needs of its diverse student population. The goal was to design a program that would provide students with a comprehensive first- and second-year experience, introducing them to university study and giving them the tools to succeed in more advanced courses and in their majors. One area of particular need was mathematics quantitative reasoning. Faculty were concerned that students could graduate with no exposure to mathematics, that work on essential skills was not being done at the beginning of the student's career where it would be most useful, and that students demonstrated poor ability to reason quantitatively. In part, this was motivated by feedback from industry that their employees struggled with this.

The University established a mathematics/quantitative reasoning requirement as an integral part of the new general education program. Briefly stated, the requirement stipulates that all students (including transfer students) demonstrate a quantitative reasoning ability early in their university career. Because this requirement would apply to all students, it needed to be flexible enough and relevant for each group. For students in the social sciences and nursing, for example, a course emphasizing quantitative analysis of real world data would be appropriate, while science majors clearly need Mathematics courses as preparation for their courses of study. A compromise of sorts was reached: students could satisfy this requirement by taking a traditional Mathematics course, or by taking Quantitative Reasoning courses that also contain significant mathematics content.

There are five colleges in the University, and each has developed its own standards for demonstrating proficiency in Quantitative Reasoning. The table below summarizes the various ways the requirement may be met.

In this article, we focus on the Quantitative Reasoning requirement for B.A. students in the Colleges of Liberal Arts, Science and Mathematics, and Nursing, as many of these students are meeting the requirement by taking Quantitative Reasoning courses. These courses follow an investigations pedagogy, and feature a variety of activities, including collaborative learning and extensive use of technology. These courses emphasize reasoning and the appropriate use of quantitative analysis rather than mathematical manipulation and computation.

The consensus of the original steering committee was that faculty input in designing, teaching, and taking responsibility for these courses would be maximized when the courses were part of specific departmental offerings, rather than in its own separate program. The Mathematics Department took the lead and developed the first Quantitative Reasoning course in 1998; they currently offer 20–25 sections per year. Faculty from across the university, in departments such as Philosophy and Academic Support, teach this course. Other departments are considering creating new courses or modifying existing ones to satisfy the requirement. One such Quantitative Reasoning course has been developed by the Political Science department, although it is rarely offered.

It is a challenge to convince faculty to teach Quantitative Reasoning courses. Initially the University had a grant to recruit and train faculty to develop and teach them. This helped build a core of faculty for the courses. Presently, it is easier to recruit part-time faculty than full-time faculty to teach the courses. The nature of the courses, which involve the integration of technology in instruction and the use of an investigations pedagogy

Students in the …	Meet the Math/QR requirement by…
College of Management	Taking a business-oriented Calculus course, taught by the Mathematics Department, as well as their own Managerial Statistics course.
College of Public and Community Service	Passing a Quantitative Reasoning exam and demonstrating that they can use numerical information to gain insight into public and community issues.
College of Nursing	Taking a Quantitative Reasoning course offered by the Mathematics Department.
College of Liberal Arts and the College of Science and Mathematics (BA students)	Taking a traditional College Algebra course or a Quantitative Reasoning course, or transferring in a higher-level course. (Waiver of the requirement is granted to students who have passed an Introduction to Statistics course taught by the Mathematics Department.)
College of Liberal Arts and the College of Science and Mathematics (BS students)	Taking or transferring in a science-oriented Calculus course

involving extensive group work, is a paradigm shift for many full-time faculty who are more comfortable teaching traditional mathematics courses. For part-time faculty, the advantage of teaching this course is that it assures them continuing work. Math Skills faculty, in addition, enjoy the challenge of teaching the course and the insight it gives them into college level expectations for their students.

Program Goals and Objectives

The working definition of Quantitative Reasoning in this program is: an ability to approach problems by means of numerical, symbolic, and visual representations of real-world phenomena, determining how to solve them, deducing consequences, formulating alternatives, and predicting outcomes. It entails analyzing quantitative information to make decisions, judgments, and predictions. The primary goal of the requirement is to motivate and enable students to use quantitative reasoning skills throughout their personal, academic, and professional lives.

The Quantitative Reasoning courses are not terminal courses; instead, they are designed to feed naturally into other courses. After completion of a quantitative reasoning course, many students take a statistics course, research methods in the social sciences, or major courses such as microeconomics. To that end, examples drawn from a wide variety of disciplines are integrated into the courses. To encourage faculty attention to these principles and to optimize student mastery, each section of a Quantitative Reasoning course is limited to fewer than 25 students

Five principles of general education must be imbedded in a Quantitative Reasoning course. Students are expected to:

- engage in critical reading and analysis;
- speak, listen, and write effectively;
- reason logically and quantitatively;
- use technology to further learning; and
- work independently and collaboratively.

The objectives for the requirement include the ability to do the following:

- Recognize and pose real world problems involving the use and/or collection of data.
- Understand and critique quantitative arguments about real world problems.
- Formulate and communicate quantitative arguments and frameworks for decision making.
- Use and make connections among the four standard modes of quantitative representations: oral/written; numerical; written; visual and symbolic.

- Generalize and apply quantitative reasoning strategies to topics outside the course.
- Write quantitative arguments clearly and concisely.

Student Placement into the Program

Entering freshmen are administered the College Board's elementary algebra ACCUPLACER test, as mandated by the Massachusetts Board of Higher Education. Transfer students take a Mathematics Department designed placement test, which uses questions provided by the Mathematical Association of America. Their score determines their placement into a developmental (non-credit bearing) mathematics course, a Quantitative Reasoning course, or College Algebra. (Students with stronger mathematics backgrounds take higher-level departmental tests for placement into statistics, pre-calculus or calculus, in which cases they are exempt from the Mathematics/ Quantitative Reasoning requirement.)

Approximately 50% of entering students, both first-time freshmen and transfers, present mathematics skills at the level of College Algebra or below. The majority of these students are liberal arts, social sciences, or nursing majors, who will not need Calculus. The Quantitative Reasoning course is often a good choice for them. Students who do intend to major in the sciences or management are advised to take College Algebra or PreCalculus instead of Quantitative Reasoning. The following flow chart summarizes the two main pathways through Mathematics courses.

Mathematics Course Flow Chart

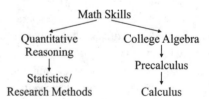

Quantitative Reasoning Courses

The challenge to the committee charged with developing the Math/QR requirement was to design a course that was an alternative to College Algebra yet covered the minimum amount of mathematics a college student should know, with a stress on analytic reasoning. The committee agreed that any course designated as a Quantitative Reasoning course must cover descriptive statistics, linear models, and exponential models or probability. In addition, use of technology (either graphing calculators or computers) must be part of the course. The course should lead into other courses, both in mathematics and in other disciplines, and should provide students with a thorough understanding of how to recognize and pose real-world problems using mathematics, how to write and analyze quantitative arguments, and how to generalize the quantitative reasoning strategies to topics outside the course.

By its design, the course should also address a challenge that has frustrated many mathematics teachers: How to teach students who are afraid of math, or who lack confidence in their mathematical abilities. In a typical semester, over 50% of students enrolled in Quantitative Reasoning courses (many of whom come from urban public schools) had previously taken developmental mathematics classes. By focusing on real world problems and by introducing concepts using real data, the Quantitative Reasoning courses shift the focus from mathematics (something that students regard as interesting only to mathematicians) to reasoning (something that cuts across all disciplines); by linking mathematics to applications, they make the mathematics meaningful.

Two Quantitative Reasoning courses have so far been developed, one in Mathematics and one in Political Science. The two courses are very similar. Because of a lack of resources, the Political Science course is rarely taught; therefore, the following discussion is restricted to the Mathematics Department's Quantitative Reasoning course.

This course is data-driven, with a strong emphasis on technology. Every class meeting is held in a computer lab, and students use the computers to gather data, to do mathematics, and to explore trends. Many incoming UMass Boston students have weak computer skills, and these courses give them valuable experience and an appreciation of the usefulness and power of technology. In keeping with the overall goals of the General Education program, students write analytic summaries, present their findings to the class in formal presentations, and work both independently and collaboratively on in-class assignments and out-of-class projects.

The Quantitative Reasoning course covers the following content:

- introduction to descriptive statistics (measures of central tendency; distributions; constructing, reading and interpreting statistical graphs; linear regression)
- linear models (average rate of change; constant rate of change; linear functions)
- number sense (scientific notation; unit conversion; rules of exponents)
- exponential models (exponential growth and decay; half-life; doubling time; exponential functions).

Exponential modeling was chosen over probability primarily to give students a broader experience of mathematical modeling. Students learn to distinguish between exponential and linear growth, and by making comparisons, they deepen their understanding of each concept.

Whenever possible, new topics are introduced using a data set or a real world motivation. For example, in the section on linear models, students examine average rate of change in the context of population growth in the United States. They then consider a variety of examples of (approximately) constant rate of change, and fit linear models to these data. When they study exponential growth and decay, they compare linear and exponential models and use Excel to project change over time. Every week, students engage in activities such as analyzing data from current news articles or the Internet, working in groups to complete in-depth projects, preparing presentations, writing an analysis of graphs and tables, and learning new techniques in Excel. In addition, the students do a considerable amount of "traditional" mathematics, such as finding slope and intercept, calculating growth rates, solving equations, and doing unit conversions.

We now present some examples of problems that students have worked on in recent semesters. Students initially find these problems very challenging because of the level of reading, the multi-step approach to the solution, and the amount of writing required. By the final exam, most students can successfully complete problems of this nature.

1. In the November 25, 2003 edition of the Boston Globe, an article ran with the headline "Colleges trail prisons in funds". The following is taken from that article.

"For the first time in 35 years, Massachusetts is spending more on prisons and jails than on public higher education, according to a report released yesterday. (The 2004) state budget included $816 million in appropriations for campuses and student financial aid, and $830 million for prisons and jails, said the report from the Massachusetts Taxpayers Foundation.

Deep cuts to state spending on higher education have left the system of state colleges and universities in 'profound' disarray, the report said, citing two eras of deep cuts that reduced state support to the same level as three decades ago when adjusted for inflation. Higher education appropriations were cut 29 percent between 1988 and 1992, and 27 percent between 2001 and 2004.

Spending on higher education dropped from 6.5 percent of the state budget at its peak in fiscal 1988 to less than 3.5 percent for the 2004 fiscal year, the report said."

Using information in the article, find the following:

a. What was the amount budgeted by the legislature for higher education in 2004?

b. Estimate the total state budget in 2004. Show your work.

c. The portion of the state budget allocated for higher education has decreased from _____ % in fiscal 1988 to _____% in fiscal 2004. Calculate the relative (percentage) change in the portion allocated to higher education between fiscal 1988 and fiscal 2004 and then write your answer using a complete sentence. Show your work.

2. The population of Haiti is approximately 9,960,000 and its landmass has an area of about 27,750 square kilometers. In contrast, the population of the United States is about 278,000,000 and its landmass is about 9,630,000 square kilometers.

a) Express each of these numbers in scientific notation:

Haiti population: Haiti landmass:
U.S. population: U.S. landmass:

b) Estimate the population density (people per square kilometer) for Haiti.

c) Estimate the population density (people per square kilometer) for the United States.

d) Compare population density of the United States to that of Haiti. How many orders of magnitude larger or smaller is the population density of the United States? Use the data to write a short paragraph comparing these two countries.

3. A Boston homeowner is currently heating her house with oil but is considering switching systems. She can choose between gas and electricity and wants to decide whether to switch. She currently spends $4,000 per year to heat with oil. Based on her best estimate it would cost $6,000 to install a gas heater and she estimates that she would pay $3,200 each year for gas. An electric heating system would cost $12,000 to install and her annual heating costs with electricity would be $2,800.

a) Identify the value and units for each of the entries in the table at the top of the next column.

b) Create a table of values in Excel comparing the three heating options for 30 years. Create a graph in Excel showing all three options on the same graph.

c) What would you recommend to the homeowner? Your recommendation should take into account how long the homeowner plans to stay in her house, and should refer to the information in your tables and graph.

	Oil	Gas	Electricity
Constant Rate of Change (slope)			
Initial Value			
Independent Variable			
Dependent Variable			

4. Job 1 pays a starting salary of $45,000 with a yearly raise of $1800. Job 2 pays a starting salary of $35,000 with a 4.1% raise each year. Write equations representing the salary at each job and make an argument about which job you would take.

Instructors teaching the Quantitative Reasoning course offered by the Mathematics Department use one of two texts: *Explorations in College Algebra* by Kime and Clark, published by John Wiley, or *Using and Understanding Mathematics: A Quantitative Reasoning Approach* by Bennet and Briggs, published by Addison-Wesley. Most of the instructors also supplement the material from the texts with their own worksheets, handouts, and web pages. The Computing Services Department at the University has dedicated one of their Macintosh labs to the course, and they provide on-the-spot support for hardware and software issues. In addition, there is an in-class assistant for each section of the course. This assistant, usually a Computer Science graduate student, Mathematics major, or former Quantitative Reasoning student, primarily works in class to help students with the computer work; the assistants also provide help when students are working on group projects and investigations in class.

Program Assessment

After establishing the Math/QR requirement, the University formed a Quantitative Reasoning Assessment Committee to evaluate and approve proposals for Quantitative Reasoning courses and to assess the effectiveness of existing courses. The current assessment model has evolved over several years of experimentation and study, and includes

• faculty reflections about the effectiveness of the course design and their teaching;

- student evaluations of the course and instructor using a committee-designed, web-based questionnaire;
- course syllabi and course web pages;
- portfolios of student work, including graded final exams, automathographies and end of semester reflections, samples of graded analytic writing about data, and graded homework assignments (portfolios are collected from new faculty and a random sample of experienced faculty);
- a sample of final exams from each section, which include a set of common final exam questions.

The portfolio review is particularly helpful for giving individual faculty feedback about their course, as well as for determining whether the general education goals of analytical reading and writing, use of technology, and mathematical content are being addressed. The committee uses the results of this assessment to suggest modifications in the course design, and to inform individual instructors about their strengths and weaknesses.

As an example, one conclusion from portfolio assessment over several semesters was that students were not getting appropriate guidance and feedback about analytical writing. This is a difficult topic to address while teaching mathematics in a computer lab, and many of the instructors did not have experience with this type of work. As a result, several workshops and discussion groups about evaluating and encouraging student writing have been offered to the Quantitative Reasoning faculty.

The use of common final exam questions is a fairly new part of the assessment, but is an important method to compare and measure student learning outcomes across different sections of the course. Instructors may choose their own text (subject to approval of the QR Assessment Committee) and they may vary the syllabus, provided they address the five principles of general education and that they meet the objectives described earlier. As a result, there is no common final exam for all of the sections of the course. Still, the committee determined that students should leave the course being able to demonstrate knowledge about certain key topics, and it should be evident that the main objectives of the course have been thoroughly addressed. For example, can a student construct and interpret a linear function using constant rate of change data? Can a student correctly analyze a complex statistical graph and write two quantitative conclusions from the graph? A set of common final exam questions was developed to measure student performance on each of the major topics covered in the course. Faculty were asked to use these common questions as a subset of all

the questions on their final exams. They were allowed, however, to grade their own finals, assigning whatever weight they chose to each of the common questions. The committee analyzes a sample of student exams using a set of holistic rubrics and makes recommendations to the instructors. Most recently, for example, instructors were encouraged to devote more time to coverage of exponential functions.

Another important assessment piece is student surveys. Similar to course evaluations, these surveys are answered by students online toward the end of the semester. Because the assessment is given in class, the response rate is very high (typically 85% - 90%). The surveys collect some demographic data and also ask questions about specific student learning outcomes for the course. Using the analysis of these surveys, the committee has modified the course content and made recommendations to the faculty. For example, when the course was first taught in 1998, only about half of the students had experience with using the Internet. By 2001, this number had grown to over 90%. As a result, faculty now spend relatively little time introducing students to the Internet. Instead, they concentrate on more advanced aspects, such as using search engines properly and assessing the validity of information obtained on the Internet.

One encouraging outcome from the student surveys is that students consistently agree with statements, "After taking this course, I have a better understanding of how mathematics is used to understand the real world" and "As a result of this course I … evaluate quantitative claims and the evidence presented in their support". Student comments on the open-ended response questions, such as "The 'reasoning' aspect of this course was the most valuable," and "This is a great class … it helped me in other classes," appear frequently.

There are other, less formal, indicators that the course is a success. Instructors who teach Introductory Statistics report anecdotally that Quantitative Reasoning students outperform the average student. With the introduction of portfolios, Quantitative Reasoning instructors have seen improvement on an individual basis. At the end of the semester, students write a reflection discussing what they have learned, how they think they will use it, and how their attitude toward math may have changed. Here are some examples of what students have written.

- Before (this course), I hated math. But after taking this course, I feel much more comfortable with difficult math problems. I feel I now have a better understanding of the basics of mathematics. This course dealt with some real life problems, which make it interesting as well as useful. I have most definitely learned things that will be useful to me in the future.

- I am not sure how much I will use this learning being a history teacher but I know I will not seem uncomfortable when the conversation turns to mathematics and its role in the world.

- I made it through a math course and surprise, surprise … I loved it and feel almost a sense of regret that it wasn't just a little bit longer.

Of course, there are negative comments. Some students are bored by the course, and should probably have taken a higher-level course; some are frustrated at having to learn the Mac platform; and some don't think that they are learning math. The most common complaint concerns the amount of work required to succeed in the course. Overall, the comments tend to be positive. The Quantitative Reasoning courses are designed to meet the needs of students who have had repeated failures in math. From the evidence gathered through student reflections and course evaluations, it appears that the courses are meeting this goal.

Challenges and Difficulties

The results from the assessment process over the past several years have been encouraging. Students in the Quantitative Reasoning courses are gaining valuable experience with the five principles of general education outlined earlier, their mathematics skills (and confidence) are better; and their ability to work with quantitative information in a variety of ways is much improved.

Nonetheless, there are several frustrations and difficulties with the course and the program. We outline these with brief commentary.

Students must satisfy the Math/QR requirement before they have taken 45 credits. However, this stipulation cannot be easily enforced by the registrar, and it is currently the case that several hundred students have "escaped" the requirement and are approaching graduation.

The student body in the QR course tends to be very diverse mathematically. It is a real challenge to the instructor to meet the needs of very weak students while keeping the better students involved in the course. This is not unique to the QR classroom, of course. The same issue arises with the use of computers; some students are quite comfortable with the software and others are not. To address this, instructors have begun using in-class assistants to provide hands-on help with computer work.

Teaching in a computer classroom has its own set of challenges. The classroom is not optimally designed, and sightlines are poor. It can be difficult to use the computers every day in a meaningful way. The computers, with ready access to the internet, are tremendously distracting to students. Some instructors do use software to block students from the internet when this becomes a problem. Overall, faculty must learn a new set of classroom management strategies.

Due to a series of budget cuts, the University has not been able to provide much support for ongoing faculty professional development and the training of new faculty to teach the course.

The course struggles with its identity. Is it a mathematics course? How much emphasis should be placed on using symbolic notation versus allowing the use of Excel to perform calculations such as extrapolations? Should the syllabus place a greater emphasis on quantitative literacy? How can faculty keep the course current and interesting, bringing in timely data and information?

These are ongoing issues. The group of faculty teaching the course contributes a large amount of extra time to discussing these and proposing solutions.

Cross Disciplinary Commitment and Participation

The Quantitative Reasoning courses have revolutionized how faculty teach and how students learn at UMass Boston. Faculty have abandoned traditional lecture-based teaching in favor of student-driven learning. They consistently seek links between the course material and current events, many have constructed resource-rich web sites, and they work together to create assignments emphasizing real data. Support for the courses has cut across traditional boundaries, as faculty from a range of disciplines came together to design and teach Quantitative Reasoning courses. This collaboration continues, as an interdisciplinary college committee assesses the courses and provides feedback to instructors.

Teaching a Quantitative Reasoning course presents many challenges to a faculty member. Most need intense training to be able to teach effectively in a computer lab. In addition, instructors must adapt to the many non-traditional aspects of the course. Many of the instructors have expanded their teaching philosophy to incorporate cooperative learning, evaluation of analytic writing, greater awareness of the use of technology and the importance of data, and a deeper understanding of challenges students face in learning mathematics.

One result of the development of the Math/ Quantitative Reasoning requirement has been the formation of a cohort of Quantitative Reasoning faculty, a community that is focused on making the course a better experience for both faculty and students. These instructors come from a range of departments and programs across the campus, including Mathematics, Philosophy, and Academic Support. The group meets before, during, and after each semester, to plan and to discuss what works; they also communicate frequently via e-mail, sharing assignments, exams, and ideas. This spirit of mutual support and collaboration has led to an "open door" policy in which many faculty freely visit one another's classes to observe, share, and give feedback. Such a community is rare on the UMass Boston commuter campus, and is an unexpected and welcome outcome of the new program.

Quantitative Literacy
Courses

Contribution of a First Year Mathematics Course to Quantitative Literacy

Aimee Ellington and William Haver
Virginia Commonwealth University, Richmond VA

Introduction

Virginia Commonwealth University (VCU) offers a first year mathematics course that is taken annually by approximately 2100 students and has the goal of making an important contribution to the quantitative reasoning abilities of these students. While no one course alone can create a quantitatively literate citizen, and many courses and programs should contribute to this development, mathematics departments can take the lead by assuring that their own courses, indeed, make a strong contribution to developing student quantitative reasoning abilities.

History of Development of Course

VCU has had a mathematics requirement in place for all undergraduate majors since the creation of the university in 1968. Until the early 1990s this requirement was fulfilled by students completing College Algebra. This course also served as a prerequisite for statistics and for pre-calculus.

In 1990, our colleague Reuben Farley was chair of the mathematics department. As he relates the history, every time he saw Ann Woodlief, Professor of English and lead advisor for English majors, she would say "tell me again why an English major needs to take your College Algebra course to graduate." In direct response to this question, a new course, Contemporary Mathematics, was created.

The department set the goal of developing a course that: would continue to serve as a prerequisite for statistics; could be taught by large numbers of different individuals, including part-time instructors and graduate students; and would provide an answer to Dr. Woodlief's question.

Bill Haver (VCU) and Gwen Turbeville of J. Sargeant Reynolds Community College taught the first pilot sections of this course. They reported on their experience in Haver and Turbeville (1995).

Course Goals

The department set the following goals for students in the materials that were submitted to the university curriculum committees:

- Students will be better able to think logically about situations with quantitative components;
- Students will be better able to make use of their mathematical, graphing, and computational skills in real situations;
- Students will be better able to independently read, study and understand quantitative topics that are new to the students;

- Students will be better able to explain and describe quantitative topics orally and to discuss quantitative topics with others;
- Students will be better able to explain quantitative ideas in written form;
- Students will improve their "number sense", learn some details of a variety of situations where mathematics is used, and become engaged and have fun doing mathematics.

In short, students should be able to deal with situations involving quantitative components that they will encounter: as students in other college level courses, particularly including statistics and the social sciences; as citizens confronted with a wide array of public policy issues; as members of the work force, teaching elementary school, reporting the news, or managing an office; and as parents, participating in the education of their children.

Student Placement

All VCU students are required to take a Placement Test. The lowest passing score (most students meet or achieve this passing level) permits students to enroll in either College Algebra or Contemporary Mathematics. Students placing at this level who are in majors requiring the study of calculus are advised to enroll in College Algebra and all others who place at this level are advised to enroll in Contemporary Mathematics. Both courses can serve as a prerequisite for statistics. Students placing at a higher level may take either of these courses, but may also be eligible to take statistics or calculus – at least one mathematics course is required for all VCU students.

Curriculum Details

The text for the course is *Excursions in Modern Mathematics*, that was modeled after COMAP's seminal text *For All Practical Purposes*. Excursions, and our course, are organized around connections between mathematics and other areas. During the course, students consider questions such as:

- What is the best way to conduct an election if there are more than two candidates? If one candidate receives the most votes (but not a majority), should that candidate be guaranteed to win?
- How can two or more parties in conflict divide limited resources? Are there ways in which two people who are divorcing can decide how to divide their possessions without going through costly litigation? How

can the legal system be advised to propose equitable distributions of estates or partnership proceeds?
- If you need to run 10 errands on a Saturday, can you save time by deciding which errands to run first? If a company is manufacturing circuit boards, how should the computer chips be placed on the board? What do these two questions have to do with each other?
- How does the size of populations grow? How does interest compound? How much money do you need to save each month to make a down payment on a house? When will the world deplete its oil and gas resources?
- What did Aristotle mean by golden mean? What is the shape of the Parthenon? Why was that shape used?

Contemporary Mathematics utilizes and strengthens quantitative skills including graphing, solving algebraic equations, percentages, proportional reasoning, 30-60-90 triangles, interval and summation notation, factorials, scientific notation, and counting arguments. However, this is not what the course is 'about'. The course is organized around meaningful topics: mathematics of voting, fair division, apportionment, routing security guards, the Traveling Salesman Problem, linear and exponential growth, scheduling, and fractals; in response to the previously described goals, the course is 'about' enabling students to encounter and understand situations that have quantitative components. However, just "covering" these topics does not, we believe, help students improve their ability to reason quantitatively nor achieve the goals listed above.

A basic assumption has been made that the best way for students to learn to communicate with others about quantitative issues is to require that students communicate with others. Similarly, it is assumed that the optimum way to enable students to learn to write about quantitative matters is to require them to write about quantitative matters.

A guiding principle of VCU's course is that approximately one third of class time should be devoted to directed instructional activities with the instructor lecturing, introducing topics, helping students review specific computational skills that will be needed, and summarizing key ideas. The other two thirds of the class time can then be devoted to actively involving students with other students completing worksheets, discussing mathematics with others, engaged in group activities, and beginning long-term projects.

Approximately 2100 students complete the semester course each year. Approximately 25 different individuals teach sections of the course; during a typical year this includes five full-time faculty, six graduate teaching assistants and 14 part-time faculty. Most students enroll in self-contained sections of 35 students. Others enroll in lecture/recitation sections. Under the lecture/recitation format, the 150-student lecture meets weekly and the 25-student recitation sections meet twice each week.

Students in all sections are expected to:

- Make weekly entries in a learning log in response to specific writing prompts;
- Work as a member of a team to develop and offer an oral presentation on a mathematical topic;
- Write two three-page typed mathematics papers;
- Undertake a relatively small independent study project culminating in a poster presentation;
- Participate in a large number of in-class activities, usually in collaboration with other class members;
- Complete four quizzes and three exams.

For the independent study project each student responds to a number of questions concerning a section of the text not previously considered in the course. Typically, in a given section of the course students will be given four possible topics to study. For example, students may be given the assignment of understanding the notion of apportionment, the details of two or three apportionment schemes, and the benefits and drawbacks of each. Other students may be given the assignment of understanding the idea of scheduling, the details of one scheduling algorithm, and question of under what conditions the resultant schedule will be optimum. After completing two preliminary reports, the students prepare a poster to use as a tool to explain the results of their study to other students in their class.

In order to support the large and ever changing contingent of part-time instructors and graduate students teaching the course, an extensive instructor's guide and a set of supplemental materials have been developed. The Instructor's Guide includes sections on In-class Activities, Learning Logs, Team Oral Presentations, Poster Sessions, Student Papers, and Long-term Student Activities. (The URL is given in the references.) A variety of grading rubrics are provided to help instructors who have limited experience grading student papers and oral presentations.

Program Assessment

The assessment outlined below is part of a long-term assessment project to determine the role of VCU's general education mathematics courses in the development of students' quantitative reasoning abilities. The details of the overall assessment plan are reported in Ellington (2003). The assessment method outlined below pays particular attention to the Contemporary Mathematics since the course has a specific focus on quantitative literacy. Similarities and differences between students who completed Contemporary Mathematics and students who completed a traditional Mathematics Course, College Algebra, are noted.

College Algebra is taught in large lecture sessions at VCU with class sizes of 100 or more, so there is little opportunity for student-teacher interaction. However, students also register for a one hour weekly session in the computer-based mathematics laboratory and are required to take a weekly quiz in the lab. Assistants are available during this hour and throughout the week to discuss students' work on the quiz and to provide free tutoring.

Bill Haver taught sections of both Contemporary Mathematics and College Algebra in the 2002-2003 school year and questioned whether students in Contemporary Mathematics would be more successful in completing the multiple-choice questions than those in College Algebra. All of the testing in College Algebra is multiple-choice; the assessment questions are the only multiple-choice questions the students are exposed to in Contemporary Mathematics. But the students in Contemporary Mathematics have the experience of regularly considering broader questions with quantitative components. As is described in the following, there was virtually no difference in the performance of the two groups of students on these assessment questions.

Assessment Questions

A series of multiple-choice questions featuring quantitative reasoning skills were designed by the authors and Reuben Farley, in fall 2001. The multiple-choice format was deemed appropriate because the questions could easily be included with the existing multiple-choice questions that make up the math placement test. Since all students who enroll at VCU are required to take the placement test, it was used as the pretest for the assessment. The questions were piloted with students enrolled in general education math courses in spring 2002. Based on the results, questions were changed, new questions were added, and others dropped resulting in a final bank of sixteen questions that cover the following topics:

- unit analysis
- interpretation of charts & graphs
- proportional reasoning
- counting principles

- general percents
- percent increase or decrease
- the use of mathematical formulas
- average
- exponential growth

Here are two examples:

1. According to an electronic magazine, online consumer spending in 2002 is projected to be $23.5 billion, up 53% from 2001. What was the level of online consumer spending in 2001?
   a. $9.9 billion   b. $15.4 billion
   c. $22.3 billion   d. $1.2 billion
   e. $11.0 billion

2. The population of a county is 100,000. A power company predicts that the population will increase by 7% per year. The county supervisors predict that the population will increase by 7,500 each year. Which group's prediction method predicts the larger population in 10 years?
   a. supervisors
   b. power company
   c. both predictions are the same after 10 years
   d. there is not enough information provided to answer the question

Interested readers may obtain a complete list of the questions from the authors.

Four different questions were included on each of the four versions of the placement test. The same four questions on each version were used in four post-test versions included as the last page of the final exams of general education mathematics courses during the 2002–2003 school year.

Assessment Participants

All students who took the math placement test prior to the 2002–2003 school year and completed Contemporary Mathematics or College Algebra during that school year participated in the assessment. As an incentive for answering the questions on the final exams, each student was given one point extra credit on his or her final exam for each question answered correctly.

Since Contemporary Mathematics and College Algebra have the same placement level, we decided to compare the assessment results of students in these two courses. Through this we hoped to determine whether the course designed to cover quantitative literacy topics, Contemporary Mathematics, is better at enhancing the development of the quantitative reasoning skills of students enrolled in the course. Or does a traditional mathematics course at the same placement level, College Algebra, help students achieve similar results with respect to their quantitative reasoning abilities?

Method of Assessment

The placement test data was used to generate a baseline percentage for each of the previously mentioned topics. The baseline represents the number of students beginning a mathematics course with an understanding of that particular topic. For each topic, the data for the questions related to that topic were combined. A statistical comparison was conducted of the proportion of students answering the topic-related questions correctly with the proportion of students who took the placement test and answered the questions correctly on the final exam. A significant result ($p < .05$) was obtained when the proportion of students answering the topic-related final exam questions correctly was statistically larger than the proportion of students answering the questions on the placement test.

Before continuing, it is important to note one feature of the placement test that had an effect on the placement test percentages. A placement level is generated by the number of correct responses on the placement test minus one-forth of the number of incorrect responses. The instructions state that it is acceptable for students to not answer any questions that they are uncertain about. As a result, several questions had a large number of no responses. A statistical comparison of the number of items left blank for each course revealed that the proportion of Contemporary Mathematics students that left items blank was the same as the proportion of college algebra students that left items blank. So both sets of placement test percentages listed below were equally affected by this phenomenon. Most topics yielded 10% to 25% of students participating not responding to items. The two topics most affected were counting principles and exponential growth with 64% and 34%, respectively, of students not responding to those items.

Contemporary Mathematics Results

Figure 1 contains the results for Contemporary Mathematics. These percentages are based on data from 399 students who took the math placement test and enrolled in a section of Contemporary Mathematics during the 2002-2003 school year.

While the distributions are not exactly even, roughly 25% of the students completed the questions on each of the four versions of the assessment instrument. The questions were divided among the four versions so that each version had a variety of questions and each version had a similar level of difficulty.

Topic	Placement Test	Final Exam
Unit Analysis	19.90	24.31
Charts & Graphs	32.24	40.32*
Proportional Reasoning	23.41	32.60*
Counting Principles	17.70	32.99*
General Percents	33.88	47.62*
Percent Increase/Decrease	15.14	26.82*
Math Formulas	28.86	44.19*
Average	36.56	57.14*
Exponential Growth	15.09	36.97*

* significantly larger percentage, $p < .05$

Figure 1. Percentage of correct responses by topic for students enrolled in Contemporary Mathematics.

Topic	Placement Test	Final Exam
Unit Analysis	17.70	23.19*
Charts & Graphs	38.02	44.35*
Proportional Reasoning	26.67	35.71*
Counting Principles	18.05	41.59*
General Percents	39.12	48.12*
Percent Increase/Decrease	15.48	28.01*
Math Formulas	29.64	46.40*
Average	37.38	56.00*
Exponential Growth	17.80	34.21*

* significantly larger percentage, $p < .05$

Figure 2. Percentage of correct responses by topic for students enrolled in College Algebra.

For each topic except unit analysis, the percentage of students answering questions on the final exam was significantly larger than the baseline percentage. The final exam percentage for unit analysis was larger than the baseline percentage, but the difference was not statistically significant. Based on this analysis, we conclude that Contemporary Mathematics did have a meaningful role in increasing the number of students with quantitative reasoning skills in these areas. We are pleased with this improvement but also are working to modify the course in order to further increase the number of students able to successfully answer quantitative literacy questions of this type.

College Algebra Results

The placement test and final exam results for College Algebra appear in Figure 2. These percentages were based on the test results of 470 students who took the math placement test and completed College Algebra during the 2002–2003 school year. On both the placement test and the final exam, approximately one-fourth of the students answered questions on each version of the assessment instrument.

For each topic, the percentage of College Algebra students answering questions on the final exam was significantly larger than the baseline percentage. Therefore, the traditional mathematics course was also a positive influence on the number of students completing the course with quantitative reasoning skills in these areas. The unit analysis percentages for College Algebra and Contemporary Mathematics were similar, but the College Algebra results were statistically significant.

Course Comparison

Since both courses achieved similar results in the placement test to final exam differences for each topic, except unit analysis, we decided to analyze the percentages further by statistically comparing percentages for both courses. First the placement test percentages (see Figures 1 & 2) for each topic were compared. The differences were not statistically significant. Therefore, both courses began with a similar number of students understanding each quantitative reasoning topic. Then the final exam percentages were compared. There was no significant difference in the percentage of students understanding each topic at the end of Contemporary Mathematics when compared to the percentage of students understanding the same topic at the end of College Algebra. Therefore, Contemporary Mathematics and College Algebra appear to have the same effect on the number of students who complete each course with a better understanding of the quantitative literacy topics we assessed.

Time Spent on Course

In spring 2003, we added one last multiple-choice question to the final exams of students in these two courses. The question was:

Please estimate, on the average, the total time you spend on this course. Include time in class, time taking tests, quizzes, and completing other projects or assignments.

a. 3 hours or less each week
b. 3–5 hours each week
c. 5–7 hours each week

Response	Contemporary Math	College Algebra
3 hours or less	13.60	19.40*
3 – 5 hours	44.48*	33.83
5 – 7 hours	35.41*	26.12
7 – 10 hours	5.38	17.16*
10 hours or more	1.13	3.48

* significantly larger percentage, $p < .05$

Figure 3. Percentage of students selecting each response to the time spent on class question

d. 7 – 10 hours each week
e. 10 or more hours each week

Three hundred fifty-three Contemporary Mathematics students and 402 College Algebra students answered the question.

Students receive three semester credit hours for the completion of each course and each class meets for two and a half hours a week. Therefore, the students who chose 3 hours or less in response to this question were admitting that they did not do much more than come to class.

We analyzed the data from this question according to class rank (freshman, sophomore, junior, senior) and grade received in the course. Neither analysis yielded any interesting patterns to report.

Course Grade

One final item for consideration in the comparison of these two courses is course grade. The number of students withdrawing from each course during the school year was quite similar (12.9% for Contemporary Mathematics and 14.6% for College Algebra). The significant difference was in the percentages of students successfully completing each course. For the 2002–2003 school year, 69.4% received an A, B, or C in Contemporary Mathematics while 43.7% received an A, B, or C in College Algebra.

We have not conducted any research which would explain these percentages. However, in course related discussions, many instructors who have taught both courses have expressed the opinion that the difference is based on the fact that students find Contemporary Mathematics more interesting and become more engaged in the course. We are heartened by the fact that the students who successfully completed Contemporary Mathematics made comparable gains in the quantitative literacy assessment when compared with the smaller percentage of students who were successful in College Algebra and that they

spend as much or more time studying than their College Algebra counterparts.

It should be noted that this assessment primarily focused on aspects of the first two goals of Contemporary Mathematics (see Course Goals above). While the main differences in Contemporary Mathematics and College Algebra appear in the four goals that could not be assessed through this series of multiple-choice questions.

One limitation of the assessment method used to date is that it relies totally on multiple-choice responses, and does not allow for analysis beyond the five response items provided for each question. We have plans to develop an assessment for analyzing student responses to open-ended quantitative literacy questions. We also believe that a lot can be learned about student quantitative reasoning skills through interviews. We have plans to set up interviews with students who have completed Contemporary Mathematics and College Algebra in which we can learn about the methods students use when presented with situations that require quantitative reasoning skills. This type of assessment may or may not yield different results.

Cross-Disciplinary Commitment and Participation

We have not been successful in developing university wide interest in developing student quantitative reasoning abilities. However, we have developed an understanding of which first year courses have quantitative components. The next stage in the development of Contemporary Mathematics is to create a student assignment that will provide a number of specific links between Contemporary Mathematics and other VCU courses. Students will then be asked to report in detail on one of these links to a course that they are currently or have previously taken.

While we currently do not have faculty in other departments participating in a quantitative reasoning program, we do have their support for our efforts. When VCU's general education requirements were revisited, the College of Humanities and Sciences added a statistics requirement for all students who were not taking calculus. Before increasing the requirement, assurance was given that the new statistics course would "be like Contemporary Mathematics". The English department strongly supported the new requirement.

Conclusions

The Contemporary Mathematics course at VCU appears to have a meaningful role in turning out students with quantitative reasoning skills. Although few impacts of the approaches taken in Contemporary Mathematics are apparent in the formal assessment activities to date, we are very pleased with the success of the course.

We are very pleased that we are regularly able to engage Contemporary Mathematics students in making use of their areas of strength outside of mathematics in this mathematics course. Many of the papers are very well written and students demonstrate that they are able to bring to bear on a topic that contains a quantitative component the same analytic skills that they may use to consider a piece of literature or an historic document. Many of the posters developed as the culminating portion of the independent study project demonstrate the artistic abilities of the large number of Arts students who enroll in this course. As these students use their artistic abilities to illuminate an issue with quantitative components, we believe that they are in a better position to consider additional situations in the future.

Probably our biggest accomplishment is the fact that we have been able to develop, and continually refresh, a cadre of short-term instructors, part-time faculty and graduate assistants who are prepared and interested in teaching a course that involves quantitative, realistic issues. Not only are these instructors invested in the topics discussed in the course, but they are committed to fully engaging students in writing, collaborative work, and independent study projects. We believe that this information concerning success with offering a quantitative literacy course of this nature to 2100 students a year, relying primarily on part-time, temporary faculty may be a worthwhile resource for other mathematics departments.

References

Haver, B., & Turbeville, G. (1995). An Appropriate Culminating Mathematics Course. *The AMATYC Review.* 16(2), 45-50.

Tannenbaum, P., & Arnold, R. (2000). *Excursions in Modern Mathematics* (4th ed.). Prentice Hall.

COMAP. *For All Practical Purposes* (5th ed.). (1991) W. H. Freeman.

http://www.math.vcu.edu/faculty/whaver/instructorsguide.html

Ellington, A. (2003). *An Assessment of General Education Mathematics Courses Contribution to Quantitative Literacy at Virginia Commonwealth University.* Mathematical Association of America, www.maa.org/saum/new_case.html.

Increasing the Relevance to and Engagement of Students in a Quantitative Literacy Course

Sarah J. Greenwald and Holly Hirst
*Appalachian State University,
Boone, NC*

Introduction

For the last fourteen years, the Mathematical Sciences Department at Appalachian has offered MAT1010: Introduction to Math as a core mathematics course for non-technical majors. This course was designed to accomplish several goals:

to engage students, alone and in teams, in solving real-life problems using the mathematics they were taught in high school;

to show students authentic, useful applications of technology, mainly using computers; and

to teach students how to write about technical information, including techniques for incorporating graphs, tables, and other mathematical structures in written documents.

In 1991, we began the development of course materials that would lend themselves to meeting these goals, and in 1993, the first edition of *How Do You Know: Using Math to Make Decisions* was published. The materials include four basic modules: physical measurement, personal finance, consumer statistics, and resource allocation. Instructors may choose to use all four or instead do three to leave time to cover additional related topics. In 1996, the course materials, including the text and the associated web pages, won first place for quantitative literacy courses in the first Annenburg/ CPB Innovative Programs Using Technology (INPUT) Competition.

In recent years, we have concentrated on keeping the course content timely and relevant, using student-centered and student-posed problems and data to ensure that students take ownership in the mathematics being studied. Our inspiration for further refinements of the course has come from sources like the NCTM *Standards* and the AMATYC *Crossroads* documents. These documents stress the use of realistic problems, fast and regular student feedback, the importance of writing, and the appropriate use of technology. We have kept these tenets in mind while refining the course.

In this paper we will describe recent enhancements we have tried in our sections to increase students' engagement in the course, including the expanded use of web-based materials, the incorporation of interdisciplinary mini-topics directed at the interests of the students in the class, and the linking of MAT1010 with other freshman programs.

Key Components of the Course

A four semester-hour core course, MAT1010 has become the mathematics course of choice for a broad variety of majors, including all of the humanities, fine arts, elementary education, and several branches of social science. We offer 22 sections of the course each semester with an enrollment of 25 to 28 students per section. Each week, the course is taught in a classroom setting for three hours and in a computer laboratory for two hours. The only prerequisite is a passing score on the mathematics placement test given to all freshmen.

Instructors include tenure-track faculty and a few adjunct instructors. Experienced MAT1010 faculty are assigned to help orient new instructors to the course philosophy and the lab component. As they gain more experience with the course, faculty may vary the content by substituting other mini-topics for either or both of the physical measurement and linear programming modules. All faculty cover personal finance and consumer statistics. Examples of mini-topics are given later in this paper.

Faculty use the "just-in-time" philosophy when covering mathematics topics in the course: All concepts are reviewed or introduced as needed to solve real-life problems, rather than using problems solely to motivate the learning of algebraic manipulations. In the measurement module, students use standard formulas from geometry and trigonometry only as needed. In the finance module, students practice percents and logarithms in the framework of interest, annuity, and loan payment calculations. In the statistics module, students review data representation techniques in an effort to handle real data, usually collected by the students about the class. In the resource allocation module, students graph and solve linear inequalities to see how others use mathematics to make decisions that affect students' lives.

Most of the labs incorporate technology to solve problems, and many have a significant writing component to reflect the "writing across the curriculum" theme of Appalachian's curriculum. In fact, MAT1010 is unique as it is the only writing course offered in mathematics or the sciences that is specifically for non-majors. Usually students are presented with a realistic situation to solve or analyze, and the accompanying write-up takes the form of a report to the poser of the problem. This report requires that technical information be appropriately presented and described. Students are given feedback and are required to refine several of their assignments over the course of the semester in order to improve their writing.

In the 2000–2001 academic year, the University performed a comprehensive evaluation of writing-designated courses via student essay testing and student end-of-course surveys. MAT1010 was assessed as were the other, more traditional freshman writing courses. The end-of-course writing designator survey results were mixed for MAT1010: Only 40% of the 650 students polled felt that the course had "helped" their writing skills a moderate amount or more. Follow-up questionnaires the next semester in several sections indicated that students differentiate between "writing" and "technical writing," with technical writing skills (incorporation of numbers, equations, tables, and graphs into reports) being helped more than "regular" writing skills by participation in MAT1010. In addition, the students were unhappy to find writing in a math course, feeling as one student put it that "that is what English is for." In recent semesters, we have worked to make our expectations regarding writing clearer to the students and to show them that the technical writing skills we can help them with are different from (and just as useful as) the skills they practice in English composition.

While the results of assessment of the writing component of the course have been mixed, the approach taken in the course has been very successful in improving students' attitudes about mathematics and about their own quantitative skills. Between 1995 and 1997, 120 sections of MAT 110 (approximately 3000 students) were given attitudinal surveys at the beginning and end of the course, and the results were gratifying. There were improvements in how students perceived their general math skills, their comfort in computer use, their beliefs about the relevance of mathematics to their own lives, their level of math anxiety, and their ability to handle word problems. One measure that did not show improvement was the students' notion that "math was a straight-forward matter of following procedures." We would have liked the students to move away from that idea, and have been refining materials to include more conceptual ideas. The same survey without the computer-oriented questions was given to students in the traditional college algebra course, which is an alternative core course to MAT1010. College Algebra students were much less positive in their views, particularly in their perceptions of the relevance and usefulness of mathematics. More information on the course design and assessment may be found in Lenker (1998).

Another source of positive feedback has been from other departments on campus. The core curriculum includes one mathematics course chosen from MAT1010, College Algebra, Business Calculus, Pre-Calculus, and Calculus I. Traditionally, departments housing non-technical majors had no specific requirements on which of these courses to take. Over the last ten years, we have seen many of majors on campus either recommend or require MAT1010 as the core mathematics course. Majors in child development, criminal justice, elementary education, sociology, and social science education all require MAT1010 as the core mathematics course. In addition, we have been asked to offer special sections of MAT1010 for the Department of Interdisciplinary Studies.

Practice and Feedback via the Web

Students are increasingly comfortable with web-based activities. We decided to exploit that comfort by using java applets and on-line quizzes in order to engage students while providing them with ways to get quick feedback and to increase their understanding of basic concepts.

Drill and Exploration via Java Applets: With the help of computer science students taking a course in java applet design, we developed a suite of applets to provide students with both drill and exploration activities. These applets may be accessed from the student area of the main course page (Hirst, online). Many are very simple drill exercises. For example, students sometimes need help choosing the correct finance formula to use in a given situation, and so we have created "guided drill" exercises like the one illustrated below. Here, the student chooses a formula, enters in the appropriate choices for the known quantities, and then calculates the formula in the usual way on a calculator. Instant feedback is given on the solution, along with the necessary calculations.

We also use many java applets that are designed to allow students to investigate concepts. For example, to discuss the various ways graphs that are accurately scaled

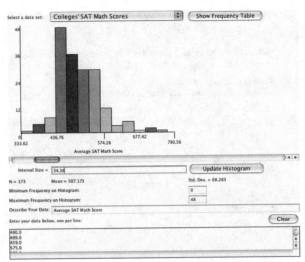

Histogram: An Interactive Exploration

can still be misleading, we use a histogram-creating java applet from the Project Interactivate[1] collection at the Shodor Education Foundation in which the students can move the slider to immediately see the effects of different choices for the interval size.

There are other drill and exploration activities available, and end-of-course evaluations indicate that students appreciate the guided drill exercises as well as the interactive learning tools.

Instant Feedback via On-Line Quizzes: Six years ago, Appalachian adopted WebCT for use by faculty interested in incorporating web-accessible materials into their courses. One of the features of WebCT that is particularly beneficial for students in MAT1010 is the automatically graded quiz. Short answer, calculation problems can be designed in template form with specified ranges for automatically generated parameters. We can create several problem forms and have the computer generate a quiz of set problem types. Each time a student accesses a quiz he or she will see similar problems with different parameter values. The students press a submit button when they are finished and the computer reports their score on each problem.

This allows for quizzes to become learning experiences, where students can take a similar quiz over and over until they get it right, each time receiving immediate feedback. Students report that they especially like this instant feedback and that they appreciate WebCT quizzes because the quizzes help to reinforce and solidify concepts.

Methods for incorporating the results of these quizzes into student course grades varies; one approach is to

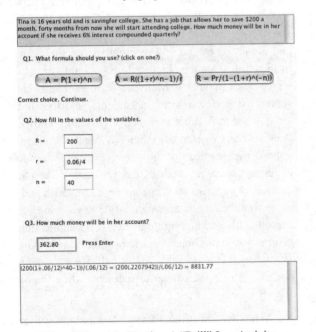

Finance Formula Practice: A "Drill" Java Activity

---

1 Project Interactivate is a freely accessible collection of java applets designed to illustrate concepts from mathematics for middle grades. Many of the activities are useful in college courses as well.

PROBLEM: 100% of what number is
            99999999999999999999?

Math common sense dictates that your answer would be

Percent Value	Correct Response	Student Response	Answer Choices
0.0%			1. smaller than 99999999999999999999
0.0%		▶	2. bigger than 99999999999999999999
100.0%	▶		3. equal to 99999999999999999999

Score 0%

WebCT Quiz Feedback

allow five retakes with the highest score recorded. WebCT automates tracking these grades and keeps records on which problems were commonly missed. The bulk of the work for the instructor is front-loaded, i.e., quizzes are much more time consuming to prepare than traditional paper quizzes, but grading is eliminated.

Mini-Topics

Since a majority of the students in MAT1010 are non-technical majors, three of the four main modules were chosen to give students math skills they might actually use, while one — resource allocation — was chosen to illustrate how others use math to influence things in the students lives. These modules remain the core of the course, but we have also developed a series of week to two-week mini-topics to show students how mathematics might be linked to or arise in their own disciplines and to illustrate that mathematics is a growing, changing subject with interesting questions that are still studied by people today.

Mathematics and the Fine Arts: Since most art and music majors take MAT1010, we have developed materials on links between mathematics and fine arts. Students explore the evolution of one-, two-, and three-point perspective, linking this to projective geometry and to Escher's misleading perspective drawings. This focus on Escher allows us to segue to geometric transformations through tilings of the plane. At this point we may also look at hyperbolic tilings through Escher's related works. Students are particularly excited by the web-based tessellation generation software we use in lab.

From music, we examine the development of instrument tuning, beginning with Pythagorean and pure tunings, in which string lengths were based on fractions of whole tones, and concluding with irrationally-based even tuning. This allows us to discuss rational and irrational numbers by investigating how the early Pythagorean and pure tuning techniques sound different from the more modern even tuning. We conclude this topic with a lab in which the students tune 100 ml graduated cylinders by filling them with water to the appropriate depth and then play them by blowing across the openings. This is usually the last topic we cover in the course, and students routinely comment on how enjoyable and easy the topic is after dealing with finance and statistics.

Coding and Secret Messages: The ubiquity of electronic information transfer motivates our study of codes and ciphers. We begin by looking at barcodes and common check digit schemes, having students bring examples to class, including product wrappers with barcodes and ISBN, checking account, and credit card numbers. This allows us to introduce the modular arithmetic concepts used by these schemes. We progress to enciphering messages with additive and multiplicative ciphers, allowing students to investigate multiplicative inverses in finite settings. We then take advantage of access to a computer algebra system for modular arithmetic of large numbers to introduce the RSA cryptosystem.

Geometry of the Earth and Universe: While geometry means measuring the earth, too often it is presented in an axiomatic way, divorced from reality and experiences. In this segment, students research problems such as the best path from Chicago to Rome, the validity of the Pythagorean theorem on a triangular plot of land between approximately Umanak, Greenland, Goiania, Brazil, and Harare, Zimbabwe, the number of stars in the universe, and the shape of space. The problems on the geometry of the earth force the students to re-examine truths from high school geometry. Many of these problems can be solved using simple string arguments, and the students are amazed to find out that their high school knowledge does not carry over to the sphere. While the problems involving the geometry of the universe are still the subject of intense research, students can understand the current theories. A segment on the geometry of the earth and universe stretches the imagination while developing visualization skills and highlighting real-world applications of geometry and its connections to art, philosophy, physics, astronomy and geography. About half of the students report that this is their favorite segment, while the others specify finance as their favorite.

What is a Mathematician? We assign each group of two students a mathematician to be studied closely and give them the references they need to complete their project. We chose the mathematicians in order to expose the students to a variety of research styles and to a survey of topics in mathematics. We selected a range of mathematicians from the 1700s until today that included women and minority mathematicians, such as David Blackwell and game theory and Ingrid Daubechies and image compression. Students prepared Microsoft PowerPoint presentations and classroom worksheets in order to engage the rest of the class with mathematics related to their mathematicians. As the class learned about the mathematics and the mathematicians from the student presentations, we highlighted the validity and success of diverse styles and the changing role of women and minorities over time. Students report that they find this segment challenging but interesting.

Working with Freshman Programs

With an enrollment of over 13,000 students, Appalachian is very concerned that students feel that they have received personal attention. To help with this, the University offers opportunities for freshmen to participate in programs that provide lots of interaction with other students with similar interests. We have made an effort to tie topics covered in MAT1010 to these programs.

Linking Courses Through Freshman Interest Groups (FIG): Faculty are given the opportunity to link courses for students with common interests through the FIG program. Several sections of MAT1010 have participated over the last few years, linking at different times with Freshman Seminar, general biology and English. For example, in 1998 a FIG group was formed for students who had laptops and the instructors from the three linked courses, MAT1010, English composition, and world civilization, met to find common themes to investigate in the courses. The students reported enjoying the experience of working with the same group of peers. The faculty were less enthusiastic about the FIG experience, citing increased behavioral problems.

Teaching in the Watauga College Program: Watauga College is a residential living-learning community offering interdisciplinary course work in the humanities and social sciences for first and second year students. In 2001, we began offering a special section of MAT1010 for Watauga College students. We cover modules on geometry of the earth and universe, mathematicians, consumer statistics, and personal finance. Throughout the course we examine what mathematics is through web-readings and examples. Watauga College students appreciate the interdisciplinary approach of the course and the chance to understand that mathematics is not just about numbers, equations or formulas.

Using Data and Information Related to the Summer Reading Program: In 1997, Appalachian instituted a summer reading program for incoming freshmen in which students were given a book to read prior to coming to campus for orientation. During orientation, students meet with faculty to discuss issues that arise in the book, and faculty are encouraged to use the book in freshman courses during the academic year. We have, where possible, utilized the summer reading book in MAT1010, usually through the use of related data while studying statistics.

While the books chosen have tended to be a mixture of fiction and non-fiction, they all have had strong social or environmental themes. For example, the first book, *In the Time of the Butterflies* by Julia Alvarez, was set amid the political repression of the Trujillo dictatorship in 1950s Dominican Republic. Correspondingly, in MAT1010 we examined economic and social data related to the Dominican Republic and other Caribbean countries from 1950 to the present. We also examined data on the role of women in politics, a strong theme in the book. Subsequent books have allowed us to examine data related to the Holocaust, the fish kills linked to the presence of pfiesteria in eastern North Carolina estuaries, the Vietnam conflict, and welfare reform. The students are not as interested in these data as we had hoped, perhaps because there is too much related to the book in their other courses.

Conclusions

Many universities have started to offer quantitative literacy courses as alternatives to college algebra for non-technical majors. We feel that we have had great success with our course, as evidenced through improved student attitudes and the adoption of the course as the required core mathematics course in many client departments. We have found that using web-based interactive explorations, on-line quizzes with instant feedback, timely topics of interest to the students, and to some extent, materials linked to other courses has increased student engagement and satisfaction. While we don't teach traditional algebra skills unless directly applicable to the application under investigation, we feel that we have not reduced the level of the content to reach these goals.

While developing material can be time-consuming, the classroom results are well worth the effort. We plan to continue refining the existing material to keep it relevant for the students, and we hope to have more interdisciplinary mini-topics to use in the future. We are currently looking at short modules on the mathematics of environmental science and on the mathematics of betting and gaming. We plan on making our ideas available to other faculty through the course website, given in the references below.

References

Alvarez, J., (1995). *In the Time of the Butterflies*. East Rutherford, NJ: Penguin/Plume Publishers.

Beutelspacher, A. (1994). *Cryptology*. Washington, DC: Mathematical Association of America.

Cohen, D., (Ed.). (1995) *Crossroads in Mathematics: Standards for Introductory College Mathematics Before Calculus*. Memphis, TN: American Mathematical Association of Two-Year Colleges.

Greenwald, S., *Geometry of the Earth and Universe* [On-Line]. www.mathsci.appstate.edu/~sjg/talks/earthanduniverse. html.

Greenwald, S. *What is a Mathematician* [On-Line]. www.mathsci.appstate.edu/~sjg/class/1010/ athematician/.

Hirst, H. *Math1010* [On-Line]. www.mathsci.appstate.edu/1010/.

Hirst, H., & Smith, J., (Ed.). (2003). *How Do You Know: Using Math to Make Decisions*. Dubuque, IA: Kendall-Hunt Publishers.

Kirtland, J., (2001). *Identification Numbers and Check Digit Schemes*. Washington, DC: Mathematical Association of America.

Lenker, S., (Ed.). (1998). *Exemplary Programs in Introductory College Mathematics*. MAA Notes #47. Washington, DC: Mathematical Association of America.

Maor, E., (1991). *What is there so Mathematical about Music?* in Applications of Secondary School Mathematics. Reston, VA: National Council of Teachers of Mathematics.

National Council of Teachers of Mathematics. (1989). *Curriculum and Evaluation Standard for School Mathematics*. Reston, VA: Author.

National Council of Teachers of Mathematics. (2000). *Principles and Standards for School Mathematics*. Reston, VA: Author.

The Shodor Education Foundation, Inc. *Project Interactivate* [On-Line]. www.shodor.org/interactivate/.

Quantitative Reasoning: An Interdisciplinary, Technology Infused Approach

David Jabon
DePaul University, Chicago IL

The Quantitative Reasoning course at DePaul University grew out of a major reexamination of the general education program for undergraduates in 1995–96. Like many universities in the 1990s, DePaul University wished to strengthen the mathematics skills of its graduates and was willing to add additional mathematics requirements for its students. The question that the faculty had to address was, what mathematical skills should an undergraduate who is not majoring in Mathematics, Science, or Business have?

Universities across the country came up with a variety of solutions. A simple and sometimes adequate approach is to require college algebra and one or more semesters of pre-calculus. While this is the easiest approach to implement, the pre-calculus material may not be very useful if one does not go on to calculus. A perhaps more common approach is to require one course from a smorgasbord of math-related courses, for example, statistics, discrete math, calculus, logic, probability. These courses might possess a special catalog designation, often a "Q"; so all students might be required to take a Q course. There are many excellent programs of this nature across the country, some with exemplary mathematics-related courses. An advantage of such an approach is that specialists often teach the courses and bring both expertise and dynamism to the classroom, but a disadvantage is that all students not take the same course and the quantitative skills of a graduate will vary dramatically depending on which Q course he or she took.

A third approach is to require all students to take a liberal arts mathematics course. For example, one based on COMAP's *For All Practical Purposes* or Burger and Starbird's *The Heart of Mathematics*, to name just two of many well-crafted texts of this genre. These courses tend to cover very interesting topics in mathematics in ways that non-majors can master and even enjoy. Some of these courses tend be to more focused on applications (such as *For All Practical Purposes)* while others emphasize problem solving. These courses can be very effective and, when required of all students, do provide a common experience for undergraduates. But the faculty of DePaul University wished to address the growing need for quantitative literacy directly by putting the focus on the interpretation and analysis of quantitative information.

A New Imperative: A Quantitatively Literate Workforce and Citizenry

In our lifetimes, there has been a vast expansion in the use of quantitative information in academic, professional, civic, and even daily life. Quantitative methods have become important in virtually every academic area, in some cases supplanting traditional methods of scholarship. In professional work, almost all important decisions must be supported by quantitative measures. Similarly, in matters of public policy, quantitative measures are essential in both making policy and evaluating its effectiveness. Even our electoral process has become extremely quantitative through the extensive use of polling and targeted advertisement. In our personal lives, we need to make numerous decisions that rely on mathematics, from evaluating the risks of medications and the results of medical tests to deciding on credit card and mortgage terms. Certainly, technology has played a role in enabling this change; technology has put tools to analyze and present data into the hands of many people, as opposed to a small cadre of highly trained specialists, and has made large data sets easy to share. But the change is much broader and is cultural at heart. An early book that portrays the shift is Darrell Huff's, 1954, *How to Lie with Statistics*. John Allen Paulos popularized it in his 1988, *Innumeracy: Mathematical Illiteracy and Its Consequences,* and its sequels. Edward Tufte examined and critiqued the visual display of quantitative information in his 1983, *The Visual Display of Quantitative Information,* and its sequels. Scholars such as Theodore Porter (1995) and Alain Desrosières (1998), have written critico-historical evaluations to put these changes into a broader perspective. Lynn Steen edited important volumes, *Why Numbers Count* (1997), and *Mathematics and Democracy: The Case for Quantitative Literacy* (2001), making a case that educational institutions at all levels must begin to address the new needs of a quantitatively capable populace and mapping some approaches. The Mathematical Association of America recognized these new needs with its influential 1996 report, *Quantitative Reasoning for College Students: A Supplement to the Standards.*

DePaul University's response to the new imperative was a Quantitative Reasoning course described below. It is designed to enable students who have completed it to:

- Make and analyze quantitative arguments expressed in numerical, graphical, verbal, or symbolic forms.

- Interpret and create graphs summarizing quantitative data.

- Understand and use reasoning involving percentage change and proportional relationships.

- Make reasoned estimations.

- Use computer tools to analyze data.

- Make simple mathematical models (especially linear

and exponential) and understand the limitations of mathematical models.

The course has college algebra as a prerequisite. Students can test out of college algebra via a placement exam. Over 45% of the undergraduate student body takes college algebra before taking the course.

As many faculty members as possible were involved in the initial development of the new requirement. Dr. Carolyn Narasimhan, Associate Dean in the College of Liberal Arts and Sciences and Associate Professor of Mathematics, provided both a vision for the quantitative reasoning requirement and a determination to make the development process truly collaborative. Faculty from all colleges were invited to a "town hall" meeting on quantitative reasoning in the curriculum. Discussion focused on the following questions:

- What should be in a foundation course in Quantitative Reasoning?

- How much can we expect from one course?

- What other components should there be in an effective Quantitative Reasoning program?

- What is the role of technology?

Beyond faculty input, institutional support was critical to the creation of the Quantitative Reasoning course. The College of Liberal Arts funded the establishment and maintenance of a computer classroom, including some staff and student support, and allowed the class size to be capped at 25. A director for the program was hired to oversee the curriculum, the labs, and faculty development. The curriculum described below was influenced by the writings cited above as well as the work of A. Rossman and K. Somers (1996) at Dickinson College, the work of D. Pierce, D. Wright, and L. Roland (1997) at Western Oregon State, and the CHANCE project.

It was decided that students can test out of the Quantitative Reasoning course requirement by taking a specific Quantitative Reasoning Examination or via placement into Calculus. In practice, very few students place out by either method. However, the faculty also decided to exempt students who have to take some form of Calculus in their major programs. Thus students majoring in mathematics, computer science, science, or business do not take the Quantitative Reasoning course at DePaul. Among the reasons for this decision: these students are required to take a substantial amount of relatively advanced mathematics in the programs already; these students are in programs that require more courses to graduate than most other programs; designing a course to meet the needs of these more mathematically advanced students as well as those with much less mathematical preparation would be almost impossible. However, most science departments and business departments have acknowledged that quantitative reasoning skills are important in their programs and require their own quantitative reasoning course, or add quantitative reasoning content to courses in their major.

Confident, Critical, and Capable

The purpose of DePaul's Quantitative Reasoning Program is to help students to become confident, critical, and capable users of quantitative information of all kinds, verbal, tabular, graphical as well as symbolic. Confidence is extremely important. The majority of students who take the course (approximately 1600 per year currently) have had difficult experiences with mathematics instruction. One of their first assignments is to write a short reflective essay giving their "math autobiography," and in their essays they often characterize themselves as "not good at math." Some sadly have chosen particular majors because they feel they won't be able to do the mathematics in, for example, science majors. Their lack of confidence in their ability to do any kind of mathematics is academically, professionally, and personally limiting, and the course directly attempts to build their confidence by giving them mathematics skills in a different, positive way.

The course also tries to develop students' criticality, primarily by making estimations and by giving them articles and graphics from the media to analyze and critique. Finding errors or even deception in published work is revelatory and empowering for most students. In assessments, students consistently state that after the course they are more inclined to read articles with quantitative information and are more apt to read it with a critical eye.

Finally, the course develops skills in handling quantitative information, especially rates, percentages, the making and interpreting of graphs, mathematical models, correlations, and basic descriptive statistics.

Technology Integration and Active Learning

A related problem to quantitative literacy is computer literacy. Many universities have put in place computer literacy requirements and computer literacy courses, but students often do not attain mastery because the computer skills are taught out of context. A key decision made was that technology would be used throughout the Quantitative Reasoning as a tool so that students would learn how to use these tools to solve real problems and produce realistic products. Thus, approximately two-thirds of the class is held in a computer lab with students working collaboratively on computer activities related to quantitative reasoning. The instructor assists the student groups as they work through the activity. The materials for the course are delivered over the Internet (found at the course website, given in the references) and student products are either Word documents or PowerPoint presentations with graphs pasted in from Excel. Excel is the main analytical tool, but students often use calculators when they see fit. The technology plays many positive roles. First and foremost, technology allows the use of real data throughout the course. Every activity and every assignment has data with a social or scientific context. Second, students are able to master the technology tools by doing realistic activities context. To use an analogy, one doesn't really know how to use a saw, until one uses a saw to cut and assemble real objects from raw materials. Similarly, one needs to use Excel in a variety of realistic contexts before one has mastery of this tool. Third, computer activities create an active, lively learning environment that is engaging for students.

Interdisciplinary Teaching and Content

Another key decision made by the faculty was that the course would not be exclusively taught by mathematics faculty. In fact, the course does not carry a mathematics prefix but rather an interdisciplinary one. Quantitative literacy skills are not unique to the mathematics faculty, and for non-majors, working with instructors who use mathematics as practitioners would be helpful. Furthermore, instructors from across the college of liberal arts bring data and examples from numerous fields creating a rich information set with wide appeal. Instructors from academic disciplines other than mathematics also tend to keep the context in focus, which helps in one of the main goals of the course, to enable students to use mathematics in realistic situations.

In the first six years (1998–2003), 82 different instructors have taught 324 sections with a total of approximately 6741 students. Over half of the instructors (45) have come from departments outside of math, computer science, and business. Specifically, instructors from anthropology, chemistry, communications, education, environmental science, geography, history, public service, physics, political science, psychology, religious studies, and sociology have taught the course. Quite unexpectedly, there has been surprising uniformity across the sections in content and approach. It is extremely rare for instructors to diverge from the main outline of the content and the primary pedagogy focusing on the collaborative computer activities.

Curriculum

DePaul University is on the quarter system, and the Quantitative Reasoning course is a one quarter course. The short duration of a one quarter course has limited the curriculum, and we believe the course could be considerably better taught over a semester with additional material. Approximately 1600 students (about 75% of all undergraduates) take the course each year. It is intended to be taken in the first year, as mentioned above, but in practice only 52% of those required to take the course do so in their first year. By the end of the second year 75% of those required to take the course have done so, with the remainder putting it off until their third and fourth years. A very small percentage, approximately 4%, of the students required to take Quantitative Reasoning place out via a placement test.

Week 1: Absolute and Relative Quantities; Introduction to Excel

Absolute quantities refer generally to raw numbers and counts; relative quantities are usually ratios of absolute quantities that normalize absolute quantities for comparison. Examples of relative quantities are rates and percentages. The first week focuses on the distinction between these two kinds of quantities, especially the importance of relative quantities. Examples of the data used are counts and rates of HIV cases by country, counts of individuals with incomes below the poverty level and the corresponding rates by states, and sports injury counts and rates. Along the way, Excel is introduced, in particular, cell references, sorting, and filling. We also built an internet-based tool to make shaded maps, so that students can take data from Excel and make and interpret their own maps. This tool is freely available over the internet. Maps for the United States, the world, the state of Illinois, the city of Chicago, and the state of Florida are currently available. This display of quantitative information in the form of maps is very common in the media and expands the use of quantitative information to the spatial realm. Students typically need instruction on how to give effective written interpretations of such maps.

Week 2: Estimation and Percentages

Estimation is a critical skill for a quantitatively literate person. One needs to estimate value in order to check the reasonableness of one's own calculations (how do you know you didn't make a small typing error?), in order to

check the reasonableness of others' calculations, and in order not to be deceived by others. Students start to develop this skill in the second week with some instruction on the topic. We give very specific guidelines: an estimate should start with some basic, commonly accepted facts such as a population figure or basic quantities such as lengths, volumes. It should include the reasoning process by which you obtain your estimate. The estimate should be expressed to an appropriate degree of precision (generally not too many decimal places). Examples of estimations students make are: how long it would take to drive across the US, how much mail is delivered in a year in the US, how many times a human heart typically beats in one day? The other major topic of the second week is the use of percentages in quantitative work. Students are asked to master five types of percentage problems that arise in everyday quantitative work: "percentage as part of a whole" problems, percent change, "percent more than" problems, successive percent change problems, and reverse percentage change problems. To help develop their criticality, students are asked to find and correct percentage errors in articles from the media. A good short example is given in the first box.

Week 3: Making and Interpreting Graphs

Graphs are essential for presenting and analyzing quantitative information. The week's focus is on learning how to make three types of graphs in Excel: pie charts, bar charts (including multiple bar charts), and XY-graphs. Students learn when each type of graph is appropriate, how to describe and interpret each type of graph, and how to critique misleading graphs from the media. Important vocabulary for describing *XY* graphs is introduced: increasing, decreasing, constant, absolute maximum, absolute minimum, relative maximum, relative minimum, periodicity, increasing at an increasing or decreasing rate, decreasing at an increasing or decreasing rate.

The January 2, 2003 edition of Nature, probably the most prestigious science journal in the world, contained the following paragraph:

"For our money, the prize for 1903 should go to King C. Gillette, who brought his safety razor to market after several years of research and development. In 1903 he sold just 51 razors and 168 blades. The next year he sold 123,648 blades, an increase of exactly 736%. Almost as meritorious was the decaffeinization process conceived by the German coffee importer Ludwig Roselius after inadvertently soaking coffee beans in salt water. He marketed the result as SANKA (for sans-caffeine)."

The paragraph contains a serious quantitative error. Find it, and give the correct value.

Week 4: Applied Interdisciplinary Module

The purpose of the fourth week is to apply the tools developed in the first weeks to an interdisciplinary topic coming from a specific area. Instructors have chosen to study data sets from ecology, political science, archeology, and economics with their students. Probably the most popular module is from economics, the Consumer Price Index and the changing value of money. Students learn about the motivation and history of the consumer price index, how it is calculated, and how to use it to compare prices in different years. The week concludes with an interesting public policy application of the ideas to the issue of the US minimum wage. Students graph the minimum wage in current dollars to produce a graph that looks like the one below.

This graph conforms to most people's view of the minimum wage: it has nominally gone up over time, with periods of stagnation due to Congressional inaction. However, in constant dollars, the graph looks like:

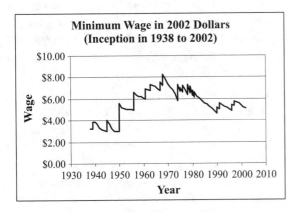

A very different story indeed. Students then critique faulty graphs of the same data from the media and finally write a quantitatively based argument either to raise the minimum wage or to keep it the same.

Week 5: Introduction to Mathematical Modeling and Linear Models in Particular

This week introduces the general concept of mathematical modeling (as a collection of mathematical techniques to facilitate predictions for planning or simulation purposes), reviews linear functions, and covers linear models. Excel is used to add simple regression lines, get their equations, and use them to make predictions. Students are introduced to the R-squared value as a measure of goodness of fit. An important idea that is emphasized in the activities is that the farther one is from existing data, the less confidence one has in predictions.

Week 6: Exponential Modeling

Students learn how to model with exponential functions in a wide variety of contexts: population growth, investments, radioactive decay, metabolism of drugs.

Week 7: Basic Descriptive Statistics and Correlation

Students learn how to determine if two variables are correlated using Excel and how to interpret the result. Heavy emphasis is placed on the interpretation of the result especially the possibility of common underlying causes for a correlation. The material covered here is in the spirit of Rossman and Chance's *Workshop Statistics*.

Week 8 and 9: Additional Applied Module or Modules

As in the fourth week, students apply the tools developed to an interdisciplinary topic coming from a specific area. Applications to finance are popular with students and instructors alike, but material on global warming, elections, and scaling laws are used according to instructor interest and inclination.

Week 10: Presentations

Week 10 is dominated by PowerPoint presentations. The most important assignment in the latter half of the course is an analytical paper and PowerPoint presentation summarizing the results of the paper. Students are asked to imagine that they are a team of presidential advisors and that they are analyzing data on a topic of public policy importance. They use data primarily from the *Statistical Abstract of the US* to determine important trends and patterns in the data. They are required to use at least three different tables and make at least one mathematical model with a prediction. The papers are usually 8–10 pages long (including the graphs) and in most sections are produced collaboratively so that the results can be presented to the class in the form of PowerPoint presentations. All students must participate in the presentation. These projects add a great deal to the course. Students get the opportunity to analyze data in free form, without the guided structure of the computer activities. They have to decide what data to use, how to graph it, and what it means. They need to make public policy recommendation based on their analysis.

Assessment Results

In addition to the standard end-of-course evaluations for each section, the program performs a mandated annual assessment project that assesses one or more of the learning goals for the course and includes (not necessarily exclusively) direct examination of student work. Assessment and evaluation of the course has shown us a number of things.

1. Students report that the active, hands-on approach which combines the technology, contributes greatly to their learning. They are asked directly on the end-of-course evaluations which parts of the course contributed the most and the least to their learning in the course; consistently, they rate computer activities using real data as the most valuable part of the course.

2. Students find the practical use of mathematics in real contexts interesting, relevant, and empowering. A common comment is "I can do math when it is approached this way!"

3. Students have surprising difficulty with percentages. Specifically, assessment has shown that the only percentage-related topic entering Quantitative Reasoning students know is the idea of calculating a number that is a percentage of another (e.g., calculating the tax on a purchase). 77% of students on a diagnostic exam had this correct. Initial performance on diagnostics on all other types of percentage problems was shockingly low: 28% on a problem involving percentage as a part of a whole, 28% on a problem involving the calculation of a percentage decrease, 14% on a problem involving the calculation of a percentage increase over 100%, and 7% on a problem involving successive percentage changes ("Recently here in Chicago, a store had a 30% sale on certain items. If you had a coupon, you could take an additional 35% off the sale price. Assuming you took advantage of this offer, by what percent would your final price be lower than the original price?") The results also showed very clearly where instruction seems to be succeeding and where not. Student performance on percentage change prob-

lems increased markedly on both the midterm and final (67% and 56%, respectively, although it should be noted that the question on the final involved additional complexity). Students also improved in successive percentage change problems (from 7% on the diagnostic to 43% on the final, an improvement but not altogether satisfactory, however.) On what we have come to call "reverse percentage problems" (e.g., "According to the official 2000 Census, the Hispanic population of the US in 2000 was 35,305,818. It rose by an astounding 57.9% from 1990 to 2000. Calculate what the Hispanic population was in 1990."), students performed extremely poorly even after instruction: 18% success rate on the midterm and 22% on the final exam.

4. Group work presents logistical and even personal challenges for students and instructors. While students generally learn more easily when working in teams, there are exceptions, especially in groups of threes, if one member participates very little. Group work sometimes lulls less capable students into complacency. We generally ask that students individually do weekly out-of-class homework to help counteract this effect. Also the production of a collaborative report and PowerPoint presentation is often a challenging, if entirely realistic, task. Contributions are not always equal, and some group members fail to show up for agreed upon meetings. It is perhaps a lesson in working with others, but sometimes an unpleasant one for the group members and at times for the instructor. The Mathematical Association of America has published several valuable books in the MAA Notes series on collaborative learning in mathematics which explore these challenges from both theoretical and practical standpoints: Hagelhans et al. (1995), Dubinsky et al. (1997), and Rogers et al. (2001). The ideas of the many authors represented in these works are informing our instructional efforts as we move forward.

5. Ten weeks is probably not enough time for a Quantitative Reasoning course. This conclusion stands out very clearly in the analysis of the final projects. Students in the more free form analysis of the final project make errors just like the ones they critiqued in the course. They forget to use rates. They make faulty bar charts and pie charts. They make errors with units (e.g. interpreting data in thousands as if it were not in thousands). If possible, a Quantitative Reasoning course should be one semester or two quarters, and further reinforced with "math across the curriculum" program.

Conclusion

The need for quantitative and mathematical skills for all our college graduates has never been greater than today. Broad societal changes have led to an increased quantification in academic work, professional work, and daily life. Algebra, while necessary, is insufficient to prepare citizens for the challenges they face as individuals and as a society. Thus universities must experiment with new curricula and new approaches to deliver it. The response of students and faculty alike to the interdisciplinary approach DePaul University has adopted to improve the quantitative literacy of students not majoring in mathematics, science, or business has been gratifying, and through assessment of student work we are attempting to refine it further.

References

Burger, E. & Starbird, M. (2000). *The Heart of Mathematics: A Guide to Effective Thinking*. Emeryville, CA: Key Curriculum Press.

DePaul University, Thematic Map Tool. qrc.depaul.edu/maptool.

DePaul University, Quantitative Reasoning Center, qrc.depaul.edu.

Desrosières, A. (1998. *The Politics of Large Numbers: A History of Statistical Reasoning*. (Camille Naish, translator). Cambridge, MA: Harvard University Press.

Dubinsky, E., et al. (1997). *Readings in Cooperative Learning for Undergraduate Mathematics*, MAA Notes 44, Washington, DC: Mathematical Association of America.

Garfunkel, S. et al. (2002). *For All Practical Purposes: Mathematical Literacy in Today's World*. New York: W. H. Freeman.

Hagelgans, N., et al. (1995). *A Practical Guide to Cooperative Learning in Collegiate Mathematics*, MAA Notes 37, Washington, DC: Mathematical Association of America.

Huff, D. (1954). *How to Lie with Statistics*. New York: W. W. Norton.

Paulos, J. A. (1988). *Innumeracy: Mathematical Illiteracy and Its Consequences*. New York: Farrar, Straus and Giroux.

Pierce D., E. Wright, & Roland, L. (1997). *Mathematics For Life: A Foundation Course for Quantitative Literacy*. Preliminary Edition. Upper Saddle River, NJ: Prentice Hall.

Porter, T. (1995). *Trust in Numbers: The Pursuit of Objectivity in Science and Public Life*. Princeton, NJ: Princeton University Press.

Rogers, E. et al. (2001). *Cooperative Learning in Undergraduate Mathematics: Issues that Matter and Strategies that Work*, MAA Notes 55, Washington, DC: Mathematical Association of America.

Rossman, A. and K. Somers, *Quantitative Reasoning: A Workshop Approach (unpublished)* 1996.

Rossman, A. & Chance, B. (1998). *Workshop Statistics*. New York: Springer-Verlag.

Snell, L. et al. (Accessed Aug. 28, 2003). CHANCE Project. www.dartmouth.edu/~chance/.

Sons, L. et al. (1996). *Quantitative Reasoning for College Students: A Supplement to the Standards*. Mathematical Association of America.

Steen, L. (2001). (ed.). *Mathematics and Democracy: The Case for Quantitative Literacy*. National Council on Education and the Disciplines.

Steen, L. (ed.). (1997). *Why Numbers Count: Quantitative Literacy for Tomorrow's America*. New York: College Entrance Examination Board.

Tufte, E. (1983). *The Visual Display of Quantitative Information*. Cheshire, CT: Graphics Press.

US Bureau of Census, *Statistical Abstract of the United States*. Washington, DC (Annual editions).

General Education Mathematics: A Problem Solving Approach

Jesús Jimenez and Maria Zack
Point Loma Nazarene University, San Diego, CA

Program Background and History

Point Loma Nazarene University (PLNU) is a Christian liberal arts institution founded in 1902. Accredited by the Western Association of Schools and Colleges, PLNU offers Baccalaureate degrees (BA, BS, and BSN) in over 40 majors and several Master's degrees. The university has a history of strong programs in the sciences, nursing and education.

Situated on the cliffs above the Pacific Ocean, PLNU currently serves 2,375 undergraduate and 795 graduate students, Because of the institution's location in a residential neighborhood, the number of students served by the university is capped by the City of San Diego. For the last several years, the institution has enrolled the maximum number of students allowed. Significant competition for this limited number of seats in the freshmen class has dramatically improved the quality of the student body.

In the early 1990s the administration of Point Loma Nazarene University decided to convert the academic year from a quarter schedule to a semester schedule. At that time, the faculty decided to continue to apply the rule that students who scored below the 35th percentile on the mathematics portion of the SAT were required to take a course in basic mathematical skills. The 35% percentile cut off was decided in the mid 1960s after correlating the data from students' SAT scores with our institutions home grown Mathematics Placement Exam.

The faculty and the administration saw the change in schedule as an opportunity to revise the general education curriculum. As part of the discussion, the faculty from the Department of Mathematics and Computer Science presented to the university faculty a summary of current policy documents (Cheney, 1989; MAA, 1989; NRC, 1989) expressing concern that students were losing quantitative ability during their college years. The university faculty, as a whole, agreed that this problem could not be ignored and that the general education curriculum should be modified to address this need. The desire was to add a course that would cross disciplines and enhance the students' quantitative skills rather than adding another traditional mathematics course to the curriculum.

PLNU is a relatively small university that de-emphasizes the use of adjuncts, the faculty is small (about 140 full time faculty members). This leads to a system of governance that is relationally based and a willingness to trust the expertise of other faculty members. Because of this strong system of trust, the university faculty made a somewhat unusual decision and tasked the Department of Mathematics and Computer Science with developing this new "cross discipline" course in quantitative reasoning and critical thinking. As a result the Mathematics and Computer Science Department used a variety of research on student learning styles to create a course focusing on developing problem solving skills. (NRC, 1989; Schoenfeld, 1985; Schoenfeld, 1987). The department named the course Problem Solving.

In the spring of 1993 one section of Problem Solving was offered, followed by another section in the fall of 1993 and by two sections in the spring of 1994. These early sections were pioneered by faculty with experience in the field of Mathematics Education. Currently we are offering six sections of the course per semester and the course is taught on a rotating basis by all full-time faculty in Mathematics. This course fulfills the general education mathematics requirement for all students who do not take calculus.

Program Goals and Objectives

One of the goals shared by faculty, though not explicitly stated in the syllabus, is to provide students with a "rigorous but gentle" exposure to quantitative reasoning. Many of the students in this class have had very little mathematics and bring some level of "math phobia" to the classroom. The catalog description and course objectives are informed by this perspective.

Catalog Description

A general education course whose major goal is to develop the ability to solve non-routine problems through dynamic processes of inquiry and exploration, logical reasoning, making and testing conjectures, and investigating implications of conclusions. A study of major concepts, methods, and applications of quantitative reasoning with emphases on active problem solving and developing connections with other disciplines.

Goals and Objectives

Problem Solving was developed in the Mathematics and Computer Science Department. It uses group discussion and team work and this is reflected in the goals set for the course. They are:

- To involve the student directly in various problem solving activities.
- To contribute to the student's ability to solve non-routine problems.
- To expand the student's methods of inquiry and exploration.

- To contribute to the student's ability to form conjectures and check implications.
- To expand the student's understanding of major concepts, methods and applications of quantitative reasoning.
- To help the student see the role of problem solving in modern society.

Placement of Students into Program

This course emphasizes problem solving in context, and this requires familiarity with several areas of the general education curriculum (political science, social science, world civilization, and others). Also, since problem solving requires endurance and patience, and is impacted by the beliefs of the problem solver, it has been our experience that students are more successful in this course if they have some "maturity." Therefore, students must have junior class standing (57 semester units or more) and show proficiency in elementary mathematics to register for this course.

Proficiency in mathematics can be shown by scoring at or above the 35th percentile on the mathematics portion of the SAT examination, by passing the Mathematics and Computer Science Department's self-developed Mathematics Placement Examination, or by passing a remedial mathematics course offered by the department every semester. Our institution has become more competitive over the last five years, with four to five students competing for every space in our freshman class. The end result is that the number of students who need to take remedial mathematics has dramatically decreased. Most of our students qualify for Problem Solving based on the mathematical knowledge that they gained in high school. Thus the skill level and background of the students in each class is quite diverse. Any student who takes calculus may choose to waive Problem Solving; therefore most of the students majoring in any of the sciences, mathematics or engineering do not take this course.

Program Curriculum

This course is the product of collaborative work among the faculty of the Mathematics and Computer Science Department. The faculty of the department had to come to a consensus on course content, teaching approach, number of units, level, and prerequisites.

Because the university desires that each student have a common general education experience, every section of Problem Solving offered follows the same textbook and syllabus (website given in the references). The textbook used is: *For All Practical Purposes* by the COMAP consortium and published by W. H. Freeman and Co. Each instructor focuses on the following chapters which are covered in the order given below:

- Planning and Scheduling
- Street Networks (Graph Theory)
- Visiting Vertices (Graph Theory, particularly the Traveling Salesman Problem)
- Social Choice (Voting Methods)
- Apportionment
- Weighted Voting
- Fair Division
- Consumer Finance (Borrowing)
- Consumer Finance (Saving)

Many of the group exercises and class examples are common to all sections and the faculty regularly share newly developed ideas (power point slides, hand outs, exam questions, etc).

The grade distribution is the same for every section:

- Three examinations (45 percent)
- A cumulative final exam (30 percent)
- Homework (12 percent)
- A group project (8 percent)
- Class participation (5 percent).

Exams and the final examination are prepared and graded by each instructor and are taken individually by each student. Each instructor also chooses a set of homework exercises; however, there is significant intersection of homework assigned in all of the sections. There is a single group project for all the sections. Groups are self-selected and can have three or four students.

Group projects have included:

1. Analyzing the weighted voting system of the Australian parliament: the students were required to find out the representative distribution for the Australian parliament and to analyze the resulting weighted voting system by
   a. computing the Banzhaf power index of each state or territory,
   b. finding the smallest quota that would make the state with smallest weight powerless,
   c. finding the smallest quota that would cause the largest weight state to have veto power,
   d. analyzing the fairness of the current system with respect to the Banzhaf power index

2. Designing an efficient route to unlock all the classrooms at PLNU. This was of particular concern to the students because at the time, Campus Public Safety could not get all of the rooms on campus unlocked before the start of classes at 7:30 a.m.

3. Vehicle routing: the students were required to create routes for bread delivery to about 25 groceries stores in the San Diego area. They were given
   a. The capacity (in bread boxes) of each truck,
   b. the addresses of the stores,
   c. the number of bread boxes each store had ordered,
   d. the amount of time they had to make all of the deliveries
   e. the requirement that all trucks had to travel no faster than the posted speed limit on each road.

   The students were required to find the minimum number of trucks and the route of each truck necessary to make the deliveries.

4. Estimating the number of Easter eggs required to fill the university's gymnasium. We expected them to consider the "packing" of the eggs rather than just approximating them with rectangular boxes. The students were also expected to approximate the volume of the gym taking into account the furniture and fixtures.

5. Analyzing the different apportionments of the United States House of Representatives that result when using different methods of apportionment.

Pedagogy

This course was developed using significant research about how people learn to solve problems (Polya, 1945; Schoenfeld, 1985) and research about group and "discovery" learning especially in mathematics (Reynolds, 1995). This work was foundational to developing the course teaching approach and also led to the renovation of a classroom specifically for this course.

At the beginning of the semester the students are told about the research that shows that academic achievement, productivity, and self-esteem improve dramatically when students work together in groups. Students are also told that this course is taught in a way that may be new to them, one that emphasizes teamwork, cooperation and support by others, rather than isolation and competition in learning. They are also reassured that much of their grade will be dependent on their own work. Further, the role of classroom instructor is explained as one of coach rather than lecturer; that there will be less direct lecturing in class than they expect, with many questions "answered" by another question asked to help each group work through their own questions and difficulties. Our fundamental belief is that students learn problem solving skills by solving problems.

Many of our students bring little experience with mathematics and a certain level of "math phobia" to the classroom. Most topics are introduced via an example or open-ended question. The solutions are described in the context of the particular problem rather than with variable-filled formulas. As students begin to recognize patterns, careful algorithmic and analytical solutions are described. Open ended group problems include the following:

1. The Restricted Final Scheduling Problem: Small State University is offering eight courses during its summer session. The table below shows with an X which pairs of courses have at least one student in common.

   The students are asked to help Small State University design a final exam schedule so that:

   a. The minimum number of rooms are used to proctor the examinations

   b. No student has to take two examinations at the same hour.

	F	M	H	P	E	I	S	C
French (F)		X		X	X	X		X
Mathematics (M)					X	X		
History (H)					X	X		X
Philosophy (P)								X
English (E)						X		
Italian (I)							X	
Spanish (S)								
Chemistry (C)								

2. The Handshake Problem: Susan and Richard (a married couple) attended a party with three other married couples (only eight people were at the party). At this party a good deal of handshaking took place, but:

   a. No one shook hands with her or his spouse

   b. No one shook hands with herself or himself

   c. No one shook hands with the same person more than once.

   Before the party was over, Susan asked the other seven people how many handshakes she or he had had. Each person gave Susan a different answer.

   The students are asked to answer the following questions:

   a. How many times did Susan shake hands at this party?

   b. How many times did Richard shake hands at this party?

   c. How many handshakes were there?

Problem Solving is taught in a specially designed room. The room holds 44 students seated in four rows of tables for two (2 ft. × 4 ft). These tables face forward so that all of the students can see the instructor, blackboard and the screen for the data projector during full class discussions. The students are seated in swivel chairs on wheels and to form groups they turn to create groups of four around every other table in the row. There is roughly five feet of floor space between each of the four rows enabling the instructor to freely move between all of the groups.

During any group discovery activity (more than half of the class each day) the instructor moves among the groups, helping students over rough spots and clarifying questions. This leads to a very high level of interaction between the instructor and student as the students are much more willing to ask questions when in a small group. Over the last ten years we have found this pedagogy to build confidence in the students so that they are more willing to take risks, "guess" at problems and be persistent in seeking solutions. Many of the students who enter the course "math phobic" leave (see survey results in Table 1 below) with a greater sense of their ability to deal with quantitative problems.

Program Assessment

In the spring of 1994 the students in Problem Solving were given an attitudinal survey at the end of the course. For a period of roughly nine years, no further formal assessment of the course was conducted. The faculty who teach the course regularly discuss the course and have modified the content over time, however no data was being collected. In response to the increasing emphasis on assessment in higher education, the department began giving the attitudinal survey again in the fall of 2003. This is a first step in assessment, with more work needed in "skills" based course assessment. The reality of teaching problem solving to 240 students every semester has made it difficult to design a skills assessment that is manageable.

In the fall of 2003 and in the spring of 2004 the students were asked about their level of agreement with the following statements.

Q1. In this class we have been directly involved in problem solving activities.

Q2. This class has contributed to my ability to solve different types of problems

Q3. This class has expanded my methods of exploration in problem solving

Q4. This class has contributed to my ability to make educated guesses and check their correctness by analyzing their implications

Q5. This class has helped me to understand major concepts, methods and applications of critical thinking

Q6. This class has helped me to see the importance of problem solving in our modern society

The bar graphs below summarize the students' responses. We use the following scale.

1 Strongly agree
2 Agree
3 Neutral
4 Disagree
5 Strongly disagree

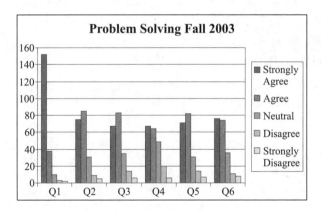

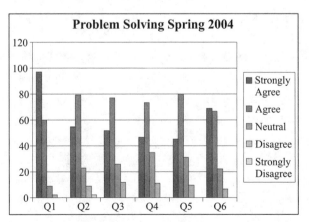

As can be seen from the data, the students report having had a positive experience in the course. In the fall of 2004, the department began to experiment with some skills based methods for assessing the course. We are currently looking at the approach described in (Charles, et al

1987) to see if they can be effectively adapted for use in a university classroom.

After reviewing this data, our department began to have conversations about the variety of mathematical backgrounds of the students in the course. A decision was made to disaggregate the data based on mathematical background. This was done in the spring of 2004. The results of disaggregating based on the number of years of High School mathematics that the student took can be seen below.

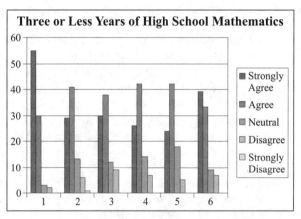

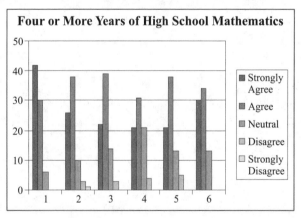

The students seem remarkably consistent in their opinion of the course in spite of the differing number of years of mathematics that they took in High School. It appears that students who took more mathematics in High School don't feel that their ability to "guess and check" improved as much as those who had less High School mathematics. More years of data will be required to determine if this is significant.

References

Baron, J. B. & Sternberg, R. J. (1987). *Teaching Thinking Skills: Theory and Practice*. New York: W. H. Freeman.

Bransford, J. & Stein, B. (1984). *The Ideal Problem Solver*. New York: W. H. Freeman.

Charles, Randall, Lester, Frank and O'Daffer, Phares (1987). *How to Evaulate Progress in Problem Solving.* Reston, VA: NCTM.

Cheney, L. V. (1989). *50 hours: A Core Curriculum for College Students.* Washington, D.C. National Endowment for the Humanities.

Curcio, F.R. (Ed.). (1987). *Teaching and Learning: A problem solving focus.* Reston, VA: NCTM.

Duncker, K. (1945). *On problem solving. Psychological Monographs 58, No. 5 Whole # 270.* Washington, DC: American Psychological Association.

Kilpatrick, J.. (1987). *"Problem Formulating: Where Do Good Problems Come From?"* Cognitive Science and Mathematics Education, edited by Alan H. Schoenfeld, pp. 123–48. Hillsdale, NJ: Lawrence Erlbaum Associates.

Krulik, S. (Ed.). (1980). *Problem Solving in School Mathematics.* 1980 Yearbook of the National Council of Teachers of Mathematics. Reston, VA: NCTM.

MAA Notes 13. (1989). *Reshaping college mathematics: a project of the Committee on the Undergraduate Program in Mathematics,* edited by Lynn Arthur Steen. Washington D.C. Mathematical Association of America.

National Research Council. (1989). *Everybody Counts: A Report to the Nation on the Future of Mathematics Education.* Washington, DC: National Academy Press.

Newell, A., &Simon, H. (1972). *Human Problem Solving.* Englewood Cliffs, J: Prentice-Hall.

Paulos, J. A. (1988). *Innumeracy: Mathematical Illiteracy and its Consequences.* New York: Hill and Wang.

Point Loma Nazarene University website. www.mcs.ptloma.edu/MTH303/303_syllabus.htm

Polya, G. (1945). *How To Solve It.* Princeton: Princeton University Press.

Polya, G. (1954). *Mathematics and Plausible Reasoning* (2 vols.). Princeton: Princeton University Press.

Reynolds, B., et. al., (1995). *A Practical Guide to Cooperative Learning in Collegiate Mathematics.* MAA Notes 37. Washington, DC: MAA.

Schoenfeld, A. (1985). *Mathematical Problem Solving.* New York: Academic Press.

Schoenfeld, A. (Ed.). (1987). *Cognitive Science and Mathematics Education.* Hillsdale, NJ:Lawrence Erlbaum.

Steen, L. A. (Ed.) (1990). *On the Shoulders of Giants: New Approaches to Numeracy.* Washington, D.C.: National Academy Press.

Wickelgren, W. (1974). *How to Solve Problems.* San Francisco: W. H. Freeman.

Quantitative Reasoning and Informed Citizenship: A Relevant Hands-on Course

Alicia Sevilla and Kay Somers
Moravian College, Bethlehem, PA

The course *Quantitative Reasoning and Informed Citizenship* was created with the help of a grant from the National Science Foundation (Grant No. 9950229) for the years 1999–2001. The course was taught for the first time in fall 2000. It was designed to address the needs of college students in the 21st century and as one course that students may choose to satisfy a requirement of the new interdisciplinary general education curriculum at Moravian College. As its title suggests, the course investigates relevant applications and is designed to help students become more informed citizens.

Background

Moravian College is a small liberal arts college that has, for the past 35 years, had a "quantitative skills" requirement. In 1968, the college instituted its "Guidelines for Liberal Education," a general education program designed to, among other things, "enhance the qualities of judgment and freedom of mind that distinguish the liberally educated person." As part of this curriculum, students were required to take one course in a category labeled "Symbolic and Quantitative Analysis." A student could meet this requirement by taking any course in the Mathematics or Computer Science Departments, or by taking Symbolic Logic, a Philosophy course.

In the mid-1980's, faculty began working on a new "Core" curriculum, a set of seven common core courses that would be taken by all students. Because of pragmatic considerations, the College was not able to institute this curriculum for all students, but for about 8 years, we allowed 25% of our entering freshmen to choose the "Core Curriculum" for general education, while the remaining 75% of students satisfied the "Guidelines for Liberal Education" that were in place since 1968. One of the seven common courses in the "Core Curriculum" was *Quantitative Problem Solving*, an interdisciplinary course developed and taught by Moravian College faculty in Mathematics, Education, Psychology, Sociology, and Economics.

Because it was not practical to maintain two curricula for the long term, a faculty committee was commissioned to design a new curriculum that captured the best aspects of both the "Guidelines" and the "Core." As of fall 2000, all entering first-year students must satisfy the requirements of a new general education curriculum, "Learning in Common" or LinC. The requirements of LinC include a course in each of four Foundational categories, six Multidisciplinary categories, and two Upper-level categories. Each student is obligated to develop an educational plan and choose a course within each category of LinC. One of the Foundational categories of LinC is "Quantitative Reasoning," which is described as follows:

> Each course in this category will develop the student's facility in quantitative reasoning through a wide variety of applications chosen from many fields and will involve the following: converting conceptual information into problems that can be solved quantitatively; using appropriate techniques for analyzing and solving quantitative problems that lead to the formation of a conclusion; creating and reading pictorial and graphical representations of data and data analysis, including those showing relationships among multiple variables; using appropriate technology as a tool for quantitative analysis; and writing and interpreting results and solutions of problems.

This description was developed by an interdisciplinary group of faculty using the *Quantitative Problem Solving* course of the Core curriculum as a model. Faculty must fill out a "course review sheet" and apply to an interdisciplinary faculty committee to have a course approved for any category of LinC. Faculty or departments that want their courses to be accepted for the "Quantitative Reasoning" category must demonstrate that the student learning objectives included in the above description are met. In addition, they must explain how they will assess what level of achievement their students have reached. Currently, nine courses have been approved to meet this requirement.

Course Goals

The course *Quantitative Reasoning and Informed Citizenship* was specially designed to meet the student learning goals of the "Quantitative Reasoning" category of LinC. It has an interdisciplinary focus and is designed to help students learn to make responsible decisions on fiscal, environmental and heath issues that require quantitative reasoning skills. Although it is offered and primarily taught by faculty from the Mathematics Department, the course was designed so that it could be taught by an interdisciplinary group of faculty. This is consistent with a practice established by a predecessor course.

The course, including student background reading materials and student activities, was developed with the help of a grant from the National Science Foundation; it has the following specific goals.

- Develop students' facility in formulating, analyzing, and solving real-world problems that involve quantitative information. Build their ability to reason quantitatively and to make numerical arguments;

- Increase students' ability to explain and interpret, orally and in writing, the results of quantitative analyses;

- Increase students' proficiency with computer software and use of internet resources in a learning environment;

- Improve students' attitudes towards quantitative reasoning tools, quantitative analysis and computers.

The course topics are organized in three sections: 1.) Using numbers, functions and graphs; 2.) Reasoning; and 3.) Statistical thinking. The course has an experiential learning focus that was inspired by successful projects such as *Workshop Statistics* by Rossman and Chance and *Mathematics for Life* by Pierce, Wright, and Roland, as well as Moravian College's Core course *Quantitative Problem Solving*. (Chromiak, et al, (1992); Rossman & Chance, (1999); and Somers, et al, (1994) have more information on these courses.) The materials developed for *Quantitative Reasoning and Informed Citizenship* consist of background materials that students read before each class, and activities that students complete in class and as homework. Most of the activities involve the use of Excel, so the course is taught in a computer classroom equipped with enough computers for students to work in groups of two. (For some activities we want students to work with a partner; for other activities some students may choose to work individually or they may work in pairs.)

Some students satisfy the quantitative reasoning requirement by taking a mathematics course required for their major, calculus for most science majors, elementary statistics for other majors. *Quantitative Reasoning and Informed Citizenship* particularly meets the needs of those students who are generally not attracted to mathematics and science and who do not have a specific mathematics requirement for their major, but any Moravian College student may enroll in the course. Although a minority, some students take this course even though they have already satisfied the college quantitative reasoning requirement with another mathematics course; they do so because of the relevant topics and they want to learn more about Excel.

Student Placement

Incoming students at Moravian College take a mathematics assessment test (designed by Moravian College mathematics faculty) when they register for their first semester classes in May before their first year. Students who have completed a calculus course in high school take a calculus assessment test, similar to a cumulative final exam in a first calculus course; students without a calculus background take the non-calculus assessment test, which is similar to a cumulative final exam in precalculus. The assessment test, together with the student's high school record and the student's academic interests, helps the mathematics faculty recommend a mathematics placement for each student. Our experience from more than ten years of using these predictors has shown them to be effective in reducing the number of course changes during the first week of classes. In addition, the number of students who successfully complete their first mathematics course at Moravian College has increased.

Each student is advised to take *Calculus II, Calculus I, Calculus with Precalculus Review, Elementary Statistics, Mathematics for Elementary Teaching, Mathematics for Design* (a course developed for Art students and team-taught by members of both departments; topics include ratio and proportion, similarity, geometric constructions with Euclidean tools and dynamic geometry software, properties of polygons and polyhedra, isometries and other geometric transformations to the plane and space, symmetry and periodic designs, projections from space onto a plane), or *Quantitative Reasoning and Informed Citizenship*. (Depending on various considerations, this recommendation may not necessarily be for their first term at Moravian.) As a requirement for graduation, all students must complete one course from the quantitative reasoning category. Students who have no specific mathematics course requirement for their major may choose any approved course to meet this requirement. However, because of the use of computer technology and the emphasis on applications, reasoning, and analysis in *Quantitative Reasoning and Informed Citizenship*, a student may be recommended to take this course when his or her performance indicators show a weakness in math. Although the mathematical topics are not advanced, this course is not a remedial mathematics course and is not perceived as such, because of its focus on applications and on interpreting results in context.

Content and Pedagogy

The first section of the course, on using numbers, functions, and graphs, contains eight topics and fourteen activities. The second section, on reasoning, contains four topics and six activities; the rest of the topics relate to statistical thinking. The list of course topics and activities given below shows how the background materials and the activities are intertwined. Two of the activities are significantly different and deserve special mention: Activity 0 on reading mathematics and Activity 5 on evaluating websites. Because students are expected to read the background materials before a topic is introduced in class, and because most of our students have not had much experience reading mathematics-related texts, we begin with an activity designed to attack this problem. Activity 0, done on the first day, involves the students in an exercise designed to help them learn to actively and successfully read mathematical materials. Although most students use the World Wide Web, many of them accept whatever they find on the web as valid and authoritative. Activity 5 introduces students to techniques designed to help them critically evaluate websites.

Activity 0: Reading Mathematics

Topic 1: Organizing information pictorially using charts and graphs
> **Activity 1**: Creating Graphs with Excel Using Class Data
> **Activity 2**: SATs and Superbowl: Creating Histograms with Excel

Topic 2: Bivariate data
> **Activity 3**: Estimating Dates and Governors' Salaries: Scatterplots

Topic 3: Graphs of functions
> **Activity 4**: Temperature Patterns: Functions and Line Graphs
> **Activity 5**: Evaluating Websites

Topic 4: Multiple variable functions
> **Activity 6**: Blood Alcohol Levels and Credit Cards: Working with more than two variables

Topic 5: Proportional, linear, and piecewise linear functions
> **Activity 7**: Calories and Rates of Change, Linear and Piecewise Linear Functions
> **Activity 8**: Major League Salaries: Rates of Change and Concavity

Topic 6: Linear and exponential models
> **Activity 9**: The Genie's Offer: Exponential Growth and Linear Growth
> **Activity 10**: Lines of Best Fit

Topic 7: Logarithmic functions and scientific notation
> **Activity 11**: Richter Scale and Logarithms
> **Activity 12**: Estimating Tax Revenues: Scientific Notation and Properties of Logarithms

The majority of the time in each class period is spent with students working on carefully constructed activities that build on and complement the background reading. While students are working on their activities, the instructor answers questions and circulates to make sure that the students are making progress and getting appropriate results, occasionally giving mini-lectures. Some activities require students to work together in pairs, and we encourage students to discuss their progress and results with one another. The format of the activities varies, but students generally will carry out an investigation and

write up their analysis, complete with interpretative explanations of their results, for each activity.

Most of the activities are completed on a computer using Excel. We chose this spreadsheet program because we felt that most of our students will have access to Excel outside of our campus and would benefit from knowing some of the capabilities of this program. Students use technology to create graphs and charts, to carry out computations and to help them understand the mathematical ideas and concepts underlying the applications. By using technology in this way, significant and realistic problems can be investigated; students can concentrate on ideas rather than computational details, and their proficiency in using computers increases. We give Excel instructions along with the activities so that students learn the details of using Excel almost without realizing it.

Here is a sample activity with instructions as we give them to students. Since this is Activity 15, students have already completed activities 0 through 14 and have learned some of the computational and graphical techniques of Excel. Hence, in this activity, some facility with Excel is assumed.

Activity 15 Ranking Cities: Ratings and Decisions

To do this activity, please work with one partner. Table 1 above gives information about twelve U. S. cities. Suppose you are considering job offers in each of these cities and want to decide, on the basis of the characteristics represented in the table (population, average January temperature, serious crimes per 100,000 population, percent unemployed, per capita income, and geographic region), which city you would most prefer. (Assume that the jobs are pretty similar, so it's the characteristics of the cities that will influence your decision.)

1. Suppose you decide on the following cutoffs for the characteristics: population, no more than 600,000; average Jan temperature, at least 25 degrees; crimes per 100,000, less than 5000; % unemployed, 5 or less. Use these cutoffs and additional characteristics if needed, to determine which city you would choose. Explain how you made your choice.

2. Retrieve the Excel file entitled "Cities" from the server. (It contains the above table.) We will look at the given characteristics one-by-one, and set up a ranking within the characteristics, based on your preferences. For the characteristic of population, set up a ranking based on a system in which the most preferred ranking receives a 10 and the least preferred gets a 1. Record these rankings for each city in the corresponding row of column H of the spreadsheet, and insert an appro-

City	Population	Ave Temp January	Crimes per 100K	% unemplyd	per capita income	Region
Atlanta	403,819	41.9	6711.5	3.80	25,563.00	Southeast
Boston	555,447	29.6	3445.9	3.40	32,150.00	Northeast
Charlotte	504,637	40.5	6847.8	3	15,586.00	Southeast
Dallas	1,075,894	45	6188.3	8.9	22,424.00	South
Honolulu	395,789	72.6	6067.4	5.4	27,259.00	South Pacific
Minneapolis	351,731	11.2	5364.4	4.8	23,284.00	North central
New York City	7,420,166	31.8	4606.7	10.8	27,039.00	East
Pittsburgh	349,520	26.7	2783.4	4.5	24,957.00	East
San Francisco	745,774	48.5	4929.2	6.4	31,262.00	West
Seattle	536,978	42.2	6286.9	3.1	35,019.00	Northwest
Tucson, Ariz.	469,446	51.1	7914.4	2.8	22,307.00	Southwest
Washington DC	523,124	35.2	4879.2	8.4	26,817.00	East

Table 1. Selected Characteristics of Twelve U.S. Cities

priate heading for column H. Explain the rationale for your ranking system.

3. For the characteristic of average January temperature, set up a ranking based on a system in which the most preferred ranking receives a 10 and the least preferred gets a 1. Record these rankings in column I of the spreadsheet and insert an appropriate heading for column I. Explain the rationale for your ranking system.

4. Choose three of the four remaining characteristics that appear in the table and that you feel could influence your decision of which city to choose. For each of the characteristics you chose, set up a ranking system in which the most preferred ranking receives a 10 and the least preferred gets a 1. Record these rankings in columns J, K and L of the spreadsheet. For each of these columns, include an appropriate column heading and explain the rationale for your ranking system.

5. Now look at the characteristics on which you have ranked the cities and on which you will base your decision. These include population, average January temperature, and the three additional characteristics you chose. Assign weights to these five characteristics, using a scale of 1 to 10, with 10 being the most important characteristic for you. Enter these weights in your spreadsheet in row 15 of columns H, I, J, K, and L. In cell G15, enter the label **weights**= . Record your five characteristics and corresponding weights here and explain why you chose the weights as you did.

6. We are now set up to calculate the **weighted sum** of the rankings for each city. The weighted sum of the rankings of a city is: (weight of characteristic 1) · (city's ranking of characteristic 1) + (weight of characteristic 2) · (city's ranking of characteristic 2) +···+ (weight of characteristic 5) · (city's ranking of characteristic 5). Enter an appropriate Excel formula in cell M2 to calculate the weighted sum of the rankings for your five characteristics for Atlanta. Record that value here. (Recall that, since we will want to calculate the weighted sum of the rankings for each city, we will want to drag down this formula, to the bottom of the list of cities. Remember to use the $ symbol in your formula for those locations of values that you don't want to change as you drag down the formula.

7. Drag down the formula to find the weighted sum of the rankings for each city in the list. List here the city with the highest weighted sum of rankings and the city with the lowest weighted sum of rankings. List at least three additional characteristics you might want to include in a ranking of desirable places to live.

8. What other types of decisions might you use an analysis like this to help you make?

9. Discuss the advantages and disadvantages of this method for helping one make decisions.

Assessment

As part of the NSF grant, we evaluated students' attitudes as well as their skill levels. To assess the students' attitudes towards mathematics and the use of technology, we administered an attitude questionnaire to all students enrolled in the course during the 2000-2001 academic year. The questionnaire was given to each student twice: on the first day of class and on the last day of class.

From the survey given to 69 students at the beginning of the courses in fall 2000 and spring 2001, it was seen that the students in the class already felt fairly confident and comfortable with mathematics. In response to the statement "I feel confident about solving problems that involve numbers," using a scale of 1 to 6, with 1 representing "Strongly disagree" and 6 representing "Strongly agree," the mean response was 4.46 and the median was 5.00. For the statement "I am able to read and understand articles involving tables of data, graphs, or reasoning using numbers," the mean response was 4.74 and the median was 5.00. The mean and median responses to these questions remained essentially the same for the post-class survey.

Paired sample comparisons of questionnaire results for the three classes during the two terms of the academic year 2000-2001 showed statistically significant improvements in the following areas:

1. Increased experience and confidence using computer programs that work with numerical data.
2. Increased experience and confidence using the World Wide Web to obtain reliable data.
3. Increased experience and confidence using spreadsheet software.
4. Increased experience and confidence using statistical software packages.

In response to the question "List three techniques you think are most useful to analyze problems involving numbers," in the post-course survey, the most frequent response was "using technology." Other responses that occurred on more than one student survey were: understanding data/analysis; being able to break down the process; graphing and chart making; use logic; good teacher/learning environment; knowledge about the subject; thinking clearly about the problem/reasoning; guess and test/check.

The results of the pre- and post-course survey on use of computers showed that all but two students rated their skill level with spreadsheet packages in the post-course survey as "Basic" or "Experienced." This compares with the pre-course survey in which 25% of the students rated their experience with spreadsheets as "None." The proportion of students who rated their level of experience with the World Wide Web as "Experienced" also increased from the pre-course surveys to the post-course surveys.

The student ratings of level of experience also increased for the application of Word Processors. (Students were required to turn in several assignments prepared on a word processor and many students routinely used word processors to prepare their daily assignments.)

A second questionnaire, the Wonderlic Basic Skills test, a standardized test that is designed to test quantitative skills, was also administered to students at the beginning and end of the course. Analyses of results of this second questionnaire revealed statistically significant improvements in the following areas:

1. An improvement in quantitative skills as measured by increased grade level.
2. An improvement in Algebra and Geometry skills.
3. An improvement of skills of solving practical applied problems.
4. An improvement in interpretative problems which require interpreting, evaluating and using quantities presented in diagrams, charts, tables, and graphs.

While the students' skills in doing mathematics improved, their confidence in their mathematical abilities did not show significant improvement. In addition, because this course is the only mathematics course that most of the students in it take, and because we don't have competency exams required for graduation, we have not measured how long this improvement lasts or if any of these competencies translate to other contexts.

Students were required to hand in written assignments based on the class activities every week. Most of these required them to interpret their graphs and solutions by writing at least a full paragraph. At the beginning of the course, most students would write short phrases and incomplete explanations. By the end of the term, 80% of the students were responding with clear and appropriate narratives that fully explained their ideas.

During the academic year 2000-2001, we taught three sections (two in the fall term and one in the spring term) of the course. The total enrollment in these three sections was 71 students. Of these, four withdrew from the course (one withdrew from college altogether) and three received a failing grade. Thus, the completion rate for this course during its first year was 93%. This is significantly higher than the completion rate for other general education mathematics courses.

Conclusion

Students who take *Quantitative Reasoning and Informed Citizenship* investigate a wide variety of problems involving applications of mathematics and reasoning. In addition to reviewing and learning mathematical concepts, in the course of working on activities, students are required to talk with one another and to write about their ideas and solutions. Students discover that in many types of problems, there is not just "one right answer". In addition, they benefit greatly from the daily use of the computer as well as writing the verbal descriptions and analyses of their work.

References

Chromiak, W., J. Hoefler, A. Rossman, and B. Tesman (1992). "A Multidisciplinary Conversation on the First Course in Statistics," *Statistics for the Twenty-First Century*, ed. Gordon and Gordon, MAA Notes, Number 26, pp. 26–36.

Dilendik, J., B. Smolansky, and K. Somers (1993). *Core: An Interdisciplinary Approach to Quantitative Problem Solving*, Bethlehem, PA: Moravian College.

Pierce, D., E. Wright, and L. Roland (1997). *Mathematics for Life: A Foundation Course for Quantitative Literacy*, Upper Saddle River, NJ: Prentice-Hall.

Rossman, A. and B. Chance (2001). *Workshop Statistics: Discovery with Data* (2nd ed), Emeryville CA: Key College Publishing.

Rossman, A. and B. Chance (1999). "Teaching the Reasoning of Statistical Inference: A Top Ten List," *College Mathematics Journal*, 30, pp. 297–305.

Somers, K., J. Dilendik, and B. Smolansky (1994). "Core: An Interdisciplinary Course in Quantitative Problem Solving," *Problems, Resources, and Issues in Mathematics Undergraduate Studies* (PRIMUS), 4, pp. 55–69.

A QL Program at a Large Public University

Linda Sons
Northern Illinois University, DeKalb, IL

Introduction

In the mid 1980s the faculty at Northern Illinois University reviewed the requirements for their baccalaureate graduates and decided that each should be at least minimally competent in mathematics. The intent of such competency was that graduates should be able to solve problems and do quantitative analysis which would be helpful in personal decision-making; in evaluating concerns in the community, state, and nation; in setting and achieving career goals; and in continued learning. To develop or determine the establishment of the desired competency for each student, a program had to be designed wherein each individual would be directed to the courses or experiences through which the minimal competency could be demonstrated or attained. In this article the program is described, and its components are discussed. In particular, the new course which set the standard for minimal competency is discussed in detail along with student reactions to the course. Also discussed are some of the program's successes and failures along with some continuing challenges the program encounters.

The Program Emerges

As a definition for minimal competency in mathematics at NIU, the Department of Mathematical Sciences proposed it consist of some computational facility and knowledge of elementary facts, facility at the interpretation of quantitative information, facility with elementary mathematical reasoning, and facility in problem solving. Graduates should be able to use mathematics in their lives and be able to solve problems, accurately and comfortably estimate answers to problems, judge the reasonableness of an answer to a problem, read charts and graphs, and ask meaningful questions concerning quantitative information presented to them. The level of quantitative reasoning expected should be commensurate with the intellectual development of a college student, while presupposing only intermediate algebra and geometry in mathematics.

In response to the question of what a college-educated person should know and be able to do, a listing of facts and capabilities emerged which became the basis for a new core competency course. The new course should introduce students to the desired patterns of thought and the mathematical resources to support them, as well as provide some practice in the thought processes. The intent was that students take the course at the start of their college career, so that they might practice the thought patterns further in other courses or activities in their college program.

The immediate problem all these developments posed was how the concept of core competency fit with the reality that many students were taking some mathematics courses for their major programs. Was it true that the entry-level courses among these were providing the envisioned level of competency which the new course would provide?

Each entry-level course was carefully reviewed so as to discern whether students could be expected to acquire as a by-product of their study of that course the equivalent introduction to patterns of thought, supportive mathematical resources, and sufficient practice in those patterns. Most entry-level courses were intended to foster development of computational facility for use in future academic work, as well as conceptual understanding of specific mathematics and its application. A look at grading standards prevalent in the department suggested that obtaining a C or better in one of these entry-level courses indicated student development beyond mere computational facility to the envisioned thought patterns of the competency. The program now became clear. Each student would be expected to obtain the foundation for the competency by taking either the new core competency course or by taking one of six other courses and obtaining therein a grade of at least C. The six other courses were: (1) Elementary Functions; (2) Foundations of Elementary School Mathematics (a course for future elementary school teachers and taken almost exclusively by students intending that career outlet); (3) Introductory Discrete Mathematics; (4) Finite Mathematics; (5) Calculus for Business and Social Science; and (6) Calculus I. Depending on potential major, each student would be advised into the appropriate course among the seven with the help of guidance from results of the department's placement test; some students needed to take college algebra before entering one of the six courses.

Continuation experiences providing practice in the thought patterns introduced in the core course would be expected in subsequent courses. These would vary according to major. Some students had additional mathematics courses as part of their major program, others had a required research methods course in the major, and still others would use the general education courses in science and statistics or the interdisciplinary category would give practice.

Design of the New Course

Besides delineating the patterns of thought to be introduced and determining the mathematical resources forming a basis for their introduction, the design of the core

competency course M101 needed to take into account many other factors. Among these were the level of the course, the prerequisites for the course, the attributes of the students, and the technology to be used. A pedagogical approach that would enable us to accomplish the intent of the course had to be devised.

While the course was to be college-level, not high school level, its prerequisites were high school level mathematics. In fact, its prerequisites of intermediate algebra and geometry were among the high school units needed for admission to NIU. But many students who would enroll in M101 would have taken the prescribed algebra and geometry a few years ago and had ample time to forget these studies. Would the course need to review?

The objectives for the course being designed would be in sharp contrast with those usually set for the prerequisite high school courses. Computational facility and knowledge of facts were the aspects of those courses that many students felt were expected of them in high school. Emphasis on problem solving was minimal in the students' background, especially problems presented in prose form, and the genuine use of the mathematics taught in high school or connections of that mathematics with every day life seldom entered the students' experience. Instead prescription problems, like age problems, mixture problems, distance problems, and coin problems were common in the students' experience, but students were often not held accountable for even being able to do these problems. What would a student with such a background do with problems like the following?

P1. Horace wants to string some Christmas lights from the top of his 6 foot ornamental light post to the top of his 25 foot flag pole. If the bases of the post and the pole are 16 feet apart on the ground, how long must his string of lights be?

P2. Roy has a lawn sprinkler which swivels with a circular motion and throws water 6 feet in each direction from its source. He has a newly seeded lawn area which is rectangular in shape—50 feet by 30 feet. His intent is to water each piece of the lawn for 15 minutes and then move the sprinkler to do another piece for 15 minutes until the whole lawn is covered. Where should he place the sprinkler to minimize his number of moves and still cover the lawn? How long will it take him to complete the sprinkling?

P3. An Army base in Germany has 7200 men. The cinema showed "Star Wars" one week and 5600 saw the film. The following week the film "Spiderman" was shown and 2840 saw it. How many could have seen both films?

P4. Larry's parents have built a new home and are planting an area in back with shrubs and bushes. He is giving them a gift of roses and flowering almonds. They need at least 25 plants to cover the area where these are to be placed. The roses come in groups of 5 for $26.73, while the flowering almonds are $4.97 each. Larry can spend no more than $200. His mother wants at least 3 flowering almonds. How many of each can he buy?

The intent for the course under design was to foster facility in interpretation of quantitative information, in mathematical reasoning, and in problem solving which would "transfer" into the life of the student. Hence the course should not be seen as merely a hurdle to jump in order to complete the baccalaureate degree. The course needed to be seen to be relevant BY the student.

Further some students taking the course could be expected to be among those who were not highly successful in their completion of the prerequisite material, or ones who, even though they were successful, did not especially like mathematics. These student characteristics could bring either anxiety or distaste to students' minds as they began the course.

Another consideration in the course design was the use of technology expected of the students. If the course was to provide transfer into the daily lives of students, what technology could they all be expected to have readily available and readily use?

The primary academic interests of students in the course could be expected to be non-scientific in focus. The technological experience of students in the course and their prerequisite knowledge of mathematics could be expected to be lower than that of students who would enroll in one of the six alternative courses which could be used to meet the competency requirement. Certainly the course was likely to have students enrolled in it who represented a wider diversity of learning styles than those who would enroll in one of the six alternative courses.

Finally, the course was not likely to be offered under ideal settings for either the teacher or the student. The limited number of teaching faculty available for the course would prevent offering the course in small individual classes meeting 3 or 4 hours per week. In fact, in order to accommodate the number of students needing the course each semester, a scheme of large group meetings handled by a master teacher supplemented by small group problem hours led by graduate teaching assistants would probably be the manner in which the course was taught.

The challenges for the construction of the new course were formidable!

Mathematical Course Content

Some thought about everyday life for a college-educated person quickly led to a listing of mathematical facts, concepts, and processes which frequently entered a person's experience. Quantitative information presented in common newspapers, magazines, and political literature used charts, graphs, elementary probabilistic and statistical terms and results from statistical testing (including hypothesis testing, confidence intervals, and survey analysis). Governmental standards, such as for measurements of water quality and air pollution, and medical test results, such as for blood composition, or for cholesterol levels are among the multiple ways statistical determinations are met in daily life. Clearly some study of statistics should be a part of the core competency course.

However, mathematical ideas and concepts which would not be considered "statistics" could also be expected to be encountered by a college-educated person. Included among these are the geometrical notions of length, area, and volume. Also prevalent could be linear and nonlinear relationships, solutions of equations and inequalities, rate of change (percentage change, slope), average rate of change, systems of equations and inequalities, optimization, and elementary logical arguments. These mathematical ideas could easily be part of problems which arise in personal business applications, in management of home and property, in comparison shopping, in executing community service projects, in exercising community leadership, or in carrying out leisure time pursuits (travel, craft work, lottery participation, etc.). They supply resources to use in solving problems, in making estimates or predictions, in interpreting or understanding situations, and in representing quantitative information. Also useful for people could be having knowledge of a general framework for problem solving, such as that posed by George Polya in his volume *How to Solve It*.

Having identified all these resources as appropriate course content, the challenge was to weave them together in a form which would be meaningful and instructive for the student.

Resources for the Course and its Outline

Many available texts for so-called liberal arts mathematics courses offered sections related to the listing of facts, concepts, and processes identified for the core competency course. However, most of these sections were rather superficial in nature from our point of view. Examples and exercises were largely mechanical in nature and seldom presented problems in life situations. Consequently text material had to be written to support the new course.

The text *Mathematical Thinking and Quantitative Reasoning* (now in third edition and published by Kendall/Hunt) exposes students to quantitative reasoning from a variety of perspectives with estimation, prediction, and interpretation prevalent throughout its pages. Examples and exercises are different from those which likely have dominated students' experiences in the past. Most problems students are asked to solve are not of a mechanical nature or intended to focus on computational skills, but interwoven throughout the exercise lists are situations which use elementary skills and facts. The student is confronted with problems presented in prose form which he/she is expected to solve without classifying them as particular types of problems, but rather as seeing them as situations to which problem solving techniques can be applied. Problem settings may have too much or too little information, thus requiring the student to learn problem formulation through clarifying or interpreting the information given. Problems for which solutions require multiple steps occur early in the text, so students become accustomed to them and develop some expertise with them. Notions such as the percentage of a quantity and the reading of charts and graphs are repeated in different settings throughout the text. To ease the transition of students from experiences which were primarily computational in character to ones which concentrate on problems presented in prose form, sections of the text were written so as to incorporate routine and non-routine problems, and exercises were split in similar manner. While the text emphasizes problem solving throughout its pages, there is a culminating unit near the end of the book which discusses Polya's framework and strategies in problem solving. These are illustrated using problems from earlier sections of the text.

To accommodate the technology which all students could be expected to have and use, the course was built around only the use of simple calculators—ones which could do elementary arithmetic and have a y-to-the-x key. (In 1988 not a large number of students had graphing calculators, but even in spring 2004 a survey in a large group meeting of 170 students showed only about 50% had graphing calculators.)

The text provides the course outline in five sections: statistics; logical reasoning; geometry in problem solving; estimation, approximation, and judging the reasonableness of answers; and problem solving. Besides graphical presentation of data, the statistics section, which occupies about one third of the course, includes measures of central tendency and dispersion, the normal curve, sampling, probability, and the nature of statistical testing. The logical reasoning part discusses inductive and elementary forms of deductive reasoning, the nature of valid arguments, common logical fallacies, and some survey analysis. The geometry section includes graphical solution of some polynomial equations, systems of equations, and systems of inequalities followed by some study of spatial relationships. The fourth division of the course involves algebraic analysis of solutions of polynomial equations, systems of linear equations, and inequalities. This fourth section also includes the function concept, the notion of average rate of change, and some error analysis (especially relative error). Finally, the fifth section, where the framework for problem solving and problem solving strategies are formally discussed, also includes enough of an introduction of the exponential function to support problems of a personal business nature.

The Teaching of the Course

The teaching of the core competency is both demanding and very rewarding. Many students develop considerably as one would hope. However, students do find the course to be different from their previous mathematics experiences. Telling them ahead of time that the course will be different offsets the fears associated with newness. Recognizing that students' past experiences with mathematics have not always been good from their point of view enables the teacher to deal with feelings of anxiety or distaste which some students may bring to the course. Students respond readily to the idea of using the mathematics they have studied previously, but some review in the context of a problem setting may be necessary to activate the students' prior knowledge.

In order to facilitate the transfer into student lives the lines of reasoning being taught, the teacher must avoid artificial situations. Further, the teacher should model the problem solving framework throughout the instruction of the course and may choose to mention it explicitly early in the course. An upbeat attitude and an appreciation for the mathematics of everyday life goes a long way towards providing students with a positive experience which translates into learning.

In order to accommodate diverse learning styles, the course is evaluated not only on hour examinations and a final examination, but also on homework performance, weekly quiz scores, and project work. The weekly quizzes usually have a question which expects explanation in writing. We use two projects which are carried out in team settings (groups of four students): one executing a statistical test and one involving personal business decisions. An individual written report is required of each student for each project.

Students Reactions

The initial reaction of most students to the course is a favorable one; they recognize that this course will be different from what they have known before, and their curiosity is touched. As the course proceeds, they note that the course is a demanding freshmen course, but at the end of it, most students view the effort as worthwhile. Some even attain higher grades than they ever did before in a mathematics class!

Students especially like the project work in the course. Both projects get praise and comments indicating understanding gained through the work. Many are amazed at how much interest they are paying on their credit cards, and some say they will stop using them.

Often students with weak backgrounds are motivated to learn elementary facts and processes through a need to know how to do an application problem. For example, some learn how to work with percentages or the correct order of operations for a calculation (computing standard deviations to compare uniformity of bowling scores does wonders).

Some students are startled by the genuine appreciation they now have for mathematics--an appreciation they never had before. One student said, "This stuff makes sense, but that algebra stuff never did." When it was pointed out that she was now using algebra, she became more excited. She followed the course with a full semester course in statistics.

Other students come back to report their use of the M101 content in other courses in the university or in extra-curricular settings. Some have returned to comment how much the course helped in their taking of the GRE.

The main detractors in the course are students who have somehow managed to put off taking it until they are juniors or seniors. These students mostly do not want to devote the time to the course which it demands. Experience has shown that those students who genuinely devote themselves to the work of the course pass the course, though an occasional student may need to take the course twice to do so. The latter situation sometimes occurs with returning students who have been out of the university for some time.

One question not heard from students in this course is, "When am I ever going to use this stuff?"

Intent and Reality

When the course was initially proposed, colleagues across campus feared the competency requirement would be too demanding a course for all students. To demonstrate the level of the course, faculty in mathematics wrote up sample problems students would be asked to do, and the fears subsided.

When the new course which set the standard for minimal competency was initially taught, members of the provost's staff feared the course would be "too easy". Certainly this did not turn out to be the case, and subsequent studies noted later in the article showed a grading standard which appeared to be fair for NIU students.

The intent for students to take their foundation course (one of the seven) at the start of their college career has met with mixed success. The realities which cause constraints are the limits on the resources of the department in both teaching power and space, the lack of a regulation governing student registration which forces early enrollment in the competency courses, and the large number of transfer students at the university.

In the fall of 2003 the total enrollment at NIU in the seven courses which could be used to meet the competency was 2457 of which 1927 were lower division students—ones who could be thought to be near the start of their college careers. The department, lacking classrooms and faculty, had to turn away a number of students while assuring them that efforts would be made to accommodate them in the spring of 2004. Since some students, because of the nature of their programs, take more than one of the seven courses, it is not easy to know precisely which students will use a specific course for the competency requirement, but approximately 18% of the student body meet the competency requirement by taking M101; 18% meet it by taking Elementary Functions; 8% meet it by taking Foundations of Elementary School Mathematics; 1% meet it by taking Introductory Discrete Mathematics; 7% meet it by taking Finite Mathematics; 34% meet it by taking Calculus for Business and Social Science; and 14% meet it by taking Calculus I. In recent years these figures reflect about a 5% increase in those using M101, a 9% increase in those using Calculus for Business and Social Sciences, and an 18% decline in those using Finite Mathematics.

In fall of 2003 the mathematics department had to cap enrollment in M101 at 480. Of these 72% were lower division students, but all students in M101 could be expected to use the course to meet their competency requirement. The juniors and seniors in M101 represent a variety of concerns: the distaste for mathematics, or the bad experiences they have had with the subject previously cause them to put off enrolling earlier, advisers in some areas within the university do not make the case for students enrolling early in their college careers (noting the opportunity for ease and success brought on by closer proximity to former study of mathematics), transfer students who are accepted without the Associates degree may know pressure from both the time delay from past experience in mathematics and from demanding potential major courses, and, of course, some students who did not satisfactorily complete an earlier registration in the courses.

Because of the constraints the mathematics department has regarding the availability of the seven courses in the fall of the year, it is difficult for the department to apply pressure on advisers who do not urge students to take their competency course as early as possible. The department has always sought to enable students to continue in the progression of mathematics courses they need in appropriate time for courses in their major or other requirements for which particular mathematics courses are prerequisite. Further the limits in teaching power and classroom space has necessitated the instruction of M101 in a less than ideal format.

Currently the M101 students are team taught meeting with a master teacher three days a week for an hour and having a problem hour one day a week led by a graduate teaching assistant (GTA). The GTA grades a portion of the weekly homework assigned and the master teacher and a grader GTA evaluate the exams, quizzes, and projects. The problem hour size is kept to 30 students or less, and the master teacher regularly meets with the GTAs and periodically observes their classes.

Each of the seven courses is assigned a course coordinator. The course coordinator is a seasoned instructor in the course who prepares the uniform syllabus for all sections of the course, advises other instructors in the course about any special needs or problems the course may have, sees to the preparation of the departmental final examination for the course, and works with GTAs assigned to the course. In M101 the course coordinator is ordinarily a professor (one of the master teachers that semester) who prepares the homework assignment sheet and project forms for all sections and helps all faculty and GTAs as needed to understand the philosophy of the competency requirement. The GTAs for M101 are hand-picked by the department's Director of Graduate Studies to be among those proven to be most able. Teaching M101 problem hours is a valuable credential for a GTA.

The continuation experiences aspect of the program still is not all it was intended to be. Those students who do take a foundation course early in their college careers will normally take courses in the general education program which use the reasoning they have studied. For those who take a foundation course which is not M101, most often their major requires continuation courses in the form of more mathematics, some statistics or computer science, or a research methods course. Those who take M101 as juniors and senior may not fully complete the program.

To encourage advising regarding the continuation experiences, it was proposed at one time to have designated with a Q in the general education course selection list, and elsewhere in the university's undergraduate course listings, those courses which represented the practice in quantitative reasoning the program envisioned. While it was seriously considered outside the mathematics department with the notion that each student would take at least one or more Q courses after the foundation course, there was serious opposition based on territorial grounds among departments.

Also, seriously discussed at one time by the University's General Education Committee was the development of a senior capstone course which would include a quantitative component. Without an obvious home it was difficult for such a course to become universal.

Assessment

A number of assessment studies have been accomplished for the program described here and the core competency which serves as a foundations course for the program.

One study is reported in detail in the MAA volume *Assessment Practices in Undergraduate Mathematics*; it focuses on the question: what hard evidence was there that the seven routes for the foundations experience possible in the program each led to at least a minimal competency? As indicated in the report mentioned, this study led to changes to some of the six courses which could be used in place of the core competency course.

Another assessment question asked was what hard evidence did we have that the students actually learned more in the core competency course than what they already knew on entry into the course. A study (done periodically) involves giving a "starter's quiz" the first week of the semester and then incorporating similar items for comparison in the final examination. The value-added tabulations usually have resulted in seeing at least a 25% improvement in student success.

Another study looked at student academic records two years after the student took M101 as a freshman and observed grade correlation. The grade in M101 turned out to be a good predictor of overall academic performance in that time frame. This suggested that the grading in M101 was not unduly harsh, but also that perhaps the level of success a student attains in foundational quantitative reasoning is a significant factor in academic achievement more generally at the level of lower division course study.

Assessment of the role of continuation experiences in our quantitative literacy program has yet to take place. However, the university conducts surveys of student satisfaction by its graduates. The results of these surveys have always turned out to be overwhelmingly favorable for the general education program and its core competencies. Also the university conducts satisfaction surveys of employers of university graduates, and these too are generally highly favorable with regard to quantitative reasoning.

Conclusion

The program discussed here has been functioning since the fall of 1988, but it is constantly tweaked with the intent of making it better. Assessment studies provide data suggesting change here or there. Ideas arise, and are explored, as to how to make the continuation experiences more meaningful and attainable for all students. The text is regularly revised so as to keep material current with student experience. The course coordinator for M101 must be a consummate educator regarding quantitative literacy; they teach colleagues, GTAs, and his/her own students. The program is also under the watchful eye of the University's General Education Committee which provides some support and expects some accountability. The form for the program follows the recommendations of the MAA report on quantitative literacy, but as suggested in those recommendations, there is always more which can be done to make the program better.

References

Sons, L., P. Nicholls, & J. Stephen (2003). *Mathematical Thinking and Quantitative Reasoning*, (5th ed.). Kendall/Hunt Publishing Co.

Gold, B., S. Keith, & W. Marion (1999). *Assessment Practices in Undergraduate Mathematics*, Mathematical Association of America.

Polya, G. (2004, reissued). *How to Solve It*, Princeton University Press.

Sons, Linda, et al. (1996). *Quantitative Reasoning for College Students: A Complement to the Standards*, Mathematical Association of America.

Quantitative Reasoning at Wellesley College

Corrine Taylor
Wellesley College, Wellesley, MA

In keeping with its mission "to provide an excellent liberal arts education for women who will make a difference in the world," Wellesley College implemented a two-part quantitative reasoning requirement in 1997. The College recognized that its students need to be proficient with mathematical, logical, and statistical tools if they are to address the many quantitative issues that arise in today's global community and in the students' own personal lives. Students also need strong quantitative reasoning skills if they are to be able to explore any academic major and pursue any career. This paper describes the Quantitative Reasoning Program at Wellesley, focusing on the evolving quantitative reasoning requirements and support of those requirements.

Early Initiatives

While the quantitative reasoning (QR) requirement went into effect just six years ago, with students entering in the fall of 1997, the College's interest in helping students improve their quantitative skills has a much longer history. Wellesley's "New Liberal Arts Program" of the 1980s included the development of courses that specifically addressed quantitative literacy. Starting in 1991, faculty from a variety of disciplines assessed the quantitative skills of incoming students, reviewed the QR content of the College's course offerings, and found numerous opportunities to enhance students' quantitative reasoning skills.

These opportunities arose in all levels of the curriculum, from helping entering students with weak quantitative skills improve those skills in preparation for introductory courses in various fields, to giving upper-level students exposure to more complex statistical analyses and mathematical modeling. They also arose in a great variety of disciplines, not only in the sciences and mathematics. In response to these opportunities for improvement, the College created its quantitative reasoning requirement and established the Quantitative Reasoning Program to support that requirement.

The Two-Part Quantitative Reasoning Requirement

Wellesley's quantitative reasoning requirement has two components: the "basic skills" component, and the "overlay" component. The requirement has maintained this form over the years since its inception, but a few details have changed. Each of the components is described in brief at first and then more details are provided about the changes that have taken place over the past five years.

A student satisfies the QR "basic skills" component either by passing the QR Assessment upon entering the College or by passing the QR basic skills course in her first year. Between 6 and 10 percent of Wellesley's entering class is required to take the basic skills course each year. In the course, students are exposed to familiar content areas (including numeracy, algebra, linear and exponential modeling, graph theory, geometry, basic probability and statistics, and formal logic) but the skills are learned as students work in a variety of authentic contexts, such as medical decision-making and personal finance. As they work with real world data, students enhance their capabilities in the six QR skill areas identified by the MAA: (1) reading and understanding quantitative information; (2) interpreting quantitative information and drawing appropriate references; (3) solving problems; (4) estimating answers and checking for reasonableness; (5) communicating quantitative information; and (6) recognizing the limits of mathematical or statistical methods.

Students must satisfy the QR "basic skills" requirement before they may enroll in quantitative courses, including most science and economics courses. In addition, each student must pass a "QR overlay course" to satisfy the second part of the QR requirement. Most Wellesley students have had only limited (if any) exposure to statistics in high school; hence, the QR overlay courses emphasize statistical analysis and interpretation of data in a specific discipline. Currently, the College offers QR overlay courses in many disciplines, including economics, political science, sociology, education, psychology, astronomy, biology, chemistry, computer science, geology, mathematics, physics, and philosophy. Some of the overlay courses are semester-long statistics courses. These include a couple of math statistics classes, a social science statistics class, and a psychology statistics class. Most of the other courses are laboratory science classes in which students collect and analyze data and present their findings in the majority of the labs.

More on the Basic Skills Requirement

In 1990 and 1991, faculty from various quantitative disciplines noted that a small but significant fraction of students lacked basic quantitative skills that were expected of students in their introductory courses. In the fall of 1991, students from three courses (chemistry, mathematics, and writing) were given an assessment of basic quantitative skills. This original assessment was developed by a physicist at another institution and had been tested for years in New York. Between 10 and 15 percent of

the Wellesley students in this pilot study did not pass the test.

From 1992 through 1996, different versions of the assessment were given to all first-year students, and consistently, just over 10 percent of the students failed the test of basic quantitative skills. In the trial years of the QR Assessment, (1991-1996) students took the assessment only once each and had little incentive to perform to the best of their ability on the assessment, as nothing was at stake. Once the QR Requirements went into effect in 1997, students were permitted two successive opportunities to take the assessment upon their arrival at the College and they had a strong incentive to do their best to pass the test. With these changes, the proportion of students who did not pass the assessment dropped to between 6 and 10 percent in any given year.

The assessment consists of eighteen questions for which the students must write out their answers; the questions are not multiple choice. Sample questions are provided in Appendix A. Students receive full credit, no credit, or half credit on each question. A score of 9.5 or better is needed to pass the assessment. Students who score between 9.5 and 12.0 are told that they may opt to take the basic skills class to improve their quantitative reasoning skills; students who do not pass the assessment must enroll in the basic skills course.

Originally, legislation did not specify when a student needed to complete the basic skills component of the QR requirement. In the spring of 1998, the College's QR Steering Committee successfully argued that a student should normally be required to satisfy the basic skills component in her first year and this change was then made to the College's bylaws. Additionally, the original basic skills course was only ten weeks in duration and was a half-credit course. The argument was made for this course to be expanded to a full semester, full-credit course, and this change also was approved, with the new full-credit course being designated as QR 140. Many quantitative courses (including all the QR overlay courses) specify that fulfillment of the QR basic skills requirement is a prerequisite.

Students who take QR 140 generally find that their quantitative skills and their confidence in dealing with quantitative issues improve significantly. High proportions of these students self-reported confidence with QR skills after completing the course. Specifically, a survey conducted by the College's Office of Institutional Research in 2000 reports that among QR 140 students:

- 83% are confident with use of spreadsheets;

- 87% are confident in interpreting graphs;

- 75% are confident in translating real world problems into quantitative terms; and
- 73% are confident with general quantitative reasoning skills.

These results are encouraging, as the students who take QR 140 are those who enter the College with the lowest demonstrated QR skills and confidence in these areas. Pre- and post- surveys are needed to measure student gains in each of these areas.

Faculty who teach quantitative courses (especially those in economics and the physical sciences) report that today's students are better prepared for the mathematical and statistical applications in their introductory courses than they were prior to the institution of the QR requirements.

More on the Overlay Requirement

The QR overlay courses are intended to teach students how numerical data are analyzed and interpreted in various disciplines. The term "overlay" indicates students may use one of the designated QR courses to simultaneously satisfy another of the College's distribution requirements (e.g., the Natural and Physical Science Requirement, the Social and Behavioral Analysis Requirement). Guidelines for QR overlay classes are as follows:

QR Overlay Classes need to Balance the Following Five Objectives

A. **Literacy.** The number of topics and the depth of coverage should be sufficient to ensure that students have the basic knowledge they need in order to function in real-life situations involving quantitative data.

B. **Authenticity.** Students should have experience in using authentic numerical data. The experience should arise naturally in the context of the course and actually advance the work of the course. Only with such experience is the literacy goal likely to be realized.

C. **Applicability.** The examples used in an overlay class should be adequate to convince the average student that the methods used in the analysis of data are of general applicability and usefulness.

D. **Understanding.** A student's experience with data analysis should not be limited to rote application of some involved statistical procedure. Rather, students should understand enough of what they are doing so that their experience of data analysis is likely to stay with them, at least as a residue of judgment and willingness to enter into similar data analyses in the future.

E. **Practicality.** The breadth of topics covered and the depth of coverage should be consistent with what an average Wellesley student can realistically absorb in a course that devotes only a part of its time to data analysis.

Minimum Exposure to the Analysis of Data

The following topics need to be addressed in a QR overlay course in order to satisfy the objectives of literacy and understanding:

A. **Framework for Data Analysis.** A QR overlay course should provide an overview of how empirical questions or hypotheses can be raised, how relevant data can be collected and analyzed to address these questions, and finally, what conclusions these data allow. Students should formulate questions that arise in the context of the course and that can be answered by analyzing data. They should then decide what type of data to collect, how to collect and analyze these data, and what conclusions these data support.

B. **Collecting Data.** A QR overlay course should address issues of data quality. Are the data representative or biased? Are the data that are collected really relevant to the question being investigated? Certain courses might stress the importance of random samples, experiments versus observational studies, blind versus double blind experiments, and so forth.

C. **Representing Data.** A QR overlay course should stress different methods of representing data, including numerical representations (tables of data), visual representations (pie charts, scatter-plots, line graphs, and histograms), as well as verbal representations (writing reasonable captions that describe a graph).

D. **Summarizing Data.** Students need to be exposed to different ways of summarizing data, including verbal summaries of data sets. They also need to study different measures of central tendency (including the mean, median, and mode) as well as different measures of dispersion (including the range, standard deviation, percentile ranks, index of diversity, and index of qualitative variation.

E. **Probability.** Because of the random component in sampling from a population, students should have some understanding of basic probability. This must include a working knowledge of how and when to use the addition and multiplication rules, the concept of conditional probability, and the vocabulary of statistical independence and mutual exclusivity.

F. **Distributions.** Students in a QR overlay course should work with examples of different distributions, including normally distributed data and various non-normally distributed data. They should know when to expect that a population will be normally distributed, and what it means for a distribution to be skewed. They should know what the mean, median, and standard deviation tell about a distribution. Finally, they should know that a normal distribution is fully specified by its mean and standard deviation and that the percentage of the population on a given interval can be determined from a table or a formula.

G. **Sampling.** A QR overlay course should discuss sampling and stress the distinction between "sampling" and "collecting data." It should introduce the notion of sample mean, and discuss why the sample mean might well vary from the population mean. The distinction between sample statistics (e.g., the mean of a sample) and population parameters (e.g., the mean of the population) should be emphasized.

Authentic Application

At least one of the following applications should be addressed to satisfy the objectives of authenticity and applicability:

A. *Issues Regarding Sampling.* An overlay course could address problems that can arise when one attempts to ascertain certain characteristics of a population by testing a sample of that population. Such issues include how one obtains a random sample and how one detects sample biases.

B. *Making and Justifying Inferences from Data.* A QR overlay course could discuss confidence intervals and hypothesis tests. It could explore how one determines whether a measured variation cannot plausibly be attributed to chance alone.

C. *Regression Analysis.* A QR overlay course could study various methods for fitting curves to data and for analyzing the deviations of the data from these curves.

Changes in the Program

Before the QR requirement was established, the College offered a handful of statistics courses and numerous laboratory science classes. While all the statistics classes and some of the lab science classes met all of the criteria, many courses needed to be retooled to meet the curricular guidelines spelled out above. Faculty from various disciplines worked with members of the QR Program to create new courses, once the requirements were in place. Today, additional courses are still being created to meet the demand for QR overlay courses.

In the spring of 2002, the College's rules were changed to allow for QR overlay classes in any discipline, not just in the sciences or social sciences. This change legitimized the sole QR overlay course offered in the humanities, Philosophy 209: *Scientific Reasoning.* It also presented the opportunity to offer more QR overlay courses that show the relevance of data analysis and interpretation in the humanities. Potential courses for the future include "Quantitative History" and "QR in Art, Literature, and Music." These courses might be team-taught by QR instructors and experts in the specific disciplines.

Offering and sustaining such classes will require coordination among instructors in the various departments and the QR Program as well as dedicated teaching units for these classes. In the meanwhile, financial support from an alumna allows for a new annual series, "Celebrating QR Connections," which explores the connections between quantitative reasoning and various disciplines. The first series (Spring 2004) explored the connection between QR and art.

As more overlay courses are created and as the professors and lab instructors for those QR overlay courses change over the years, it is increasingly important that there be oversight of and continued guidance for these courses. Members of the QR Program are committed to meeting with department chairs and instructors of QR overlay courses at least annually to ensure the continuing quality of these existing courses.

The QR Program's new web site makes it easier for faculty to review the overlay guidelines. Communication about QR overlay courses has been improving, but can be richer, still. One planned improvement is for an annual workshop of all Wellesley QR overlay instructors (and potential ones), so instructors may share ideas and resources with each other. In this workshop, not only would instructors work together toward improved curricular materials for existing QR overlay courses, but they would also have the opportunity to plan new overlay courses (including interdepartmental ones), modules, and workshops.

Final Remarks

Wellesley College's Quantitative Reasoning Program has provided support for the quantitative reasoning requirements since the fall of 1997. The form of those requirements was years in the making and the details of those requirements have been evolving over the past five years. The two-part requirement ensures: (1) that students have the basic QR skills needed to enroll in quantitative courses throughout their college career and to address the quantitative issues that arise throughout their lives; and (2) that they understand, in depth, how data analysis is conducted in a specific discipline and they can apply these advanced skills in other areas.

New courses, new workshops, and improved forms of communication are under development presently to further strengthen the QR Program and to ensure that Wellesley students can apply strong QR skills in solving the many quantitative challenges presented in today's society.

Reference

Wellesley College Quantitative Reasoning Program. www.wellesley.edu/QR

Appendix A

Sample Problems from the QR Assessment

1. A commercial artist needs to rent some high-quality photographic equipment to reproduce her artwork. She considers two types: the first costs $400 to rent plus $2.50 per copy, while the second costs $150 to rent plus $5.00 per copy. (a) Which is less expensive to rent if she only needs a few copies? (b) How many copies would the artist need to make before the other type of equipment is less costly?

2. Children with elevated lead levels in their blood are typically given iron sulfide to displace lead from vulnerable brain receptors. Iron sulfide is sold as a liquid to be taken orally, with a concentration of 15 milligrams (mg.) iron sulfide for every 0.6 milliliters (ml.) of liquid. If a child needs 75 mg. of iron sulfide per day, how much of the liquid should be taken?

3. The cost of first-class mail has changed several times in the last few years. On June 30, 2002, it went up from 34 cents to 37 cents. (a) By what percentage did the cost of first class mail increase on June 30, 2002? (b) Suppose the costs of providing mail service have increased by 5% since June 30, 2002, and the US Postal Service wants to just cover the cost increase with another increase in the price of first-class postage. What feasible price should it charge for a first-class stamp?

4. The following table presents 1996 data on public school employees by occupation (in the rows) and sex (in the columns). Numbers reported represent thousands of employees.

	Male	Female	Total
Official, Administrator	31	19	50
Principal, Assistant Principal	55	45	100
Classroom Teacher	506	1,529	2,035
Other Professional Staff	60	203	263
Teachers' Aides	38	327	365
Clerical, Secretarial Staff	6	252	258
Service Workers	304	330	634
Total	1,000	2,705	3,705

Officials, administrators, principals, and assistant principals are considered to be "school leaders." (a) What proportion of male public school employees serve as school leaders? Express your answer as a fraction, as a decimal, *and* as a percent. (b) What proportion of school leaders are male? Again, express your answer as a fraction, as a decimal, *and* as a percent.

5. From 1970 to 1990, Sri Lanka's population grew by approximately 2.2 million persons every five years. If the population in 1970 was 12.2 million, find a formula for P, Sri Lanka's population (in millions) in terms of t, the number of years after 1970.

Appendix B

Overlay Courses as of Fall 2003

ASTR 109   Our Place in Space and Time

ASTR 206   Basic Astronomical Techniques with Laboratory

BISC 109   Human Biology with Laboratory

BISC 111   Introductory Organismal Biology with Laboratory

BISC 111X   Introductory Organismal Biology with Laboratory

BISC 201   Ecology with Laboratory

CHEM 111   Introductory Chemistry II with Laboratory

CHEM 120   Intensive Introductory Chemistry with Laboratory

CHEM 231   Physical Chemistry I with Laboratory

CHEM 232   Physical Chemistry for the Life Sciences with Laboratory

CHEM 261	Analytical Chemistry with Laboratory
CS 199	Simulation, Probability, and Statistics
GEOL 102	The Dynamic Earth with Laboratory
MATH 101	Reasoning with Data: Elementary Applied Statistics
MATH 220	Probability and Elementary Statistics
MATH 251	Topics in Applied Mathematics
PHIL 209	Scientific Reasoning
PHYS 202	Modern Physics with Laboratory
PSYC 205	Statistics with Laboratory
QR 180	Statistical Analysis of Education Issues
QR 199	Introduction to Social Science Data Analysis
SOC 212	Sociology and Demography of the Family

This description of Wellesley's QR Program, especially of the QR overlay guidelines, incorporates the writings of various members of the College's QR Steering Committee, past and present.

Advising, Assessment, and Other Issues

Designing a QL Program to Match Student Needs and Interests

AbdelNaser Al-Hasan
*Mount Mary College,
Milwaukee, WI*

Introduction

Mount Mary College (MMC), located in metropolitan Milwaukee, is Wisconsin's oldest Catholic college for women, enrolling 600 full-time undergraduate, 600 part-time undergraduate and 175 graduate students.

Historically, the college has not had a mathematics course requirement for the baccalaureate degree. In the past two years, a liberal arts core task force had been working to design a core to meet the needs of women in the 21st century based on the mission and vision of the college.

This paper will describe the steps taken by both the Department of Mathematics/Computer Science and the college as a whole in introducing a Quantitative Reasoning (QR) program at MMC that will meet the challenges facing women graduating from MMC.

Program History

In summer 2002, the Department of Mathematics/ Computer Science received support from the college to examine the effectiveness of all remedial math courses as part of the department's involvement with the MAA PREP Workshop: Assessment at the Departmental Level. The initial goals of this examination were to determine the effectiveness of the two lower-level remedial math courses and advise the college on how to better serve students in fulfilling the college's current math competency requirement. Examination of the enrollment records from the last five years revealed that more than 60% of students admitted to MMC are in need of remedial courses in the mathematics department. We also found that only about 25% of students enrolled in the remedial courses continued with the algebra sequence, and less than 2% of students who continued with the algebra sequence enrolled in precalculus.

This data revealed that the majority of our students experience a course below precalculus as a terminal course. Given the fact that some graduates of MMC never take a math course if they pass the math competency exam, the department felt that in order for the college to better serve all MMC's students, a mathematics requirement is needed. However, before such a change can take place, revision of current courses and possible creation of new courses is needed as well. In light of the new data and other departmental recommendations, the Department of Mathematics/ Computer Science restructured the offering of its lower division courses and aligned the curriculum to better prepare students for the mathematical challenges facing them in everyday life.

Concurrently, the college was reviewing the current core and trying to revise it while maintaining the mission and vision of the college. MMC's core is based on the concept of liberal arts education as a formative and transformative process, as well as one that provides breadth in perspectives and the development of certain skills. Since MMC did not have a mathematics requirement, the core task force members asked the Department of Mathematics/ Computer Science for direction. A copy of the 1995 report of *The Mathematical Association of America's Committee on the Undergraduate Program in Mathematics,* was provided to all members of the core task force. They concentrated on the term "quantitative literacy program" and initial recommendations in spring 2003 indicated that each student should be quantitatively literate and thus each MMC student must take a math course at MMC.

Many departments have shown their commitment to a quantitative literacy program. The program was planned to begin its implementation in the Department of Mathematics/ Computer Science Department as early as fall, 2003 with participating departments to start their implementations in fall 2004.

Program Goals and Learning Objectives

It was evident that in order for this program to be a success it must have goals and objectives that meet the mission and vision of the college and be designed based on the need of MMC's student population. The Department of Mathematics/Computer Science believes that QR for all our graduates will not be gained by taking a specific course or courses in the department but through the realization of how important skills learned in the department can be applied in identified QR courses taken in their own field of study.

The following goals and learning objectives for this program were created to parallel the recommendations of the 1995 CUPM Report and also fit the mission of our college. Students who are quantitatively literate are able to

1. Interpret mathematical models such as formulas, graphs, tables, and schematics, and draw inferences from them.
2. Represent mathematical information symbolically, visually, numerically, and verbally.
3. Use arithmetical, algebraic, geometric and statistical methods to solve problems.
4. Estimate and check answers to mathematical problems in order to determine reasonableness, identify alternatives, and select optimal results.

5. Recognize that mathematical and statistical methods have limits.
6. Recognize the importance of mathematical skills learned in the mathematics department in future QR courses in own field.
7. Understand the uses and limitations of technology.

Curriculum Details

As mentioned above, the Department of Mathematics/ Computer Science felt that revision of current curriculum and creation of new courses were needed for students to appreciate the usefulness of mathematics courses and subsequent courses taken within their own field of study. The core task force recommendation consists of taking a math course as part of the general core requirement set for all MMC students. However, the specific course may vary from student to student depending on their math placement score, degree requirement, and math transfer courses.

Major programs at MMC that require students to study specific mathematical content are biology, business administration, chemistry, dietetics, and merchandise management. In addition, art and design, art therapy, behavioral sciences, English, communication, fashion, foreign language, graphic design, history, interior design, justice, music, nursing, occupational therapy, philosophy, and theology, require only a general math competency. For the latter majors, the Department of Mathematics/ Computer Science devised a foundation course called Quantitative Reasoning (QR). For all other majors, the department revised the content of its algebra sequence to be more of a modeling approach without sacrificing skills.

With this in mind, the department adopted the following specific learning goals for its program:
1. Be able to construct a logical argument based on rules of inference and to develop strategies for solving quantitative problems.
2. Be able to make sense of numbers that a person encounters in the real world.
3. Be able to interpret statistical information.
4. Be able to develop an understanding of basic probability relative to real world situations.
5. Be able to interpret mathematical models of real world situations.
6. Appreciate the role of mathematics in the real world, in particular, the use of mathematics in politics and business.

To help students reach these goals, the department devised the following new courses.

MAT052: Basic Math Skills, 1 credit. This course, bearing elective credit and not core credits, is designed for those students with minimal mathematical skills. Students will be placed in this course based on their math competency score with a pass/fail grade. Upon passing the course, a student will enroll in either MAT 101 pre-algebra or MAT 103 quantitative reasoning depending on which course is required in her/his major.

MAT101: Pre-algebra, 3 credits. This course is designed for those students with weak math skills whose major requires an algebra course.

MAT103: Quantitative Reasoning, 4 credits. This course is designed for students who will be taking only one math course in the Mathematics/Computer Science Department and who have weak math skills. This course will serve at least 40% of all MMC students. It is a survey course that combines critical thinking and mathematical skills applicable to personal and social issues. Topics include logic and problem solving; number sense and estimation; statistical interpretation and basic probability; interpreting mathematical models; and further applications to the use of mathematics in politics and business.

These were added to the set of pre-existing courses: MAT105: Intermediate Algebra, MAT111: College Algebra, MAT207: Basic Statistics (with prerequisite of MAT105: and MAT216: Elementary Statistics with prerequisite of MAT111. The only course that will not satisfy the MMC's QR requirements is MAT052.

The Department of Mathematics/Computer Science believes that the above seven courses will be sufficient as a starting point to meet the goals and objectives of the new core requirement.

Cross-disciplinary Commitment and Participation

A critical step of the development program will be when participating departments identify at least one QR course in their department. Students will be informed by their department of the skills learned in the mathematics/computer science course(s) and how important these skills are to their success in QR course(s) within their field. The Behavioral Science and Business Administration Departments will be participating in such a program.

The Behavioral Science Department indicated that they would like BES/PSY majors to take MAT101 as a prerequisite for their QR course, BES310: Behavioral Science Statistics. Students entering BES310 need to perform basic math operations and to understand the order of operations, be able to interpret graphs and tables, understand and be able to work with fractions, decimals, percents, perform basic operations with negative numbers and have a sense of numbers. The following list will be provided to all students declaring a behavioral science major before enrolling in MAT101.

Students will be asked to collect and insert material such as exams, quizzes, homework, and projects into a folder relative to the above list. The assessment notation will be a value of 0–3 score for the level of attainment. The numerical value has the following meaning:

3 – Exceptional knowledge level of content area
2 – Expected knowledge level of content area
1 – Improved knowledge level of content area
0 – Inadequate knowledge level of content area.

At the conclusion of the semester, the student is expected to self assess her knowledge level relative to the contents covered in the math class taken, by placing a numerical value 0-3, in the right column under outcome. Students will be asked to bring this grid to the advising session and the advisor will give some feedback regarding the student's progress.

We believe that this process will allow students to self assess their progress towards taking a QR course within their department. Students will have the opportunity to discuss strengths and weaknesses with their advisor before registering for a QR course in the department. If a student's knowledge of a particular content area is 0 or 1, a worksheet on that particular content area will be provided to that student to increase the knowledge level to at least 2. The Behavioral Science Department began implementing these changes in fall 2004.

The Business Administration Department indicated that all of its students must possess reasonable quantitative skills in order to be successful in their studies and professions. Business administration, accounting, and marketing majors are required to successfully complete (grade C or better) MAT111. The business/professional communication major is required to successfully complete (grade C or better) MAT105. The business faculty advised the Department of Mathematics/ Computer Science that most of its courses are QR courses. They strongly believe that all its majors must be able to understand financial relationships, financial ratios, present and future values, as well as to incorporate models into decision making and to be able to present analyses and decisions logically, concisely and completely. They also believe students enrolling in MAT101, MAT105, and MAT111, will become better citizens if they value the mathematical skills and logical rea-

Student self assessment form

Name_____

Course_____

Content
Outcome

Number sense

Operations with negative numbers

Understanding the order of operations

Operations with fractions

Operations with decimals

Operations with percents

Interpretation of graphs

Interpretation of tables

Understanding the meaning of a variable

Be able to solve equations

soning developed in math courses and used in subsequent QR courses. The Business Administration Department will monitor students in two courses: BUS211: Financial Accounting (with MAT111 as prerequisite) and BUS216: Understanding Business Statistics (with MAT105 as prerequisite).

A list of math skills will be developed in late fall to be given to students declaring a business administration major during the spring advising session. This list will concentrate on skills learned in MAT101, MAT105, and

MAT111. The list will be similar to the one created for the Behavioral Science Department; however, some students will be monitored in more than one math class.

Since many topics will be recurring in all courses, we are hoping to see a positive increase in outcome. For example, solving linear equations, a student will be exposed to this concept in MAT101, MAT105, and MAT111, a positive increase will be expected if a student enrolled in all three courses. The implementation started in the fall of 2004.

Student Placement into the Program

The diagram below illustrates the admission of each student into the program.

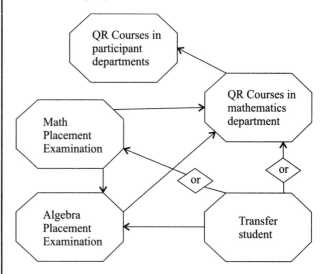

Because the Behavioral Science Department has its own QR course (BES310), it has indicated that their students will be only required to complete MAT101, rather than continue through completion of MAT103.

Other departments such as nursing are requesting input from the Department of Mathematics/Computer Science regarding student placement in either MAT101 or MAT103.

Program Assessment

The Department of Mathematics/Computer Science will:
- Give students in MAT052 pre-and-post math placement tests. Data collected will inform the department of the level of skills gained by students finishing the course.
- Students in MAT101 will be given pre-and-post math placement tests. The expectation is that students will score at least 70% on the math competency exam upon finishing the course. Students will also self as-

sess relative to the math skills given to them by their own department.

- For MAT103, the main QR course in the Department of Mathematics/Computer Science, students will be asked to collect homework problems, projects, or exam problems during the semester demonstrating the fulfillment of the learning goals set forth for this course. Students will reflect on these problems during the semester and these problems will count as an exam grade towards the final course grade.

- Students in MAT105: Intermediate Algebra and MAT111: College Algebra, will self assess relative to the list of math skills given to them by their own department.

Participating departments will:

- Identify course(s) in their department as QR courses

- Identify math skills used in the above course(s) that are covered in prerequisite math course(s) taken by students

- Students will be given a list containing such skills as soon as a major is declared with these departments and before enrolling in math course(s)

- Instructors teaching such QR course(s) will collect data on the success of students relative to the skill list and its application to the field, using methods similar to that described in the previous section.

- Data will be monitored annually and communicated to the Department of Mathematics/Computer Science

The Department of Mathematics/Computer Science and the participating departments will look at the data collected at the end of the 2004/2005 academic year to determine if curriculum revisions, the creation of new courses, or student placement adjustments are needed.

Conclusion

The main focus of this program is for students to realize the usefulness of the mathematical skills learned in the Department of Mathematics/Computer Science to their own field of study. By providing students with a skill list that relates directly to their personal interest, we are hoping to see the following outcomes in the next couple of years:

Attitude — A positive attitude towards math courses

Anxiety — Lowering math anxiety towards math courses.

Communication and Productivity — Increase communication between students and faculty teaching math courses. Since students need to understand how to assess themselves on a particular math skill, we are hoping that they will be asking questions concerning this skill and thus increase their productivity in math courses and subsequently in QR courses in their own field.

Participating Departments — Departments need to realize that our students need to become more quantitatively literate. We are pleased to have two departments participating in this program. The goal is to involve all departments, making this QR program a college wide program not limited to particular departments.

Reference

Committee on the Undergraduate Program in Mathematics. (1996). *Quantitative Literacy for College Literacy*, MAA Reports 1 (New Series), Mathematical Association of America, Washington, DC.

Quantitative Literacy as an Integral Component of Mathematics Curriculum, Case at North Dakota State University

Doğan Çömez and
William O. Martin
*North Dakota State University,
Fargo, ND*

Introduction

In recent years the quantitative skills of students at every level have been the focus of discussions in both public and academic circles. The mathematician J. A. Paulos brought increased general visibility to the issues with his books, *A Mathematician Reads the Newspaper* (1995) and *Innumeracy: Mathematical Illiteracy and Its Consequences* (1988). Others, such as Steen (1997, 1998) and Kirsch and Jungeblut (1986), have also examined quantitative literacy and called for changes in education to improve the situation. As happens with any issue of such wide interest and debate, an important part of the discussion is the very definition of quantitative literacy. Recently, in *The Case for Quantitative Literacy*, Steen, et al (2001) summarized several perspectives on quantitative literacy. The MAA's project SAUM (Supporting Assessment in Undergraduate Mathematics) includes some work focused on this important matter.

We believe that quantitative literacy should not be separated from general literacy in mathematics. In our view, quantitative literacy should be addressed as a part of our aims to increase mathematical literacy at all levels. Assessment activities at North Dakota State University (NDSU) reflect this perspective.

The Mathematics Department has developed a comprehensive assessment process that examines student learning in (a) services courses, (b) the major, and (c) the masters and PhD program. The most ambitious component, established in part with external funding, examines the introductory mathematics courses in conjunction with the NDSU general education program. Assessment of the undergraduate and graduate programs involves many of the department's faculty. All components of the project are designed to minimize extra demands on all participants, including students and faculty, to provide useful information for participants as well as to the Department and University, and to focus on assessment as an integrated part of departmental activities rather than an "add-on" activity done primarily for external purposes.

This is reflected in the department's goals for student learning, one of which is "Students will recognize phenomena and be able to abstract, generalize, and specialize these patterns in order to analyze them mathematically." It is in this connection that the department emphasizes quantitative literacy in its service, as well as major courses. Consequently, the assessment tools utilized reflect this component as an integral part of the program to be assessed. In this way, the assessment of quantitative literacy is not done as a separate activity. It is one essential component of our assessment program, reflected in the choice of assessment rubric and other tools. Below, we will describe this aspect of our assessment program in more detail.

The important distinction of our approach, in contrast to many other quantitative literacy programs, is that our assessment does not begin with an attempt to define a single set of core quantitative skills that are important for every person. Instead, we start by asking which skills are seen as important to individuals in specific settings, then we examine the extent to which our programs seem to have developed these essential capabilities. In our assessment activities we focus on three general capabilities:

1. Analyzing and interpreting data (in various forms or context), reasoning carefully and logically to reach sound decisions

2. Using mathematical concepts in real-world settings to model, put in mathematical context, develop strategies to solve, and interpret the outcome meaningfully

3. Critical and logical thinking

Later in this paper we provide a collection of examples from tests given as part of our assessment program to illustrate how we emphasize these three elements.

Assessing Quantitative Literacy

The NDSU Quantitative Assessment Project has been assessing the quantitative readiness of "rising juniors" for several years. The goal is to determine whether students beginning their upper-division undergraduate studies have the quantitative skills necessary for success in their chosen courses as well as readiness to comprehend the real world mathematical challenges occurring around them daily. (More details of the process can be found in Martin and Bauman, 1999.) This is accomplished by working with instructors of junior level courses from across the campus (for example, in agriculture, communications, business, psychology, engineering, science, mathematics). Instructors are heavily involved in writing custom-designed tests that will measure whether their students have:

- Prerequisite skills that are essential for success in the course.

- Skills that the instructors expect students to have on entry to the course.

- Knowledge that will not be covered in the course except for possible quick review

- Knowledge demonstrating readiness to comprehend the real world mathematical problems.

It is important to note that the junior-level courses in which the students take the tests are not themselves the focus of our assessment. Instead of looking at the quantitative skills developed by a particular mathematics or science course, we are examining whether students possess prerequisite quantitative capabilities identified as crucial for success by the instructor of the junior level course when students begin that course. The students' skills were probably developed over many mathematics, statistics, and other courses in school and college. When we find that students have difficulty with a particular concept, one of our first tasks is to decide where and when the student might have had the opportunity to develop that knowledge.

The tests are given to students in the class early in the semester, are scored by mathematics graduate students, and then are returned to students within a week or two. Results of the tests are summarized in reports that are given to the course instructor so that the instructor and the students learn early in the semester the extent to which students have the expected skills needed for the course.

These tests are conducted in a variety of courses with small to medium class sizes of 30-45 students. Participating courses have included:

- *Quantitative Methods and Decision Making*, offered by the Department of Agricultural Economics

- *Operations Management*, offered by the College of Business Administration

- *University Calculus-III* (multivariable calculus)

- Introduction to Differential Equations

- *Mechanics of Machinery*, offered by the Department of Mechanical Engineering

- *Research Methods*-I, offered by the Department of Psychology.

Some of these courses, such as University Calculus-III and Introduction to Differential Equations, have multiple sections or were tested in multiple semesters. The table at the end of this section summarizes the number of students involved in the last three academic years.

Copies of recent individual course reports can be accessed from the table in the department assessment website. The reports contain considerable information about student achievement, their academic backgrounds in mathematics and statistics, and instructors' quantitative expectations in a variety of courses.

While the focus of our project is on "rising juniors," students at all levels may participate in the assessment depending on when in their individual programs they take the course. The majority of students who take the exams are in their second or third year of college. Although our focus has been on more quantitative disciplines, we have

Courses	2000–2001		2001–2002		2002–2003	
	Fall	Spring	Fall	Spring	Fall	Spring
Research Methods-I		44	55	34	58	41
Quantitative Methods and Decision Making	46		41			
Operations Management		30		88		72
University Calculus-III	105	183	63	151	181	44
Introduction to Differential Equations	119	140	104	147	163	
Mechanics of Machinery		33	48		37	43

assessed in NDSU Mass Communication and Psychology courses that have no or minimal mathematics and statistics prerequisites. Bill Martin also worked on a similar project at University of Wisconsin-Madison (Bauman and Martin, 1995); there the quantitative literacy assessment program assessed in many fields that had low level quantitative expectations, such as Journalism, Teacher Education, Consumer Studies, and Introductory Biology for general education. We mention these courses to emphasize that our methodology can be used—in fact, was designed to be usable—in a broad spectrum of courses ranging from non-technical to highly technical.

Examples

At the end of this paper are eight examples of questions asked in the courses assessed. In each example, the success rate of the students and the degree of success (as a percentage of the total number of students taking the test) are also indicated to give a sense of what we learned from these tests. Every problem is rated holistically A-E, with A meaning *completely correct*, B indicating *basically correct with a minor error*, C indicating *flawed response, but quite close to a correct solution*, D means *that student took some appropriate action, but far short of a solution*, and E indicating *no response or nothing relevant to the problem*.

Example 1 was given to students taking *University Calculus-III* and *Operations Management*. The latter course is offered by the College of Business Administration (prerequisite *Introductory Statistics* and *College Algebra*). It covers managerial techniques for manufacturing and service operations. The problem illustrates our focus on quantitative literacy in terms of the skills and capabilities required in the chosen discipline. This problem examines the ability of students to interpret graphical information in the context of a real-world situation. The given percentages, based on students who attempted the problem, refer to the proportion who answered in the stated way.

So, for example, 30% of the students "Accurately estimated lower bound (x-intercept)" while 40% "Gave the exact upper bound." For this problem, under one third of the students who took the test demonstrated an overall understanding of the problem (just 30% of the responses received an A or B rating).

Example 2 has been used in a variety of courses (here, the students were in an introductory Agricultural Economics course, the same question in a little modified form was asked of students in *Research Methods-I*, offered by the Department of Psychology, with prerequisite College Algebra and Introductory Statistics). The problem represents a standard, real-world way of representing data that we found many people are unable to correctly interpret. The difficulty correctly interpreting these data often surprises course instructors who assume that the representation is widely understood. This example requires students to analyze data and to use mathematics in a real life setting, two of the three general capabilities we mentioned in the introductory section, above.

Example 3 was given to students in *Operations Management*, offered by the College of Business Administration, and to students in *Introduction to Differential Equations*, which is a first course in ordinary differential equations and their applications (with prerequisite single-variable calculus). The example tests students' ability to extract information from a graph. This situation is a natural setting for one of the most elementary applications of first-order linear differential equations. In comparison to many items we use, this class had relatively high success rates on this problem with 93% essentially solving the problem correctly (a rating of B allows for a minor error in the solution, but we consider that the student understood the problem).

Example 4 was given to students taking *Operations Management* and *Quantitative Methods and Decision Making*. The latter is offered by the Department of Agricultural Economics (prerequisite *Applied Calculus*, the calculus course for Business and Social sciences).

This question is another example that asks students to interpret tabular data, a task that is important in a wide variety of courses. Furthermore, students are challenged to reason carefully and logically to reach sound decisions while using mathematical concepts in a real-world setting and interpret the outcome meaningfully.

Example 5 was used in *University Calculus-III* and *Mechanics of Machinery* and is offered by the Department of Mechanical Engineering (prerequisite *University Calculus-II*, and *Introductory Linear Algebra*). This problem requires no computational skills, only an understanding of the connections between a function and its derivatives. It places little demand on memory, instead examining the students' ability to think logically and use their basic grasp of fundamental concepts of differential calculus in a situation that is likely to arise, for example, in the modeling of an engineering problem. Students who took this test had successfully completed one full year of regular calculus, so one might hope that success rates would be quite high, above the 62% rate that we found.

Example 6 has appeared on many tests, such as for students taking *University Calculus-III* and *Mechanics of Machinery*. Again, it focuses on students' understanding of basic concepts from first-year calculus and requires no recall of specific integration techniques. The problem forces students to think logically and use their basic grasp of fundamental concepts of integral calculus in a situation likely to arise in many applied settings.

Example 7 has also been used on many tests, including *University Calculus-III* and *Mechanics of Machinery*. The problem does require more algebraic and computational skill than the previous two. This is a standard application of differential calculus, so one would expect that all students who successfully completed first year calculus (typically with B's) would have high skills of the sort required by the problem. However, we have often found that success rates are very low, as indicated for this particular administration (less than one third of the students could solve the problem, even allowing for some minor errors).

Example 8 is typically used in courses that require students to have completed 2–3 semesters of regular (engineering and science) calculus. Students are required to use the fundamental properties of the differential calculus concepts without explicit algebraic information on the function under study. As with the problems in Examples 5 and 6, it does not require any special computational skills and instead focuses on interpretation involving core concepts of introductory calculus.

The feedback loop of the assessment program is flexible. After exam results are compiled, initial feedback goes to the instructor of the course in which the test was administered, not to the instructor of a prerequisite mathematics/statistics course. So, if students do poorly on a *Quantitative Methods and Decision Making* test, the initial feedback is a conversation between us and the instructor of the *Quantitative Methods and Decision Making* course. The focus is on identifying the significance of the low performance. This analysis could include examining the mathematics records of the students who took the test to see what their grades were in prerequisite courses. Only after this initial analysis of results do we consider, with the collaboration of the course instructor, what to do with the findings.

The feedback loop for this project does not follow a set pattern in each case. In one case, students may have a weak mathematics background indicated by lower course grades. The problem may be that the department, such as Agricultural Economics, might need to emphasize to their students the importance of doing well in prerequisite courses. In another case, such as a differential equations course, students may have had predominantly A's and B's in prior courses. In such a case, one suspects either a disparity in grading and learning in those courses, or that skills learned for a short term to successfully take course tests do not persist over the longer term so that they are still available a semester or year later.

Conclusion

These examples illustrate our view of quantitative literacy as a somewhat broader concept than is often found in the literature. Rather than focusing only on basic mathematical and statistical skills that are required for informed citizenship, for example, to read and understand the newspaper, to handle finances, and for other tasks in our daily lives as in examples 2 and 4 above), we view quantitative literacy in terms of the quantitative skills and capabilities that an individual requires in their chosen profession or program of study.

The difficulty of adopting this broader definition is immediately apparent: Rather than being a set body of knowledge applicable to all, quantitative literacy becomes a variable that depends on the individual. Some (for example, engineers, scientists, and actuaries) require considerably higher or more technical quantitative skills than others (for example, social workers, and physicians). Our method of assessment is a reflection of this broader view of quantitative literacy as the quantitative skills that the individual requires for success in their chosen field. Instead of trying to design a single instrument that measures quantitative literacy in any setting, we devise tailored instruments that reflect the quantitative requirements of particular settings.

Although the procedure is more complex, we believe it also provides much better insight to the quantitative readiness of a broad range of college students. Because we do not depend on one test or assessment tool, the instruments are not trivial for those with highly technical backgrounds; nor are they impossible for those who have lesser needs for high level mathematics and statistics in their program. The process is more collaborative and collegial and less threatening than external methods, supporting and depending on faculty involvement; we call this process faculty-driven. It has been our experience that most faculty welcome this opportunity to review, discuss, and try to improve the quantitative capabilities of their students so that they are better prepared to succeed in their chosen fields of study and believe that it has the desired positive effects.

References

Bauman, S. F., & Martin, W. O. (May 1995). Assessing the Quantitative Skills of College Juniors. *The College Mathematics Journal, 26*(3), 214–220.

Martin, W. O., & Bauman, S. F. (1999). Have our students with other majors learned the skills they need? In B. Gold, S. Keith, and W. Marion (Eds.), *Assessment Practices in Undergraduate Mathematics,* MAA Notes 49. Washington, DC: Mathematical Association of America.

Kirsch, I.S. & Jungeblut, A. (1986). *Literacy: Profiles of America's Young Adults*, Princeton, N.J. Educational Testing Service.

Paulos, J.A. (1988). *Innumeracy: Mathematical Illiteracy and Its Consequences*, Vintage Books, New York, NY.

—— (1995). *A Mathematician Reads the Newspaper*, Doubleday, New York, NY.

Steen, L.A. (1997). *Why Numbers Count: Quantitative Literacy for Tomorrow's America*, New York, NY. The College Board.

—— (1998). *Numeracy: The New Literacy for a Data-Drenched Society*, Educational Leadership, 57:2, 8–13.

Steen, L.A, et al. (2001). *The Case for Quantitative Literacy*, MAA, Washington DC.

Example 1

The function on this graph gives the profit, $P(x)$, made by an agricultural chemical company in a week if they make and sell x bags of fertilizer. They are able to produce **at most** 2500 bags of fertilizer each week.

(a) Use the graph to determine the range of weekly production levels that would be profitable for this manufacturer. ***Explain how you arrived at your answer***.

Accurately estimated lower bound (x-intercept):	*30%*
Gave the exact upper bound:	*40%*
Gave a correct written explanation, e.g. noting that profitability corresponds to positive function values	*35%*

(b) Use the graph to estimate the number of bags that should be produced and sold each week to earn the largest profit.

Accurately estimated x value corresponding to maximum:	*95%*
Incorrectly stated maximum profit (around $35,000) rather than the number of bags that give a max:	*5%*

Degree of Success:	*A 25%*	*B 5%*	*C 5%*	*D 65%*	*E 0%*

Example 2

A Media professor asked the 126 students in his class whether or not they read *Time* or *Newsweek* the previous week. The students' responses are summarized in this table:

		Time	
		Yes	No
Newsweek	Yes	41	23
	No	52	10

(a) How many students said they read *Time* the previous week?

Selected correct numbers:	*15%*
Gave correct total:	*20%*

(b) How many students did not read either magazine the previous week?

Selected correct numbers:	*85%*

(c) How many students said they read at least one of the news magazines the previous week?

Selected correct numbers:	*30%*
Gave correct total:	*50%*

Degree of Success: A 20%   B 0%   C 20%   D 60%   E 0%

Example 3

A nurse has recorded a patient's pulse rate every 15 minutes. His readings are recorded on this graph. Use the information from the graph to answer the following questions.

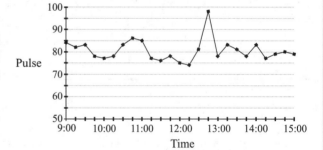

(a) What was the highest pulse rate recorded between 9:00 and 15:00? When did it occur?

Estimated highest rate correctly (97, 98, or 99 are good estimates)   93%
Correctly gave time at which highest rate occurred (12:45)   87%

(b) What was the lowest pulse rate recorded between 9:00 and 15:00? When did it occur?

Estimated the lowest rate correctly (73 or 74 are good estimates)   93%
Correctly gave the time at which the lowest rate occurred (12:15)   87%

(c) **Estimate** the patient's average pulse rate between 9:00 and 15:00. Explain how you got your answer.

Attempted exact computation (not wrong, but unnecessary   67%
Gave estimate in range 78-82   87%

(d) Shortly after checking the patient's pulse one of the times, the nurse remarked that he may have counted incorrectly. Which observation appears like it could have been incorrect? Give a reason for your choice.

Identified 12:45 reading with some appropriate comment   80%

Degree of Success: A 60%   B 33%   C 7%   D 0%   E 0%

Example 4

A television station tracks the viewing of its station by 1000 households. The average number of these households that have a television set tuned to the station during various viewing periods are given in this table:

Time Slot	Spring	Summer	Autumn	Winter
Late afternoon	380	350	450	500
Prime time	410	420	450	440
Late evening	240	250	270	290

(a) On average throughout the year, how many of the 1000 households tune to this station during Prime time?

Selected correct numbers from table	*100%*
Attempted to use correct method to compute average	*93%*
Gave correct average number	*93%*

(b) During which viewing period (season and time slot) do the fewest households tune to this station? Give the average number of households tuned in at this time.

Identified correct viewing period	*93%*
Gave correct number of households	*60%*

(c) During which season does the station have the highest average number of households tuned to their broadcasting?

Identified correct season	*80%*
Attempted to calculate average(s) (not necessary)	*13%*

(d) A market researcher found that an average of 1.7 people are watching the television when it is turned on. Assuming this pattern holds for the station during all viewing times, how many people in these 1000 households on average watch the station during the highest viewing period (season and time slot)?

Used correct viewing period (season and time slot)	*73%*
Attempted correct method to compute average number	
of viewers during this viewing period	*73%*
Obtained correct number	*80%*

Degree of Success: *A 40%*   *B 27%*   *C 33%*   *D 0%*   *E 0%*

Example 5

Here is a sign chart for a function $y = f(x)$ and its first and second derivatives, f' and f''.

	$x < -1$	$x = -1$	$-1 < x < 1$	$x = 1$	$x > 1$
f	$+$	does not exist	$+$	0	$-$
f'	$+$	does not exist	$-$	0	$-$
f''	$+$	does not exist	$+$	0	$-$

(a) Sketch a possible graph for a function that satisfies the conditions in this table.

    Appropriate graph for $x < -1$:   *63%*

    Appropriate graph for $-1 < x < 1$:   *63%*

    Appropriate graph for $1 < x$:   *75%*

(b) For which values of x is the function *decreasing*?

    Gave correct interval where f is decreasing: *63%*

    Degree of Success: *A 25%*   *B 37%*   *C 19%*   *D 19%*   *E 0%*

Example 6

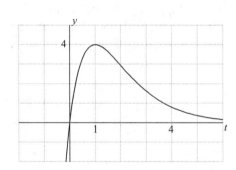

Estimate the value of this integral as accurately as possible from the graph of $y = f(t)$:

$$\int_0^4 f(t)\, dt$$

Used grid to estimate area: *71%*

Used rectangles to estimate value: *0%*

Used trapezoid rule to estimate value: *0%*

Used Simpson's rule to estimate value: *0%*

Method used not apparent: *0%*

Gave reasonable estimate: *53%*

Example 7

A cylindrical aluminum can (see figure) is to contain 500 ml. (cubic centimeters) of apple juice. These formulas may be useful as you answer the following questions:

Volume of cylinder $= \pi r^2 h$ Area of rectangle = length $\times$ width

Area of circle $= \pi r^2$ Circumference of circle $= 2\pi r$

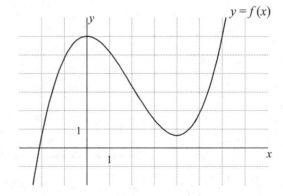

(a) Express h, the height of the can, as a function of r, the radius of the circular top of the can.

Correctly expressed h as a function of r: 75%

(b) Express A, the surface area of the can including the side and the circular top and bottom, as a function of r, the radius of the top.

Exhibited rule for area of side of can: 94%
Exhibited rule for area of top and bottom of can: 81%
Derived function for surface area in terms of the radius: 63%

(c) Find the radius that gives the smallest possible surface area for this can.

Found derivative of function from question 3b: 50%
Attempted to find the zero of the derivative: 38%
Found the zero (any exact or approximate form of the answer is alright):   31%
Confirmed this is a local minimum, e.g., using second derivative

     Degree of Success: A   6%   B   25%   C   25%   D   44%   E   0%

Example 8

Here is the graph of a function $y = f(x)$.
Use the graph to answer these questions:

$y = f(x)$

(a) Estimate $f'(4)$.

     Sketched tangent line at each point (not necessary):   31%
     Commented on local minimum and/or horizontal tangent at $x = 4$:   0%
     Stated $m = 0$:   94%

(b) Estimate $f'(2)$.

     Observed that gradient at $x = 2$ is negative: 6%
     Estimated at $x = 2$, $-3 < m < -1$:   56%

(c) On which interval(s), if any, does it appear that $f'(x) < 0$?

     Gave correct estimate for interval: 94%

     Degree of Success: A   56%   B   31%   C   13%   D   0%   E   0%

A Case Study of Assessment Practices in Quantitative Literacy

Rick Gillman

Valparaiso University, Valparaiso IN

Introduction

As we develop and implement quantitative literacy programs, it is important to remember to design efficient and informative assessment plans. To accomplish this, we need to understand what the goals of our program are, as well as the context within which the program exists.

This paper describes the assessment efforts of the quantitative literacy program at Valparaiso University. As we begin describing this program, it should be noted that it is not a complete QL program as described in Quantitative Reasoning for College Students: A Supplement to the Standards. As you will see, it was designed to address the first component - remediation - of the three described in the volume.

After a description of the historical development of the course and a typical unit in it, various assessment goals are described. For each of these goals, there are descriptions of the assessment measures used over the past seven years to determine the effectiveness of the course at reaching the goal. These measures may give the reader some ideas for tools that he or she can use on their own campus.

In a final section, there is a discussion of what we have learned at Valparaiso, both about assessment techniques and about our success.

A History of MATH110: QPS

In the fall of 1996, the Department of Mathematics and Computer Science at Valparaiso University began offering MATH110: Quantitative Problem Solving. The course was designed and implemented in response to concerns about the quantitative skills of students taking general education courses in the sciences and other disciplines. In particular, faculty in the Department of Chemistry and the College of Nursing have serious concerns about student preparation for specific courses that they offered.

The initial stipulation made by these faculty members was that students be required to take the pre-calculus course that was already being offered by the Department. The Department resisted this, noting that the pre-calculus course was designed for students who intended to follow it with a calculus course. It also noted that both national and local statistics showed the extreme difficulty of successfully doing the requested remediation. (The Department also suggested that the student preparation issues were an admissions problem, not the department's problem.)

MATH110 was the compromise solution between requiring pre-calculus and doing nothing. Quantitative Problem Solving (QPS) is a 4 credit pass-fail course that counts towards graduation, but does not fulfill any general education requirement. While reviewing topics from intermediate algebra, the primary purpose of the course is to teach problem solving skills in a small group context.

The decision to focus the course on problem solving skills was in response to several factors. These included the recognition of the failure of traditional methods mentioned above, our understanding that the literature suggested that problem solving in context was the real issue rather than skills, and an attempt to make the course somewhat attractive for faculty to teach.

A placement exam was implemented to identify students who should be taking the course; beyond this course, the placement exam relies heavily on the student's choice of major for placement recommendations. Prior to this, placement had been based on a relatively simple decision tree using student provided information about their selected major and his or her SAT/ACT scores. The Department selected, and continues to use, the COMPASS test published by ACT. Between 10% and 15% of the students entering the University each fall test into QPS.

The exam is more successful than our previous system of placement in that we are able to identify students with significant quantitative deficiencies. In recent years, we have had more difficulty with false positives – students placing into QPS when the other indicators (GPA, courses taken, SAT scores) suggest otherwise. While not a serious problem, this does put a larger burden on the advising process because these students need individualized attention.

A Typical Unit in QPS

QPS is organized around units consisting of problems on a common theme. In general, the students are responsible for reviewing arithmetic or algebraic skills outside of class using the Introductory Algebra Software published by Quant Systems. In class, students work in small groups to solve problems utilizing the skills that they reviewed outside of class.

There is no required text for the course. The students construct a portfolio of problems and solutions over the course of the semester and the instructors frequently motivate this effort by telling students that they are building their own reference text for the future. Students work on an evolving list of problems that the faculty members have identified as interesting and appropriate for the course.

One of the (faculty's) favorite units in QPS is the unit on ratios, proportion, and percents. Before the first day of the unit, students will have independently completed the appropriate review modules on percents, ratios, and proportions. During the first session of the unit, students work in small groups exploring the exchange rate between Canadian dollars and US dollars. While this is initially easy to do, the problem becomes more complicated when they are asked to modify the exchange rate to include the differing sales tax rates in two specific locations.

The following session, the students are asked to solve a problem posed in the Arlo and Janis comic strip. The comic strip asked readers to determine Arlo's real age when told that his is on July 26 of his metaphorical year (the springtime of my life, May/December marriages, etc…). Readers are told that the metaphorical year has 365 days and that Arlo's life expectancy is 74.9 years. The problem becomes interesting as students begin to work in different units (days, hours, years/day, months/year) and different forms (decimals or fractions). As they work through understanding the metaphor, the unit analysis, and the arithmetic, the students begin to understand the subtleties of the problem. When they share their answers, they are quite surprised to find that working in different units and making different rounding decisions can make as much as six months difference in Arlo's age. For homework, they are asked to determine where they are in their own metaphorical year.

The final session in this unit has the small groups comparing the age of the universe (approximately 10 billion years) to a 24-hour day. The primary mathematical tool that they need is a basic understanding of scientific notation, which they had reviewed in an earlier homework assignment. They are frequently astonished to discover that the time elapsed since agriculture has been discovered corresponds to less than one half of one second!

Assessment Goals

Two distinct assessment goals soon became apparent. The instructors in the course were primarily interested in determining if they had improved the specific problem-solving skills and study habits of students enrolled in the course. The more general University community was interested in determining if the course improved the performance of students in general and if it increased the retention rate among this population of students.

We will discuss attempts at assessing each of these two goals in the following sections.

Assessing Problem-Solving Skills

Midterm Assessments. It was quickly decided that the course would have a midterm assessment and a final assessment (which look suspiciously like tests to the students). Since this course is not graded, these assessments can be used to focus on identifying student growth areas and items that need additional instructional attention.

These assessments consist of problems that look and feel similar to problems that they had been working on over the previous six or seven weeks. For example, for the ratio and proportion unit, students are asked to determine the time of day that corresponds to their own age using the metaphor from the Riddle of the Sphinx (What walks on four legs in the morning, two in the afternoon, and three in the evening?)

On each individual problem, approximately 60% get the question completely correct, with another 25% making specific technical mistakes. (In the example above, students typically determine that they've lived ¼ of their life and get an answer of 3 hours — forgetting that the day specified begins at 6:00 am and so the correct response should have been 9:00 am.)

Roads to War. This pattern of 60/25/15 repeated itself in a new assessment device implemented during the past year. For a last homework assignment, students were asked to explore the Roads to War problem (Bransford, 2000), which asked them to transfer solution method from one problem to another. Nothing similar to this problem or its context had been done previously in the course.

In the Roads to War problem, students are told the story of a general who wished to capture a fortress located at the center of a network of roads. The roads had been mined so that only a small number of soldiers could use a road at a given time. The general accumulates his soldiers at the fortress by sending small groups simultaneously down many different roads. The students are then immediately asked to help a doctor determine a course of treatment for a patient that has a tumor that can only be treated by a laser of high intensity, but surrounding tissue will be damaged by the high intensity of the laser.

Sixty percent of students were able to make the transference of method: treat the patient by focusing multiple lower intensity lasers from different directions. A typical student response of this type is:

> I was given the Roads to War Problem. I was to find a way to destroy a tumor in the stomach using rays and at the same time avoid destroying the healthy tissue. I have decided to pinpoint the tumor and blast a multitude of low intensity rays at the tumor at once. This is so the healthy are left intact and the tumor is slowly destroyed. [Accompanying picture shows rays hitting the tumor from many directions.]

Another 25% offered solutions that might be more practical medically (i.e., treat over time), but did not involve the transfer of method we were looking for. A typical response of this type was:

> A method that you could use is using a lot of small doses of rays over a period of time. They should send a little to the area (in increments) and then when all of it works together, it will do the same thing as a large dose, but without so much destroying of tissue.

The remainder of the students gave highly divergent answers.

Written Reflections. Throughout the entire course, students are taught to write out solutions to problems rather than simply giving answers. It is a natural extension of this idea to have them writing personal reflections on what they believe that they learned in the course. Here are excerpts from several reflections from this past year:

> One good thing about the class was a part I found very frustrating. I don't think that the profs answered one question that I had. They always made me figure it out which I guess is a good thing.

> The only part of this course that was truly helpful was the computer modules. They taught me a lot about math. It took me through equations and helped me to figure out algebraic expressions. The modules did help me with some of the formulas in class. The use of tables and setting up problems helped a lot because application problems are harder for me.

> Using a variety of different problems I found my skills improving as the course progressed. I feel tremendously more confident when presented with a word problem. The only thing that I don't feel I got from this class is a strong base that will make things such as the assessment test easier.

> I think that I could have learned more in a traditional class setting.

> In this class I have realized different strategies of how to solve and pick apart the steps of a problem. While doing this I have used the knowledge that I have obtained in the past. The computer modules were very helpful in reviewing basic algebra.

Faculty Journal. Since the inception of QPS, it has been taught using co-instructors. During the first several years of the course, the instructors kept a journal of their experiences.

On a typical day, one of the instructors acted as the principal instructor while the other observed and offered reflective comments on the class. This instructor was responsible for keeping the journal, which recorded the activities of the day, including interesting student responses to problems, new questions that were posed in the course of the discussion, and basic information about attendance.

The journal provided a method of offering consistency across multiple sections of QPS, identifying difficult or interesting problems, and skills that needed additional attention.

Unfortunately, as the set of problems used in QPS became standardized and the instructors taught QPS several times, the journal became less and less effective at offering new insights about student learning difficulties and progress. The instructors have not kept a journal for the past three years.

Anecdotal Stories. Some of the students enrolled in QPS actually take other mathematics courses in subsequent semesters, therefore, the instructors have opportunities to talk with them, or at least observe them, after the end of the semester. Student comments about QPS during these conversations and observations are sometimes revealing. For example, when asked what the most important thing she learned in QPS, one student thought for a moment and then said "patience". Another student was observed managing her small group's activities (a skill taught in QPS) and writing extensive solutions to problems in a Finite Mathematics class.

General Performance and Retention

Until very recently, at Valparaiso University, prerequisites for given courses were interpreted as advising statements and recommendations rather than exclusionary statements. Thus, even though completing QPS (or testing out of it) was a prerequisite for all of the courses that met general education requirements in the sciences, approximately 1/3 of the students who tested into QPS did not actually take the course. This provided a comparison group to use in investigations of general student performance and retention

Subsequent Courses. The first attempt at this type of assessment occurred after the end of the first year of QPS. The transcripts of all of the students who tested into the course were examined for courses having a QPS prerequisite. It turns out that a statistical comparison was not possible because of the diversity of options that the students had. They were scattered across 20 courses, none of which had a large enough population to apply these meth-

ods. However, examining the grades by course did suggest that the students who had completed QPS showed less variation in their grades.

GPA and Retention. During the 2001 academic year, the Office of Institutional Research conducted a study of students who had begun in the 1997 and 1998 classes. It examined the GPA's and retention rates of these students. In this study, the average GPA and retention rate of students who had tested out of QPS are 2.58 and 77%. For students who tested into QPS and successfully completed the course, the corresponding numbers were 2.02 and 67%. Their average GPA was just above the 2.0 that students needed to stay in the University in good standing. In contrast, the students who either failed QPS or did not take it had an average GPA of 1.65 and a retention rate of 57%. The difference in these latter two retention rates is significant at a .05 level.

It should be noted that the GPA's include those of students who were not retained at the University. Among those students who were retained at the University, all of the GPA's rose, and the gap between those successfully taking QPS and those who should have taken QPS narrows significantly: 2.82 and 2.77 respectively. The study also showed that students who tested into QPS, whether or not they successfully completed the course, were about 12 credits behind the other students in their course of study. All of this suggests that QPS may play a role in the retention of students at the University, but does not significantly impact student GPA's.

Pre- and post- tests. This past fall, we had students enrolled in QPS retake the placement exam at the end of the semester. We intended this to be a simple measure of improvement in the mathematical skills of the students, and we found that only 46% were able to test out of QPS after taking the course. The surprising information came in data that we did not think to look at ahead of time. The COMPASS exam also provides scores in three subcategories of problems - pre-algebra skills, basic arithmetic skills, and miscellaneous skills.

It was immediately obvious that the initial subcategory scores of the students who failed to test out of QPS on the post-test were significantly lower than the initial scores who tested out of QPS on the post-test. This was across all three subcategories. Further, the post-test subcategory scores of these same students (those who didn't test out of QPS the second time) did not change from the pre-test to the post-test. Even more surprising was the fact that the pre-test subcategory scores of the students who tested out of QPS on the post-test were essentially the same as those of the students who chose not to enroll in QPS even though it had been recommended.

At the end of the academic year, we reviewed the GPA's and retention rates for all of these students. Although the sample sizes are small (36 students failed the post test, 31 passed the post test, and 37 did not take the course), the data suggests that taking the course has a significant impact on the GPA and retention rates of the students who tested out of QPS on the post-test as compared to those students who did not elect to take the course (3.00 vs 2.73 and 90.6% vs 80.0%). Those students who failed the post-test had a lower GPA than the students who did not take the course, but a higher retention rate (2.50 and 87.5%, respectively).

We will continue to gather this data.

Conclusion

From all of this assessment data, several conclusions can be drawn about the QPS course that is offered at Valparaiso University and also about the assessment of quantitative literacy programs in general.

Quantitative Problem Solving. The data suggests that QPS is at best modestly successful at improving the quantitative problem solving skills of the students enrolled in the course. However, the data does suggest that the students who are successful in QPS either have a skill set, or learn a skill set in QPS, that significantly helps them to succeed at the University generally.

Assessment. The examples above suggest that there are several different methods of assessing your goals, whatever they may be. Four particular observations stand out from this case study.

Know what it is you want to assess. As it turns out, only one of the assessment measures described above speaks directly to the problem that led to the implementation of QPS. The initial problem at VU was the fact that some students were having difficulties in general education courses requiring some quantitative skills. While we can say something about how students' quantitative skills have improved and something about how successful they are generally, we can not show an impact on their performance in specific subsequent courses.

Discussions with the Office of Institutional Research indicates that the data needed here — specific course grades for specific students — can be obtained with some effort. However, they indicate that it is probably not worth the effort because of the resulting small sample sizes and cohort differences. This leads directly to the next conclusion.

Be aware of variations in the population. Particularly at smaller institutions, any statistical study is affected by small populations. These studies can be affected by aggregating data such as two matriculating cohorts with different beginning levels, or by ignoring the question of retention. Unfortunately, disaggregating the populations simply makes the sample sizes even smaller. Similarly, the comparison group referred to on the previous page may have un-identified traits distinguishing them from QPS students even while they have comparable placement scores, standardized test scores, and high school performances.

Use multiple assessment measures. While it is clearly advantageous to have a specific assessment measure identified before starting a program, it is also clear from our examples that having a variety of measures will increase the confidence that you have in your conclusions. Look carefully at the information that you gather; it may be valuable in ways that you did not originally anticipate.

Be prepared for the results. One of the most discouraging outcomes of our assessment is the ambiguity of the results. There are faculty members, both within the department and without, who would like to declare QPS a failure, but cannot do so. Conversely, there are faculty members, both within the department and without, who would like to declare QPS a complete success, but cannot do this either.

References

Bransford, J. et al. (2000). *How People Learn: Brain, Mind, Experience, and School*. National Research Council.

Johnson, J. (1996, October 20). *Arlo and Janis*. Chicago Tribune.

Sons, L., et al. (1996). *Quantitative Reasoning for College Students: A Supplement to the Standards*. Mathematical Association of America.

—— (2002). *Introductory Algebra*, Quant Systems, Charleston, SC.

—— (2003). *Compass/ESL Version 3.2*. ACT Educational Technology Center.

The Quantitative Literacy Requirement at Alma College

Frances B. Lichtman
Alma College, Alma, MI

Alma College is a selective, residential, liberal arts college located in Alma, Michigan, devoted exclusively to the education of undergraduate students. The College enrolls about 1,200 students primarily from Michigan and also from 20 states and 12 foreign countries. Biology, Business, Education, History, and Psychology are the majors that attract the largest percentage of students.

Admission requirements historically have included a minimum of three years of high school mathematics. However, until recently, students could graduate from the College without further study in the computational and mathematical sciences. In fall 1997, an important change was made in the core curriculum requiring freshmen to complete a non-remedial course in the computational and mathematical sciences.

The requirement is entitled *Computational and Mathematical Sciences* to imply that courses in disciplines other than mathematics are applicable. Although the disciplines provide different contexts, the overarching goal of the requirement is to provide students with experience in mathematical problem solving. As stated in the academic catalog, all Alma College graduates should be able to:

- interpret mathematical and computation models (e.g. formulas, graphs, tables, algorithms).
- represent computation and mathematical information (e.g., symbolically, visually, verbally).
- solve problems and accomplish tasks using algebraic, geometric, statistical, computational or algorithmic methods.
- assess mathematical and computational results in fields of application.
- recognize limitations of computation and mathematical processes, techniques and methods.

A student's entry point into the mathematics curriculum is determined by math placement, which is based on standardized test scores (ACT Math and AP Calculus), math background, and performance on the placement examination. Students whose ACT Math scores are at least 30 are exempt from placement examinations. Students whose ACT Math scores are between 24 and 29 take placement examinations covering topics in algebra. When ACT Math scores are less than 24, students are tested on arithmetic skills as well as algebra. Entering students are placed into one of the following math groups, each of which offers courses tailored to students' preparation:

Group 1: Basic Core Mathematics
Group 2: Basic Algebra
Group 3: Liberal Arts Mathematics
Elementary Statistics

Group 4:   Pre-calculus
           Liberal Arts Mathematics
           Elementary Statistics
Group 5:   Brief Calculus
           Calculus I
           Pre-calculus
           Liberal Arts Mathematics
           Elementary Statistics
Group 6:   Discrete Mathematics
           Calculus II
           Brief Calculus
           Calculus I
           Liberal Arts Mathematics
           Elementary Statistics

The final course selection is made in consultation with a student's academic advisor.

The computational and mathematical sciences requirement can be satisfied by successful completion of mathematics courses in Groups 3 through 6 or those more advanced. The courses in Groups 1 and 2 are considered to be remedial and are mandatory for students who place at those levels. Students placed in Group 1 must, upon successful completion of Basic Core Mathematics, enroll in Basic Algebra the following term. Under-prepared students, consequently, need two or three courses to fulfill the requirement.

Overlapping courses in placement Groups 3 through 6 are intended to provide the flexibility to take into account a student's major academic background, and temperament. Pre-calculus is recommended only for students planning to study calculus. Students placed into Group 6 may enroll in Calculus II only if they have AP credit in Calculus I or permission from the Department of Mathematics and Computer Science.

The courses Liberal Arts, Mathematics, and Elementary Statistics, options in each of Groups 3 through 6, are appropriate for students with varying levels of preparation

The Liberal Arts Mathematics course presents a variety of contemporary mathematical topics that reveal the power and relevance of mathematics in today's world. Based around the textbook *For All Practical Purposes*, by COMAP, students study concepts such as identification numbers, transmitting information, planning and scheduling, weighted voting systems, fair divisions, and apportionment.

There are two statistics courses that fulfill the requirement, one offered by the Department of Mathematics and Computer Science and the other offered by the Psychology Department. The courses both include data analysis, de-

sign of surveys and experiments, inference techniques, regression, correlation, and analysis of variance. Unlike the psychology course, the Department of Mathematics and Computer Science course attracts students from diverse disciplinary backgrounds and uses broad-based applications. One component of the course is a research project in which students design studies, collect and analyze data, and submit written reports.

Other courses that fulfill the requirement include Mathematics for the Elementary Teacher, a sophomore course, and Beyond the Third Dimension, both at the Group 3 level. Computer science courses with prerequisites of placement in Group 4 or completion of Liberal Arts Mathematics satisfy the requirement, as do more advanced computer science courses. The Philosophy Department offers Symbolic Logic, which has a prerequisite of Discrete Mathematics or completion of an introductory logic course.

Beyond the Third Dimension is a reading and writing course about the fourth dimension. The course involves readings selected from both mathematical and non-mathematical literature and several invited speakers from disciplines other than mathematics. Built around Thomas Banchoff's *Beyond the Third Dimension,* with readings from Plato and Swift, students study topics such as the geometry of the binomial theorem, tessellations of *n*-space, and perspective views of the hypercube. Writing is a major component. A detailed description of the course is available in Putz (2001).

Placement Data

At the time of placement testing, students report their academic backgrounds in mathematics. The majority of entering students have completed a course in pre-calculus or functions; approximately 25% have completed a course in calculus. A small number of students have been admitted to the College without the mathematical background stated in the formal admissions criteria.

During the past ten years, the proportion of entering students who have had mathematics courses in twelfth grade has been decreasing while the mean ACT Math score has remained at about 24. During the same period, the proportion of students placed into developmental mathematics courses has been increasing.

It was hypothesized that the timing of a first course in algebra might help explain the completion rate of twelfth grade mathematics. Student-reported data from fall terms 1997 through 2003 indicated that more than half of the entering students in each year had completed a course

MOST ADVANCED COURSE*
FALL 2003

All Entering Students (*n* = 358)

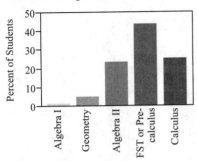

Students with No 12th Grade Math (*n* = 136)

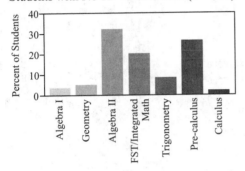

*Data does not include international students.

Math in 12th Grade, Fall Term

Placement in Groups 1 and 2, Fall term

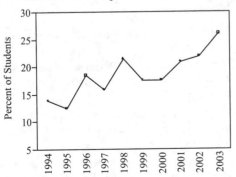

in algebra prior to ninth grade, however, no trend was found.

Completion Data

This section will focus on students who fulfilled only the minimum computational and mathematical sciences requirement and who, if not obligated, may not have taken a course in this area.

The classes of 2001, 2002, and 2003 were the first to include graduates who were required to fulfill the quantitative literacy requirement. It applied to 205 students in the class of 2001, 285 students in the class of 2002, and 276 students in the class of 2003. Three hundred seventy-four, 49%, of the aggregate (n = 766) completed only one non-remedial quantitative course. Statistics was the most prevalent choice, followed by Liberal Arts Mathematics and Mathematics for the Elementary Teacher.

A student's major or minor often prescribed the selection of a course. Statistics was required for majors and minors in Business, majors in Psychology, minors in Psychology who planned to teach, and students with minors in Public Health. Elementary Education majors needed to complete Mathematics for the Elementary Teacher.

Of the 374 graduates, 29% (220) completed one course in the computational and mathematical sciences that was not designated by their majors or minors. These graduates most frequently selected Elementary Statistics or Liberal Arts Mathematics. The latter has been attracting an increasing proportion of students who have the discretion to select any quantitative course.

Students who completed Beyond the Third Dimension or Symbolic Logic had also taken other quantitative courses. Ten graduates, majoring in Business, Elementary Education, Psychology, and Communication, had taken the course Beyond the Third Dimension, taught in alternating spring terms only. All had completed a statistics course; two were math minors. Symbolic Logic was selected by six graduates, five of whom majored in the social sciences and one who majored in Biochemistry. Other courses taken by students who completed Symbolic Logic included Statistics, Liberal Arts Mathematics, Calculus II, and Introduction to Computer Programming.

All of this information is graphically presented in the following tables.

Discussion

Students whose math placement was in the remedial courses typically completed the quantitative literacy re-

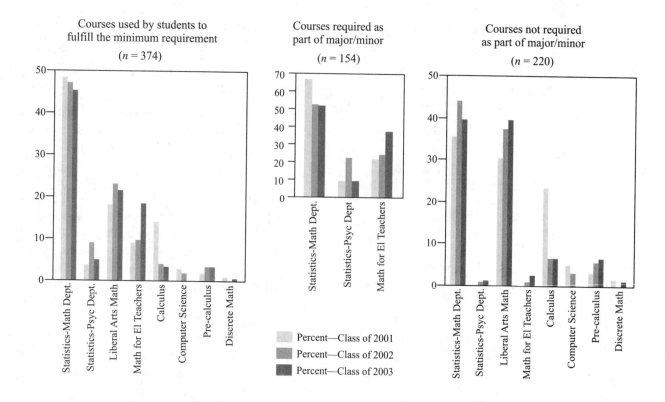

Courses used by students to
fulfill the minimum requirement
(*n* = 374)

Courses required as
part of major/minor
(*n* = 154)

Courses not required
as part of major/minor
(*n* = 220)

Percent—Class of 2001
Percent—Class of 2002
Percent—Class of 2003

quirement with applications courses rather than those that emphasize theoretical mathematics. While there was the potential that the presences of these students in applications courses would lead to a weakening of the curriculum, this has not occurred.

The requirement, in conjunction with the large number of students needing remediation, has increased the proportion of credit hours in mathematics dedicated to remediation from approximately 7% in the years immediately preceding implementation to about 17% at present. With rare exception, adjunct faculty is responsible for teaching developmental courses.

Conclusion

Requiring that students complete a course in the computational and mathematical sciences is the first step towards a quantitative literacy program as described in the MAA report, *Quantitative Reasoning for College Graduates: A Complement to the Standards*. Remediation is implicit in the requirement and necessary for about one-fourth of our entering students.

Most students who have no quantitative courses prescribed by their majors or minors select applications

courses rather than those that emphasize theoretical mathematics.

For our students to be quantitatively literate, they will need further experiences that apply and deepen their foundational understanding. In the future, we will need to develop a curriculum that includes the study of mathematical problems in courses that forge connections between mathematics and other disciplines. At Alma College, this might best be initiated by members of the Department of Mathematics and Computer Science partnering with faculty outside the discipline who are interested in developing a quantitative reasoning component for their courses.

References

Banchoff, T. F. (1990). *Beyond the Third Dimension*. New York: W. H. Freeman.

COMAP. (2000). *For All Practical Purposes, Mathematical Literacy in Today's World*. New York: W. H. Freeman and Company.

The Mathematical Association of America (1998). *Quantitative Reasoning for College Graduates: A Complement to the Standards*. MAA Online.

Putz, John. (2001) Going out on a Limb: Reading and Writing about the Fourth Dimension, PRIMUS, v.11 no. 1.

Traveling the Road Toward Quantitative Literacy

Richard J. Maher

Loyola University Chicago, Chicago, IL

History of the Program

Like most Jesuit institutions, Loyola University's College of Arts and Sciences has had a core curriculum for many years. In the fall of 2002, the university decided to begin work on a common core curriculum for all its undergraduate students. In January, 2003, the administration formed a seventeen member Core Renewal Steering Committee consisting of twelve faculty, three staff, one student, and the Associate Provost. This committee was charged with determining…

what a graduate of Loyola University Chicago should know, appreciate, and be able to do regardless of his or her college or undergraduate major.

After nearly a year of consultation with administrators, alumni, faculty, staff, and students, the committee delivered its first major report on November 21, 2003. This report listed four educational goals and several learning outcomes associated with each goal. A Quantitative Literacy component was included in this report, which was approved by the university's Board of Trustees on December 5, 2003. This report in turn formed the basis for the committee's second major report, concerning the structure of the core, which was completed on May 10, 2004, and approved by the Board of Trustees on June 4, 2004. The Steering Committee is now working on the remaining steps in the process, including generating course proposals, developing program assessment plans, and determining faculty development needs. The plan is to implement a university-wide core curriculum for students entering during the 2005-06 academic year. This new core curriculum will apply to all the undergraduate programs offered by Loyola University Chicago, which includes the College of Arts and Sciences, the School of Business, the School of Education, the School of Nursing, and the School of Social Work.

Mathematics has always been a part of the core curriculum of the College of Arts and Sciences. The three mathematics courses now offered for core credit for students not majoring in chemistry, mathematics, physics, or statistics, (Fundamentals of Statistics, Finite Mathematics, and Elements of Calculus I) have been offered as service courses for over forty years. Their contents have evolved over the last twenty years or so to the point where these courses are *de facto* quantitative literacy courses. (Note: Students who major in chemistry, mathematics, physics, and statistics now are viewed as meeting their core curriculum requirement in mathematics within the College of Arts and Sciences through the extensive mathematics requirements that are a part of their majors.) Now that quantitative literacy is to be a part of the undergraduate education of all Loyola students, the role of these courses will be re-evaluated in this new context. The department may also develop one or more new courses as well.

Program Goals and Learning Objectives

The quantitative literacy requirement is one of the knowledge-based requirements that make up the new university-wide core curriculum. Each of the fifteen courses used to satisfy a knowledge requirement must also integrate *knowledge* with *foundational skills* and, if possible, *values*. As indicated below, these three general areas contain several components. [Note: The numbers in the KNOWLEDGE column denote the number of courses required in that area.]

KNOWLEDGE
Artistic(1)
College Writing Seminar (1)
Historical (2)
Literary (2)
Philosophical (2)
Quantitative Analysis (1)
Scientific Literacy (2)
Social/Cultural (2)
Theological (2)

VALUES
Civic Engagment
Diversity
Justice
Spirituality/Faith

FOUNDATIONAL SKILLS
Communications
Critical Thinking
Ethical Awareness
Information Literacy
Quantitative and Qualitative Analysis and
    Research
Methods
Technological Literacy

Each Knowledge-based component has learning outcomes and competencies associated with it. For example, each Knowledge-based course must reinforce the development of one or more Foundational Skills. The four courses in the Philosophical and Theological components must contain at least one course in ethics. All students must complete at least one course addressing each of the core curriculum Values. Finally, a one-semester College Writing Seminar is required as part of the Knowledge

component of the core.

The following details relate specifically to the quantitative literacy requirement.

Learning Outcome

Demonstrate understanding of quantitative analysis. Quantitative analysis enables one to understand and analyze quantitative information presented in various formats. It involves reasoning by symbolic, numerical, or geometrical means; determining various ways to solve problems; and predicting possible consequences.

Competencies

By way of example, Loyola graduates should be able to:

a) Represent and interpret quantitative information symbolically, graphically, numerically, verbally, and in written form.

b) Recognize the limitations of mathematical and statistical models.

c) Develop an understanding of the nature and history of mathematics, its role in scientific inquiry and technological progress, and its importance in dealing with issues in the public realm.

d) Develop an understanding of the rudiments of statistics, including sampling and hypothesis testing, and the uses of statistical reasoning in everyday life.

Student Placement Into The Program

Beginning with the fall, 2005–06 semester, all undergraduates entering Loyola University Chicago were required to meet the core curriculum requirements outlined above. No core curriculum course may have a college level prerequisite, except where a proficiency level must be demonstrated or a developmental course is needed. At the present time, all undergraduates entering the College of Arts and Sciences are required to take a Mathematics Placement Test. The results of this test determine the chemistry, computer science, mathematics, and statistics courses for which the students are eligible and the registration process blocks students from registering in courses for which the test indicates they are unqualified. The department designed this test after our experience with various standardized tests proved unsatisfactory. The test has been effective (fewer drops and failures) and since the fall 2005–06 semester it has been administered to all entering undergraduates.

Placement in the quantitative literacy courses depends on the results of the Mathematics Placement Test. The proficiency level required for enrollment in either

Fundamentals of Statistics or Finite Mathematics is lower than that required for Elements of Calculus I. The first two courses require the material typically taught in a second year course in high school algebra, while Elements of Calculus I requires a precalculus course. The new Core Curriculum allows students who do not exhibit the required proficiency to take any needed prerequisite courses.

Placement also can be affected by the requirements of the major departments. At the present time, students majoring in Psychology or in the School of Social Work are encouraged to take Fundamentals of Statistics while Biology students are required to take Elements of Calculus I (and II). Students majoring in the School of Business also are required to take Elements of Calculus I. When the university-wide core requirements take effect, it seems likely that students in the College of Arts and Sciences, the School of Business, and the School of Social Work will continue to take the same courses that they do now. Most students in the School of Nursing probably will opt for Fundamentals of Statistics while enrollments of students in the School of Education will most likely be split between Fundamentals of Statistics and Finite Mathematics.

Curriculum Details

Fundamentals of Statistics

In the past, this course was mostly computational and there often was a good deal of overlap with courses offered by other departments. For example, we covered many of the same things that social science and business majors were doing in their methods courses. At the same time, nobody ever discussed to any great extent how there is much more to statistics than number crunching. After discussions within the department, with the departments of psychology and sociology, and with the School of Business, we decided to introduce more "whys" into Fundamentals of Statistics. We also found that using *Statistics* by Friedman et. al., allowed us to structure a course that would deal with the "whys" as well as say enough about the "hows" to make it a solid statistics course. This approach also fits in nicely with the needs of the humanities students, who enroll with increasing frequency in this course.

The learning objectives of this course include:

1. Having a basic knowledge and understanding of standard statistical terms and tools, including their uses and their limitations;

2. Being comfortable with data sets and the various parameters used to describe them;

3. Understanding the differences between random studies and observational studies and their respective outcomes;

4. Being able to evaluate claims and assertions that are supported by statistics;

5. Recognizing the problems inherent in surveys and sampling, including sample choice, bias, and non-response;

6. Understanding the meaning of and differences between association, correlation, and regression.

Some faculty devote a good deal of time to discussing what is involved in setting up and testing hypotheses and what the results really mean. Others prefer to spend additional time on polls and surveys or on various aspects of regression and correlation. Group work and, occasionally, projects may be a part of this course. Projects, when they are used, often involve sampling student opinion on issues that affect campus life; much of the emphasis here is on obtaining a representative sample.

Finite Mathematics

When first offered, this course covered topics such as logic and truth tables, number systems, equation solving, manipulations with matrices, and perhaps some elementary linear programming and game theory. Over the years it has evolved into a kind of "Mathematics in the Real World" course that uses a good deal of mathematics in its presentation. Adopting the COMAP text several years ago gave instructors the flexibility to explore some interesting topics whose study requires a fair amount of mathematical sophistication.

The learning objectives of this course include:

1. Having the ability to analyze patterns in data and the interactions among systems;

2. Understanding basic models and their applications in areas such as the environment, growth, and economics;

3. Being comfortable with the basic notions of graph theory and its applications in such areas as planning and scheduling, task organization, and optimization;

4. Being familiar with coding and its applications in communications, identity codes, and the internet;

5. Having a basic knowledge of voting theory and its potential applications and implications in social choice procedures.

Some faculty spend additional time on graph theory and linear programming while others devote time to codes, how they are used, and how they can be deciphered. Still others focus on the mathematics of social choice, particularly voting theory. Group work and projects are popular in this course. One recent project involved studying the snow removal plan of a Chicago suburb to see if it could be improved. Another one used material covered in class to decipher some interesting codes that the students had not seen previously. Throughout this course, the students get to use mathematics, some if it quite advanced given their backgrounds, in everyday settings and actually understand what is going on.

Elements of Calculus I

This course formerly was "Calculus Light," with an enrollment consisting mostly of biology majors. As such it satisfied neither the students taking it nor the faculty teaching it. In the mid 1980s there was a movement to include more applications in the course, although initially many of them were contrived and included almost as an afterthought. The advent of calculus reform showed how it was possible to teach courses driven by meaningful problems and applications. We currently use one of the Hughes-Hallett texts and find that it meets our needs very well. In fact, the School of Business now requires its students to take this course instead of a separate business calculus course that we formerly offered.

Some of the learning objectives of this course include:

1. Obtaining a strong background in the methods, techniques, and applications of differential calculus;
2. Obtaining a basic knowledge of anti-derivatives and the Riemann Integral along with their applications;
3. Becoming familiar with non-trivial applications of differential and, to a lesser extent, integral calculus in the life sciences, the social sciences, and business.

Each semester, faculty cover a variety of examples from business, the life sciences, and the social sciences. They also try to incorporate at least one in-depth application. However, there is less flexibility in this class since it is the first course in a sequence and there is a significant amount of material to be covered in the first semester. One application that generates a good deal of student interest involves analyzing how to minimize the cost of making a can or a 55-gallon drum. In the latter case, *Problems for Student Investigation,* offers an interesting presentation. Another involves using the census figures for the United States from 1790-2000 to discuss population models and their limitations. A third shows how the standard, and artificial, example of finding the best path using both a side-

walk and a parkway to get to a bus stop can, with a bit of effort, be adapted to determine the most economical way to construct a pipeline across a wetland.

General Comments

The learning objectives of all three courses are shaped in part by their roles as both service courses and as core curriculum courses. There may be some modifications as we adjust to the university-wide core curriculum and we are actively considering what steps might need to be taken.

At the present time, students are free to enroll in any course for which they are qualified by the placement test. We anticipate that this will still be the case under the university-wide core curriculum. Enrollments in Fundamentals of Statistics now consist primarily of social science majors, although the percentage of humanities majors increases each year. A small number of students are from the School of Business. We expect that most students from the School of Nursing will enroll in this class under the new core program, as will many from the School of Education. The Finite Mathematics classes now enroll students from both the humanities and the social sciences (for example, psychology majors are required to take two mathematics classes). The quantitative literacy requirement will no doubt generate additional enrollments from the School of Education. At present, roughly 90% of the students in Elements of Calculus I are from either Biology or the School of Business. This percentage should not change significantly when the university-wide core curriculum is implemented.

Program Assessment

The present core curriculum for the College of Arts and Sciences contains no formal assessment process. We do a variety of things to determine how well our department is addressing the needs of students within the college. For example, we compare our own impressions of what we are accomplishing with what faculty at other schools do in similar settings and with what appears in the literature. We also receive student feedback through teacher evaluations that are designed to elicit written comments and we discuss our activities with the departments that we serve. We can use this information to address issues of interest that arise from time to time. Nonetheless, it is somewhat ironic that we are using qualitative measures to evaluate the effectiveness of quantitative literacy courses.

All of this will change when the university-wide core curriculum takes effect. One of the requirements of this new core is to measure the effectiveness of each department's efforts to meet the required goals and outcomes of each knowledge component of the core. In particular, this means that a formal process will be developed to assess the effectiveness of the quantitative literacy component. Exactly what form this process might take is unknown at this time, but one proposed model, in the early stages of discussion, would work with the following data:

- Grade(s) in quantitative literacy course(s);
- Grade(s) in course(s) that use or reinforce quantitative literacy;
- Input from instructors in courses — not necessarily core courses — that use or reinforce quantitative skills;
- Performance on a computer generated test taken during the senior year, perhaps view in comparison with a benchmark test given during the first year, that evaluates quantitative abilities.

If this model is chosen, this rough outline would be molded into an actual assessment process.

Cross-Disciplinary Commitment and Participation

As was noted earlier, each Knowledge-based course in the new university-wide core curriculum must reinforce the development of one or more of the Foundational Skills and address, if possible, one or more Core Values. The core also defines quantitative abilities as a Foundational Skill. It seems likely that the contents of two or three of the core courses offered by other departments will reinforce quantitative skills. On the other hand, a number of non-core courses offered by the Departments of Biology, Chemistry, Natural Science, Physics, Political Science, Psychology, and Sociology within the College of Arts and Sciences will build on the quantitative literacy requirement. A similar comment applies to courses within the Schools of Business, Education, Nursing, and Social Work. We also anticipate that there will be inquiries from

departments not currently using quantitative methods as to how they might be employed in their disciplines. The university-wide core curriculum is intended to be exactly that: university-wide. As a result, departments across the university will be encouraged to incorporate quantitative knowledge and skills into their curricula. The faculty development program that is being developed to support the university-wide core will play a large role in this area.

As was noted earlier, the Core Renewal Steering Committee is now working on the remaining steps needed to implement the university-wide core by fall, 2005-06. But the core is a reality and quantitative literacy is a part of it. More important, it will not exist in isolation. The structure of the core insures that quantitative literacy, like all the other core components, will be integrated into each undergraduate student's course of study. This approach can only work to the benefit of our students as they enter the world that awaits them after graduation.

References

www.luc.edu/corerenwal/intro.shtml

www.luc.edu/corerenwal

www.luc.edu/corerenwal

www.luc.edu/corerenewal/overview.pdf

www.luc.edu/corerenewal/universitycorecurr.pdf; Section D, p. 4

Freedman, D., R. Pisani & R. Purves (1998). *Statistics*; (3rd ed.). W.W. Norton.

COMAP, (2003). *For All Practical Purposes*. (6th ed.). W. H. Freeman.

Hughes-Hallett, D., et.al., (2002). *Calculus, Single Variable*, (3rd ed.). Wiley.

Ramsay, J. (1993). "Optimal Design of a Steel Drum", in *Problems for Student Investigation*, M. Jackson, & J. Ramsay, Editors, MAA Notes 30, MAA.

—— (1993). Designing a Pipeline with Minimum Cost, in *Problems for Student Investigation*, M. Jackson, & J. Ramsay, Editors, MAA Notes 30, MAA.

Quantitative Literacy Course Selection

Carrie Muir

University of Colorado,
Boulder, CO

Introduction

Since 1999, I have been the undergraduate advisor for the Mathematics Department at the University of Colorado at Boulder. According to the job description, I would split my time between teaching math courses and advising math majors. Much to my surprise, from the very beginning I also had requests for advising from humanities and social science students, as well as calls for help from advisors in those fields: the problem? course selection.

I had never really considered selecting a mathematics or related course as a potential problem for general liberal arts students. As an undergraduate, I was a math major, so I had no trouble of my own. My friends with other majors also had little or no difficulty. The courses approved for the general education mathematics requirements were both limited and sequential. The only real choice might be between first semester calculus and general statistics.

I have spoken with colleagues, both in academic advising and in mathematics, from various institutions about their undergraduate experiences, and have found most are similar to my own. Requirements were usually some set number of credit hours in mathematics, selected from a simple, ordered list. In such traditional programs, course placement and course selection in math are one and the same.

However, like many liberal arts schools, the College of Arts and Sciences at CU-Boulder does not have a pure mathematics requirement. While some schools have gone to a combined natural science and mathematics requirement, others have gone to a broader quantitative literacy requirement. Our College of Arts & Sciences has taken the latter path, with a requirement titled Quantitative Reasoning and Mathematical Skills, or QRMS.

Liberally educated people should be able to think at a certain level of abstraction and to manipulate symbols. This requirement has two principal objectives. The first is to provide students with the analytical tools used in core curriculum courses and in their major areas of study. The second is to help students acquire the reasoning skills necessary to assess adequately the data which will confront them in their daily lives. Students completing this requirement should be able to: construct a logical argument based on the rules of inference; analyze, present, and interpret numerical data; estimate orders of magnitude, as well as obtain exact results when appropriate; and apply mathematical methods to solve problems in their university work and in their daily lives. (CUB Catalogue, 2003.)

As with any broad quantitative literacy requirement, the courses which satisfy the QRMS requirement are not in tidy sequences of mathematics courses, where placement determines selection. At CU Boulder, the courses available to students for fulfilling this requirement fall into four main categories. First, there are traditional mathematics courses, such as College Algebra, Precalculus Mathematics, Introduction to Statistics, and several flavors of calculus. Second, there are discipline specific mathematics courses, such as Mathematical Tools for Economists, Mathematics for Secondary Educators, and Finite Mathematics for Social Science and Business. Third, there are less traditional mathematics courses, designed especially for the QRMS requirement, such as Quantitative Reasoning and Mathematical Skills, The Spirit and Uses of Mathematics, and Mathematics for the Environment. And finally, there are non-mathematics courses, such as Quantitative Research Methods, Physics of Everyday Life, Order, Chaos, and Complexity, and Telecommunications.

It may seem surprising that a course titled Telecommunications would fulfill the QRMS requirement. Here is the course description from the 2003–2004 catalog.

> ECEN200 (3). Telecommunications 1. Covers the Internet and World Wide Web. Also introduces the main concepts of telecommunications, electronic publishing, audio, video, coding information theory, cryptography, data storage, and data compression. Approved for arts and sciences core curriculum: quantitative reasoning and mathematical skills.

The material on coding, cryptography, data storage and data compression clearly fall into realm of quantitative literacy.

With so many choices, students should surely be able to find a course to fit their interests and level of preparation! So why were the students having such trouble?

The Students

The mean and median ages for CU-Boulder full-time undergraduates are 20.3 and 20. Therefore, our students tend to be traditional college-age. A random sampling of students in spring 2002 and fall 2003 QRMS courses indicates that the majority of students in these classes are freshmen. A survey of the College's academic advisors supports this indication. A student trying to select a QRMS course is likely to be a 17- or 18-year old freshman.

Students admitted to CU-Boulder in Arts & Sciences are expected to have passed three years of mathematics in high school, and to have completed second year algebra. Few students come in with a deficiency in mathematics. Students' high school backgrounds vary by major, of course. Surveying advisors from across the college, I found that students in arts, humanities, and social science divisions were unlikely to have taken more than the minimum required mathematics, while undecided students and those in the natural sciences were likely to have taken through a precalculus course.

Coming straight out of high school, many students have never had to make a course selection on their own. If they have chosen courses, it was from a limited list of options. No wonder the CU-Boulder catalogue can look overwhelming.

In addition, young college students have generally not achieved what Chickering and Reisser (1993) call *instrumental independence*: "the ability to carry on activities and solve problems in a self-directed manner and the freedom and confidence to be mobile in order to pursue opportunity or adventure." These students may have weak decision making skills and may rely heavily on authority figures. When an Arts & Sciences student at the University of Colorado is preparing to register, the primary authority figure is his or her academic advisor.

While the "typical" student in Arts & Sciences who is struggling with QRMS course selection is a traditional aged freshman with a non-science major, other types of students also have difficultly, and may be the "typical" case on other campuses. Older students may be paralyzed with fear when confronted with the very idea of a math-related course, not having taken any mathematics in many years. Students who intend to pursue a science or engineering major, but who aren't sure which major, may have a hard time deciding which variation on calculus to choose. For any student working on a difficult course selection, academic advising is of critical importance.

The Advisors

In recent years, many institutions have been giving increased attention to academic advising, expanding and reshaping the services available to students. According to Celeste Pardee (2000), three models for providing advising are quite common. The first is a decentralized model, where services are provided by individual academic departments. The second is a decentralized model, where all academic advising is provided by a single unit. The third is the shared model, a blending of the centralized and decentralized systems. The College of Arts & Sciences at CU-Boulder uses a shared model, and so will have many characteristics in common with institutions using any of the three types of system.

Every Arts & Sciences student at CU-Boulder is assigned a professional academic advisor, determined by the student's major. If a student has multiple majors, s/he will have an advisor for each major, one of whom will be assigned as the student's primary advisor.

The advisors are hired to specialize in a particular major, or a few related majors. The advisor for a given department generally has a masters degree in that field or a closely kindred field. The advisors specializing in undecided students are slightly less likely than other advisors to have completed a graduate degree, perhaps because they do not advise students in a particular major. Advisors in the natural science departments are slightly more likely to have finished a PhD than the rest of the advisors.

Just like their students, advisors' mathematics backgrounds vary by division. Advisors in the arts, humanities, and social sciences have generally taken through a college algebra or statistics course, although a few have not taken a math class since high school. Advisors for undecided students have usually taken a college statistics or calculus course, and natural science advisors have usually taken at least one course beyond the calculus. While the variation in educational background by division is to be expected, it leads to an interesting result: *the advisors with the weakest mathematics backgrounds are advising the students with the weakest math backgrounds.* This correlation can cause problems when it is time for a student to select a QRMS course.

Advisors who are thoroughly familiar with QRMS course options and who have spent many years advising can likely overcome a weak mathematics background with practical experience. Unfortunately, there are few Arts & Sciences advisors who have that many years of experience. At the time of this writing, the amount of Arts & Sciences advising experience ranged from three months to 20 years, but the average across the board was about 4.5 years. To my surprise, I found variation in advising experience by division. Advisors working with arts, humanities, and undecided students average about three years experience, while natural science and social science advisors average about five years. High turnover among advisors is a problem faced by many schools for various reasons: faculty who take on advising as a short-term service or teaching assignment, staff given inadequate training, and advising done primarily by undergraduate "peer advisors," to name a few.

The Various Solutions

I have tried various measures to make QRMS course selection easier for the students and their advisors. All of the variations have been an improvement on the previous situation, i.e. no support available. The resources I have devised break down roughly into two categories: advisor training and resources, and student resources.

Advisor Training and Resources

The initial version of advisor training involved individual consultations. When an advisor encountered a particularly difficult placement situation, s/he would call or e-mail me for assistance. I would work through the case with the advisor, and use that case as a model for how to deal with other students. I hoped that by working through a few cases with each advisor, I could train everyone to be an expert in the issues that arise for their particular major.

At first, the consultations worked very well. The sessions were in depth and highly personalized. However, as the number of math majors grew, I had less time to spend on consultations. Furthermore, the high turnover rate among advisors meant I was frequently starting from scratch with a department, so I decided to move on to group sessions.

The first group training session I offered was suggested by the director of the Academic Advising Center. She asked if I would give a brief talk on course placement during the advisors workshop held before freshman orientation. I put together an overview of the mathematics courses most often taken by freshmen, and made a flyer reviewing some key points about each course.

The pre-orientation session was very popular with the advisors. They were able to go over information and ask questions right before helping freshmen select courses. They were also able to hear questions from the other advisors, and find out about courses their majors rarely took. The flyer was also a big hit; many advisors told me that they taped it up right next to their desks.

As popular as the pre-orientation session and flyer may have been, I was still getting a lot of questions from advisors. It became obvious to me that neither piece was sufficiently in-depth. The high advisor turnover rate was also a problem again; too many new advisors had to wait many months before the next workshop.

Making the sessions more in-depth was fairly easy. The Advising Center director allowed more time for my session during the pre-orientation workshop, so I could dig a little deeper with the advisors. I also switched from a one-page flyer to a roughly 20-page booklet. Instead of mentioning a few key points about each course, the booklet went in-depth into each course: what kinds of grades should a student have earned in various prerequisite courses in order to be ready, the format of the course, the intended audience for the course, student resources available for each course, etc. I included more courses in the booklet than in the flyer, expanding the list to include all first-year mathematics courses and a few popular non-mathematics courses approved for QRMS.

The booklet also included several reference sections for which I had seen a need. One of these references was a glossary of common mathematical terms, to aid advisors in reading course descriptions and matching graduate/professional school requirements to CU-Boulder course offerings. Another reference I added was a chart of suggested courses for students with interests in particular careers. Other reference sections included what to do with a student who needs calculus but isn't ready, different places for students to find help with mathematics courses, and a table of courses with similar content to each other.

The new sessions were a big improvement. They kept the most successful parts of the original sessions, but added enough material to let advisors feel more comfortable with course suggestions. The booklet was even more successful. However, I ran into practical problems. After one year, there was no longer enough time available during the pre-orientation workshops for my extended session. The level of detail included in the booklet required semester updates. Such updates meant a new copy for every advisor every term, a very expensive proposition in a time of campus budget cuts. And it was still hard to get information out to new advisors.

Time restraints demanded the pre-orientation sessions return to the shorter version. But I did not want to lose the chance to share additional information. I also wanted a chance to catch the always-present new advisors. I found two solutions. First, I give very short talks to the advisors throughout the semester. The group meets weekly for full staff meetings; about once per month, I mention some particularly timely issue relating to student placement in QRMS courses or student success in mathematics courses. Secondly, I send out e-mail memos to the full advising group. The memos let me go into topics from the meeting in more depth, or just send out reminders as appropriate.

I was able to overcome the problems with the booklet by transferring it to the web. The Arts & Sciences advisors have a secure web site, which houses the internet version of the booklet. Now the booklet is always available to any advisor, and can be updated as frequently as needed. Changing the booklet from a printer-friendly format to a web-friendly format took quite a bit of time in the beginning. In the long run, I have saved time, paper, and money through the ease of updates.

Student Resources

In the beginning, the students had a few basic resources: the college catalogue, their academic advisors, and myself. Natural science students needed little or no help with QRMS course selection, as their majors determined how much calculus they would have to take. The remaining students seemed to find very little help in the catalogue. A list of courses is only useful to someone who can understand the differences among those courses. Depending on their major, the student might be able to get help from their advisors; if not, they wound up in my office.

At this stage, I did one-on-one consultations with any student who asked, just as I did with advisors. As word got out that there was a math advisor, the demand for such consultation quickly became greater than I could possibly manage, even if it were my only task. I began to limit student consultations to brief e-mail questions, and as the college advising staff became more knowledgeable, I encouraged students to talk to their own advisors. The e-mail consultations were still more than I could handle, so I needed to develop some resources for student use, much as I had developed the booklet for advisor use. I began with a simple frequently asked questions section on the undergraduate math web site. It included the list of courses approved to fulfill QRMS with direct links to the course suggestions, a version of the suggested courses by possible career I had developed for the advisors, and the list of resources for help in mathematics courses.

With those resources on the web, and with the advisors now more confident in suggesting QRMS courses, I stopped doing student consultations entirely. But I was still not satisfied with the resources available to students. I wanted some way to be able to give an individual suggestion to any Arts & Sciences student, without taking too much time away from the math majors and minors, and without requiring a magic wand. The answer once again came through the web.

Over the course of a year, I worked up a list of every possible combination of up to two majors and one minor/concentration/certificate an Arts & Sciences student could have. The list got very messy, especially as I allowed for the possibility of a major or minor in a different college. Once I was confident the list was fairly complete, I came up with a course suggestion for every combination. The process was akin to doing a one-on-one consultation with a student for every combination.

With technical assistance from another math department faculty member, I took the list of major/minor combinations and course suggestions and turned them into an online decision tree. The student selects up to two majors and one minor/concentration/ certificate. Undecided students can select a broad field of interest instead of a major, such as fine arts or natural science. Once the student has selected his/her fields of study, they are given the course suggestion I chose for their combination of fields. Here is a sample result.

> Based on your responses, you might consider the course MATH1310: Calculus 1 with Computer Applications to fulfill the Quantitative Reasoning requirement of the Arts & Sciences core curriculum.

> If you do not feel prepared for a calculus course, or do not meet the prerequisites, then you might consider the course MATH1150: Precalculus Mathematics.

> You should be sure to discuss your options with your academic advisor. To identify your advisor(s), or to make an advising appointment, please click here to go to the main Arts & Sciences Advising site.

At present, only screens which suggest a calculus course include mention of a preparatory course. All other QRMS courses require only the three years of high school mathematics expected of all incoming freshmen. However, I would eventually like to include questions about a student's mathematics background in the decision tree.

The second sample result which follows makes it easy to see the basic template for the response screens.

> Based on your responses, you might consider the course *ECEN 1200-Telecommunications 1* to fulfill the Quantitative Reasoning requirement of the Arts & Sciences core curriculum.

> You should be sure to discuss your options with your academic advisor. To identify your advisor(s), or to make an advising appointment, please click here to go to the main Arts & Sciences Advising site.

The student resources and advisor guide that I have created can be seen on line. The URL's are given in the references.

Conclusions

I have presented the various solutions I developed as a progression, as if working towards a final, perfect system. However, devising tools, training, and resources for quantitative literacy course selection should be considered as an ongoing process. A model that works well one year may need to change the next, to fit changes in general education requirements, available courses, or faculty and advising structures. And a model which I tried and found a poor fit for my college may be ideal for your school.

When trying to help liberal arts students and academic advisors with quantitative literacy course selection, awareness, patience, and flexibility are very important. Mathematics departments, and other departments which teach quantitative literacy courses, need to keep in touch with the rest of the campus. We need to be aware of when students are having difficulties, and try to find the cause of each problem. We need to be patient with both students and colleagues, remembering that mathematics is not their field. We also need to have patience with ourselves, and be prepared for a long process when developing course placement resources. And finally, we need to be flexible, willing to try a variety of methods for helping with course selection until we find a mix that works well.

References

Chickering, A. W. & Reisser, L. (1993). *Education and Identity, Second Edition*. San Francisco: Jossey-Bass Inc.

Pardee, C. F. (2000). "Organizational Models for Academic Advising". In *Academic Advising: A Comprehensive Handbook*, Gordon and Habley, eds. San Fransisco: Jossey-Bass Inc

Muir, C. (2003). Student Resources. spot.colorado.edu/~carriem/ advising/qrms.

Muir, C., (2003). Advisor Guide. spot.colorado.edu/~carriem/ AAC/Guide.html

University of Colorado at Boulder Catalogue 2003–04. Boulder: University of Colorado at Boulder, 2003.

About the Editor

Rick Gillman, Professor of Mathematics and Chair of the Department, has been at Valparaiso University for 19 years. He did his undergraduate and masters work at Ball State University before completing his Doctorate of Arts at Idaho State University in 1986. He has publications in a range of journals including *Math Horizons* and the *CUR Quarterly*. Rick's research area is in combinatorics, with a particular interest in applied problems that can engage undergraduate students. He was the founding director of VU's annual Celebration of Undergraduate Scholarship. Rick is the editor of *A Friendly Mathematics Competition*, which chronicles the first 35 years of the Indiana College Mathematics Competition. Rick is a member of the MAA, the Council on Undergraduate Research, and the NCTM. He is active in the MAA at the section level, having served the Indiana Section of the MAA as its Student Chapter Coordinator, Public Information Officer, Secretary-Treasurer, and Chair. He is currently Governor for the section. At the national level, Rick has served as a member of the MAA's Membership Committee, and as chair of the MAA committee on Quantitative Literacy. He was a founding officer of SIGMAA QL.